"The best account I've read of the St. Louis Cardinals' improbable championship season of 1934. . . . "
—Russ Smith, *Wall Street Journal*

"The 1934 St. Louis Cardinals were not nice guys. But then, a lot of early ballplayers weren't. They tended to be scrappy, not-very-educated kids with tempers who would do about anything to win the game they weren't paid a whole lot of money to play. The 1934 'Gashouse Gang' took this general profile to a higher level, with odd birds like Dizzy Dean, nasty fellows like Leo Durocher and Joe Medwick and fine players like Frankie Frisch and Pepper Martin, who somehow put all their talents together for a great season. Heidenry outlines, with a mix of respect and bemusement, just how they all survived it, while making it clear why it proved so difficult to replicate."
—*New York Daily News*

"The book places its baseball in the context of the Great Depression, yet any chapter will give readers an upsurge of energy as they relive the season with this gang."   —*Library Journal*

"*The Gashouse Gang* is . . . a nostalgic return to a time and place where ballplayers had names like Heine Meine, and big, rawboned country boys chewed tobacco when they weren't chewing up the basepaths—blue-collar baseball at its best."
—*Palm Beach Post*

"Heidenry . . . carefully researched newspaper accounts, player biographies, and baseball histories for the anecdotes and game accounts that provide the substance for another highly readable slice of baseball history. . . . A memorable, engaging account of a great baseball team made up of many of the game's most colorful characters."
—*Booklist*

"Among the annual proliferation of baseball books, this one will stand out for the quality of the writing and the facinating story it tells of the famous Gashouse Gang of St. Louis and their triumph in the 1934 World Series over a very good Tigers team. This is the likes of Dizzy Dean, Pepper Martin, Frankie Frisch and Joe Medwick rollicking through a different era and defeating The Tigers of Hank Greenberg, Charlie Gehringer, Mickey Cochran and Goose Goslin. Good stuff. Good book."

—FAY VINCENT, former commissioner
of Major League Baseballl

"The Gashouse Gang is a solidly researched and warmly told account of that team and season, with a special focus on star hurler Dizzy Dean. . . . Other Cardinals who come alive in Heidenry's well-written text are Leo Durocher, Pepper Martin, Frankie Frisch, Joe Medwick, and Dean's younger brother, Paul."

—*Bookpage*

"Heidenry draws on plenty of sources—including contemporary newspaper reports—to offer a balanced picture of the team, and even discloses that its 'Gashouse Gang' nickname was not pinned on the team until 1935 . . . [T]his is certainly a credible look at baseball at the height of the Great Depression."

—*Tampa Tribune*

The Gashouse Gang

the

GASHOUSE GANG

How Dizzy Dean, Leo Durocher, Branch Rickey,
Pepper Martin, and Their Colorful, Come-from-
Behind Ball Club Won the World Series—and
America's Heart—During the Great Depression

JOHN HEIDENRY

PUBLICAFFAIRS
New York

Designed by Timm Bryson

Library of Congress Cataloging-in-Publication Data
Heidenry, John.
  The gashouse gang : how Dizzy Dean, Leo Durocher, Branch Rickey, Pepper Martin, and their colorful, come-from-behind ball club won the world series-and America's heart-during the great depression / John Heidenry.
      p.   cm.
  Includes bibliographical references and index.
  ISBN-13: 978-1-58648-419-4 (hardcover : alk. paper)1. St. Louis Cardinals (Baseball team)—History.   2. World Series (Baseball) (1934) I. Title.
GV875.S3H45 2007
796.357'640977866—dc22

                                                                2006036914

10 9 8 7 6 5 4 3 2 1

PBK ISBN: 978-1-58648-568-9

To my uncle
Lawrence M. Morrison,
a member of the 1934 Knot Hole Gang

Thank you, Larry, for everything

Contents

PREFACE

The year 1934 was among the most extraordinary in U.S. history, and the baseball season that year was among the most storied in the annals of the sport. In that year, a squad of quarreling, slovenly, brilliant misfits known to legend and lore as the Gashouse Gang—and officially as the 1934 St. Louis Cardinals—captured the imagination of a country in the throes of desperate social unrest and turmoil unlike anything it had ever experienced before, outside the battles fought on American soil, or has since.

The same could be said of the Gashouse Gang. They were the unique product of a particular time and place—mostly men who had known extreme poverty and hardship in the South and West, with a few hard-nosed kids from eastern states thrown in for variety. Among their number were a couple of ex-sharecroppers, a pool shark, a handsome dandy who worked as a Hollywood double in the off-season, a grease-stained third baseman who liked to drive his midget auto racer around a track before a game, a surly outfielder who punched any of his own teammates if they looked at him in the wrong way, and even a couple of college kids. Collectively, as the Gashouse Gang, they were the creation of a pious, nonimbibing Methodist who would not even watch them play on a Sunday because his religious principles forbade it.

Who could have thought up such a cast of characters, or the thrilling story of their pennant drive—when, just to make things even more interesting, their star player decided to go on strike and even made a bonfire of his uniform to show how mad he was at the way he was being treated by management?

Yet the 1934 Cardinals were more than just unusually colorful ballplayers. To a man, they were among the finest athletes ever to play the game. The story of their achievement has never been fully chronicled until now.

As occasion warrants, the world outside baseball occasionally intrudes in the course of this narrative. Yet every page lives and breathes the spirit and day-to-day reality of that soul-trying time.

As the 1934 season got under way, the Depression had just reached rock bottom, and a new mood had begun to take hold of the country. In January, President Franklin D. Roosevelt had asked Congress for $10.5 billion to advance recovery programs over the next year and a half. That same month, Congress had passed the Gold Reserve Act, giving the president the power to devalue gold deposits in the United States. The country returned to a modified gold standard, with a devalued dollar. As public confidence increased, the hoarding of gold all but ceased, paper currency and gold flowed back to the banks, and deposits rapidly increased. "We have nothing to fear but fear itself," Roosevelt had told the nation during his inauguration the previous March, and he reiterated that message in his popular Fireside Chats, broadcast over the radio. Finally, people were beginning to believe him.

The year 1934 is also synonymous with massive unemployment, mile-long bread lines, and the westward migration that began when Oklahoma, Kansas, Texas, and Arkansas turned into a giant Dust Bowl, and the skies would darken under a cloud of dust half a continent long. John Steinbeck described in his novel *The Grapes of Wrath* the great Dust Bowl drama that was unfolding while the Gashouse Gang fought its epic battles on baseball fields on the other side of the country: "And then the dispossessed were drawn west—from Kansas, Oklahoma, Texas, New Mexico, from Nevada and Arkansas, families, tribes, dusted out, tractored out. Car-loads, caravans, homeless and hungry; twenty thousand and fifty thousand and a hundred thousand and two hundred thousand. They streamed over the mountains, hungry and restless—restless as ants, scurrying to find work to do—to lift, to push, to cut—anything, any burden to bear, for food."

As Charles C. Alexander noted in *Breaking the Slump: Baseball in the Depression Era,* the 1930s were also the heyday of a small but determined U.S. Communist Party, which as early as March 1930 organized a rally in New York's Union Square that brought out thirty-five thousand demonstrators. "If the smell of revolution (and sometimes tear gas) was in the air for much of the thirties, what was perhaps even scarier for middle-class Americans who had worked hard to accumulate savings was the epidemic of bank failures—4,377 in all—from 1930 to March 1933."

During this era of profound social upheaval, baseball remained the undisputed great American pastime, and it is fair to say that the heroic feats of many of the players in that time offered welcome relief from the hardships of daily life that were the lot of most fans.

Baseball's golden age was also coming to an end, and 1934 would be its last year. The immortals of the game—Ty Cobb, Walter Johnson, Lefty Grove—were all or mostly gone now, and the 1934 season was also the last hurrah of the greatest of all ballplayers, Babe Ruth. Unable to find a managerial job that suited his personality, talent, and pocketbook, the Babe gracefully exited from the game at the end of the season.

Ruth had been the very personification of the decade before 1934—the Roaring Twenties. He loved New York's nightlife, chorus girls, champagne. Yet his outsize personality and almost superhuman ability had also helped save baseball from itself. In the wake of the so-called 1919 Black Sox scandal, when eight players of the Chicago White Sox were accused of throwing the World Series against the Cincinnati Reds, the game was suffering from declining attendance and a serious credibility problem. Ruth's bat changed all that. His magnificent achievements as a slugger brought renewed interest in the sport, and helped to restore its appeal.

In 1934, the man waiting to take Ruth's place as the most talked-about baseball personality of his time was a brash, twenty-four-year-old upstart brimming with self-confidence and pitching genius who sometimes liked to refer to himself in the third person, in that soft, self-deprecating, semihumble Arkansas twang of his, as Ol' Diz. At other times, when he was feeling a little less humble, he called himself the Great Dean. The world knew him as Dizzy Dean, and he was one of the true originals not only of baseball, but also of American popular culture.

There has never been a personality in the world of sports quite like Dizzy Dean, and the 1934 season was not only the finest showcase of his awesome talent as a pitcher, but also the stage when his instincts and abilities as America's most fascinating and unpredictable public figure were in full flower. We shall not see his like again.

I almost got to see the Gashouse Gang play, but not quite. A little more than a decade later, my father took me for the first time to Sportsman's Park in St. Louis, where I grew up. That dilapidated wooden structure, so different in every way from modern stadiums, remains for me a memory prism for peering into a part of the past.

In *The Gashouse Gang,* I have gone back in time to a year when my parents, uncles, and aunts were young and still single, and a visit to Sportsman's Park was a special treat. Like those of millions of other Americans, their lives were a struggle for survival. Yet they had something that we today do not have: They had the privilege of watching the Gashouse Gang, one of the greatest ball-clubs of all time, play baseball. I almost saw it all as a boy, sitting in the grandstand and enjoying a Cardinals game in Sportsman's Park a few years later. This book is my time machine, enabling me to roll back the years and see the Gashouse Gang play for myself.

THE
IMPOSSIBLE
DREAM

Branch Rickey was the most brilliant strategist in the history of baseball. A military metaphor perhaps best describes him, for this otherwise genial, convivial, devoutly religious Sunday school teacher was ruthlessly competitive and, like a field commander in the heat of battle, cold-bloodedly analytical. In 1919, he had been given the charge of a small, ragtag band of men whose mission was to defeat a foe with much greater resources both in manpower and wealth. As the new general manager of the St. Louis Cardinals, he had to find a way to send his squad onto the battlegrounds of baseball—Ebbets Field, Wrigley Field, Baker Bowl, the Polo Grounds—and make sure, first of all, that they were not quickly annihilated. That had been the fate of past Cardinals teams all too often. Season after season stretched out like an eternity as the lowly St. Louis squad loitered among the damned in the bottom tier of the second division.

A Methodist so pious he would not even attend a baseball game on a Sunday, Rickey wanted his team of chronic losers not merely to prevail over their National League opponents. He dreamed a dream that was even more impossible. The law of averages said that the Cardinals, like most other teams, might theoretically someday win a pennant. Yet in the hard world of professional baseball, it was a simple fact that most championships—and the biggest profits—were mostly garnered by teams in New York, Philadelphia, or Chicago, because they had the money, swagger, population, and muscle to acquire the best talent year after year.

Rickey, like the Napoleon of baseball that he was, aspired to something much bigger than an occasional championship season. He wanted an empire, and a long row of pennant flags fluttering above the stadium that was to serve as his court. He wanted players who were not mere foot soldiers in the baseball wars, but immortals whose names would be remembered for as long as the game was played.

Meanwhile, though, in the summer of 1919, he had a serious and seemingly insoluble problem on his hands. His St. Louis team was not merely in debt. It was poverty-stricken and spiraling down into the lower depths of do-or-die desperation. Ever since assuming his post that January, he had worked several conjuring tricks just to field a squad of nine able-bodied and reasonably talented men. Not having even enough money to buy new uniforms, he had scoured the city's sporting goods stores, purchasing exactly enough uniforms for home and away games to give each player only one more-or-less matching set. He also made sure that, while on the road, the Cardinals always roomed in the cheapest hotels.

Moreover, only about a dozen of the players from the 1918 season even looked good enough to patch up and repair. The rest he simply refused to re-sign, or traded away.

Rickey's plight, which was only exacerbated by the team's precarious finances, was the Cardinals' simple lack of genuinely competitive talent. In some respects, the two dilemmas were interchangeable. A little cost cutting here and careful budgeting there might enable him to acquire an exceptional player now and then, especially since he also had a reputation as having one of the best eyes in the game for spotting ability and aptitude in a young athlete before he had fully developed his skills. (Sportswriter Jim Murray was later to remark of Rickey, "He could recognize a great player from the window of a moving train.") But one or two good men were simply not enough to build an empire. St. Louis was just too small a baseball market to provide the buckets of black ink necessary to acquire the abundance of talent that the clubs in the big cities could afford.

As a result, the man who would be Napoleon had been put in charge of some of the worst foot soldiers and inept officers currently impersonating professional ballplayers. All the evidence suggested that he was going to meet his Waterloo before his campaign had even begun.

Then one day in the summer of 1919, the thirty-eight-year-old Rickey sat down to dinner with three fellow baseball executives at a restaurant on 110th Street and Broadway in New York. Their conversation sowed the seeds for a vision gradually dawning on Rickey over the course of the next few days that not only saved his career, and the St. Louis Cardinals franchise, but also profoundly changed the way Major League baseball was played.

In fact, during Rickey's career, the game of baseball was to undergo several radical innovations, and some of the most revolutionary were proposed by Rickey. If Babe Ruth, the archetypal soldier on the field, dominated the sport in the twenties with his masterful displays of great power, Rickey was to succeed him in the following decade, though mostly behind the scenes, as baseball's most indomitable and revolutionary figure. His acumen and foresight regarding baseball, viewed both as a business and as a season-long strategic enterprise, were without rival. In one of the most amazing stories in the annals of all sports, Rickey did build his empire, and the most extraordinary team he created was the 1934 St. Louis Cardinals. Perhaps ultimately this is his story.

Yet it has many beginnings and a roster-full of other larger-than-life characters competing for attention. And so, before the tale of Rickey's empire building can be resumed, and his predicament fully appreciated, it is necessary to begin at the beginning, and then weave together all of the other strands in this singularly stirring and quintessentially American epic.

———

Rickey's great-grandfather was David Brown. After he married a young Pennsylvania woman named Hannah Hubbard, she was disowned by her family because Brown drank whiskey. Taking his wife and child, and a cart with a yoke of oxen, he journeyed by raft down the Ohio River to Sciotoville, near Portsmouth, Ohio, in 1819, and built a log cabin there. The couple had eight children. The house was in a settlement called Duck Run.

Jacob Franklin Rickey, called Frank, who preferred temperance to whiskey, was Branch Rickey's father. He married Emily Brown, a descendant of David and Hannah Brown, in 1874. A bull of a man who liked to wrestle as a pastime, Frank Rickey also helped to build the Duck Run Free-Will Baptist Church. Frank and Emily were originally Baptists but gravitated to Methodism. Their second child, Wesley Branch, was born on December 20, 1881, and named in honor of John Wesley, the founder of Methodism. Emily, the oldest, was born in 1875, and Frank came later, in 1888.

The Rickey family lived in a small wood-frame farmhouse just a few feet from a creek called Duck Run, which had given the settlement its name. The farm was five miles distant from Lucasville, the nearest town, with a population of only 150. On Sundays, the family traveled to Lucasville for church, singing hymns along the way. During the school year, the Rickey children walked to and from school in Lucasville each day. Branch and his brother, Frank, also frequently accompanied their father on hunting expeditions, shooting rabbits, squirrels, and quail. When Branch was twelve, the family moved to Lucasville and attended the Flat Woods Methodist Protestant Church, but kept the farm as their source of income.

Rickey first learned the basics of baseball when the children from Duck Run got together four or five times a summer to compete with children from other communities, including Dry Run, its bitter rival. They used rocks for bases, and each team was responsible for bringing a baseball.

A solidly built boy who eventually grew to five feet nine inches, Rickey batted left-handed with fair power. His running speed was about average. As a player, he was also merely average. What he excelled in was enthusiasm for and love of the game, and a keen appreciation of its multiple challenges.

After Rickey finished high school, he was unsure what to do next. The family had no money to send him to college, nor would he have qualified anyway because the Lucasville school was not even certified to grant a high school diploma. Encouraged by his family and friends, he took an examination to become a grammar school teacher, readily passed it, and later found a position in Turkey Creek. Each day he rode his bicycle eighteen miles from home to school, and then back again. In Lucasville, he also began dating a young woman named Jane Moulton, the only woman he ever courted, whose father owned the local general store.

A few years later, Rickey took the entrance examination at Ohio Wesleyan University just outside Columbus, and passed.

Friends helped him to prepare for the test by loaning him books and tutoring him. Like a young Abe Lincoln, he studied all night by kerosene light, after teaching all day. One of the texts he studied was a Latin text, since Latin was a requirement at Ohio Wesleyan. Meanwhile, his courtship of Jane Moulton was not faring well; her family was considered well-to-do, whereas the Rickeys were poor. Other young men courting her had not only money, but an education. Rickey, though, had set his sights on college and on Moulton, and he was not to be deterred. He repeatedly asked her to marry him, and just as often she declined.

In the spring of 1901, after the end of the school term, young Rickey packed his bags and left for Delaware, Ohio, where he took the entrance examination and was accepted into Ohio Wesleyan's preparatory school. He had saved sixty-two dollars from his teacher's salary. Stuffed into his canvas bag were a catcher's mitt and baseball shoes. When not attending classes, he waited on tables at a restaurant to pay for his keep. He also tried out for the school baseball team and qualified as its first-string catcher. Diligent in his studies, he was admitted that fall into the university proper.

As passionate about football as he was about baseball, Rickey also earned a spot that first semester on the football team. He proved to be such an exceptional player that, by season's end, he had become something of a campus hero and was even named to an all-star team representing all Ohio colleges.

As a scholar, though, the backwoods freshman got off to a somewhat uncertain start. As he later told St. Louis sportswriter J. Roy Stockton:

> I thought I was some stuff when the Latin teacher called
> on me the first day. We were starting Virgil, and I sang of
> arms and the man, and went on singing, undaunted by

snickers from classmates. Finally, the professor stopped me. "Mr. Rickey," he challenged, "where in the world did you learn that brand of Latin?"

"From *Grove's Elementary Latin*, sir," I answered. The snickers turned into roars of laughter. How was I to know that the Grove who wrote that book and the Professor Grove in the classroom were one and the same?

Although he had mastered Latin vocabulary and grammar, Rickey had no idea how to pronounce the august sentences in the *Aeneid*.

In the spring of 1902, Rickey was playing his second season with the Ohio Wesleyan baseball team when he and several of his teammates caught the eye of the manager of the Portsmouth Navies, a semipro team that was closely monitored by professional scouts. The college did not prohibit students from playing semipro ball for money, and Rickey accepted the offer to play for the Navies for twenty-five dollars a week. In the fall, he was back in school, and once again playing halfback for the football team.

Then disaster struck. A faculty adviser for student athletes informed them that Ohio Wesleyan had joined the Ohio Conference of Colleges. All student athletes were required to sign a form attesting that they had never dishonored their amateur standing by playing for money. Rickey, unable to sign the form in good conscience, resigned from the team. Yet the story of his honesty soon swept the campus and earned him even more accolades. Semipro and even professional football teams heard the tale and came calling. Rickey's exclusion from college athletics seemed to be working in his favor. A team from Shelby, Ohio, a pioneer pro football franchise and one of the forebears of the National Football League, signed him up at a salary of a hundred dollars a game.

Yet misfortune continued to plague him. After only a few games, Rickey suffered a broken leg. In fact, though, the setback turned out to be yet another instance of good luck following upon bad. The management had become so impressed by the young athlete's analytical skills that he was immediately invited to become the team's coach. Not only did he accept, but that spring he was also asked to coach Ohio Wesleyan's baseball team. With the salaries he earned from his two coaching jobs, he was able to finish the school year.

A decisive moment in Rickey's life, and a foreshadowing of his decision in 1947 to integrate Major League baseball by signing the young Jackie Robinson to the Brooklyn Dodgers, occurred during the college baseball team's first practice session that spring. Charles Thomas, a young black student, showed up during tryouts. Some of the players murmured in protest, but Rickey was adamant that he be given a chance. Thomas not only made the team but also was eventually accepted by his teammates. All went well until the Ohio Wesleyan team traveled to South Bend, Indiana, for a baseball game with Notre Dame. Though the other players were allowed to register, the hotel desk clerk told Thomas, "We don't allow Negroes here." Notre Dame University itself did not object to Thomas's presence on the ball field.

Rickey consulted with the hotel manager and asked whether Thomas could stay with him in his own room. Reluctantly, the manager agreed. Up in the room, Thomas tearfully rubbed his hands furiously, saying, "If they were only white. If they were only white."

In the early years of the twentieth century, many ballplayers lived an almost nonstop itinerant existence, and Branch Rickey was no exception. In the summer of 1903, he signed on as a catcher with a minor league team in Dallas. The following year, he graduated from Ohio Wesleyan. In 1905, the St. Louis

Browns signed him up, and he caught for them that year and the next. Then, in the fall of 1906, Rickey returned to Ohio Wesleyan University to coach the football team. That same year, he finally succeeded in marrying Jane Moulton, the woman of his dreams. In the summer of 1907, he was crouching behind the plate for the New York Highlanders, who later became the New York Yankees. In a game against the Washington Nationals—later the Senators—he set a dubious record by allowing the Nationals to steal thirteen bases against him in a nine-inning game.

One May evening in 1908, Rickey happened upon a speaker standing in front of a railroad depot in Delaware, Ohio, who was giving an antitemperance speech. As a devout Methodist, Rickey was profoundly affected by two issues that would continue to play a major part in his life: the evils of alcohol and racial intolerance. Already, the Methodist lecture circuit featured speakers, strongly influenced by the evangelical fervor of British Methodism, who were denouncing the mistreatment of black Americans. Other injustices that weighed heavily on the Methodist conscience were child labor and the lack of a living wage for working people.

After listening to the speaker at the depot for a few minutes, Rickey gathered a small crowd around him and spontaneously launched into a harangue about the menace posed by liquor. The response was enthusiastic. A few days later, he received an invitation from the Anti-Saloon League to give a lecture in Chillicothe, Ohio, for ten dollars plus expenses. He accepted, and again met with a rousing reception; and for the rest of the summer, he and Jane roamed the state, stopping regularly at small towns, where Rickey preached against alcohol and polished his ability to parry hecklers. In the fall, he worked on the

William Howard Taft for President Committee, while also attending night classes at Ohio State and running the university's athletic program.

Early in 1909, Rickey's health visibly began to fail. He always looked haggard, was racked by a spasmodic cough, had lost a significant amount of weight, and felt constantly fatigued. He was also often kept awake by night sweats. After he began coughing up blood, Jane Rickey insisted that he consult a doctor—who, in the event, grimly informed Rickey that he had contracted tuberculosis.

With the help of a Methodist bishop, Rickey and his wife immediately traveled to the famed Trudeau Sanatorium in Saranac Lake, New York, for treatment. The only known "cure" at the time was complete rest and exposure to dry, clean air. Throughout the remainder of the year, he and Jane spent their days taking long walks, picnicking, playing bridge, and doing nothing that required exertion. To gain weight, Rickey also reluctantly followed doctor's orders and drank beer with his meals. By autumn, his health had returned, tests revealed that his lungs showed no sign of tuberculin, and he was discharged.

Back in Lucasville, Rickey took stock of his life. He was twenty-seven, with two hundred dollars in savings. He was a recovered consumptive, and he was without a job. After reviewing his options, he and Jane decided that he should enter law school, since the legal profession would provide him with stable employment. Jane was to remain in Lucasville, looking after their young children. Rickey moved to Ann Arbor, Michigan, and entered the University of Michigan Law School.

Rickey managed to complete the three-year course in two years. Yet the lure of athletics proved irresistible. Though his health and age now prevented him from playing either football or baseball, he coached the university's Wolverines baseball team during this period. A young man named George Sisler was both a pitcher and a phenomenal hitter on that team, and under Rickey's guidance he was to blossom into one of baseball's greatest players.

After graduating, Rickey opened a law office in Boise, Idaho, but the venture proved a failure and he returned to Michigan. In 1913, he was hired as the executive assistant to Robert Lee Hedges, owner of the St. Louis Browns. It was during this period that his legendary gift for recognizing talent, as well as his ruthless aptitude as a businessman, began to mature. Sisler was by now playing semipro ball, having signed a contract at age seventeen, while still underage. A year later he repudiated that contract in order to preserve his college eligibility. The Pittsburgh Pirates had acquired his contract, but Sisler signed with the Browns in order to play for his former college coach, Branch Rickey. The National Commission, the sport's highest tribunal before the establishment of a baseball commissioner, ruled that Sisler was the Browns' property because he had been underage when he signed his semipro contract. Late in the 1913 season, Rickey also became the team's manager for the final twelve games of the season, and he remained in that post for the next two full seasons as well. But the quality of the players was poor, and Rickey proved to be no better as a tactician than he had been as a player. In both years, the Browns finished under .500.

———

Mrs. Helene Hathaway Robison Britton was a striking, wealthy woman who lived on Lindell Boulevard, popularly known in St. Louis as Millionaires' Row, in a mansion that faced directly on Forest Park, the setting in 1904 of the World's Fair, and now a 1,371-acre public park. A well-known society hostess who always dressed in the height of fashion, she was also a militant advocate of women's right to vote. In 1914 she inherited the St. Louis Cardinals from her uncle Stanley Robison. Club officials called her Mrs. B., and sometimes Lady Bee. Mrs. B. installed her husband, Schuyler Britton, as president of the team, but also took an active interest in its affairs. Schuyler, with Lady Bee's blessing, named Miller Huggins, a former second baseman with the Cincinnati Reds who had joined the Cardinals in 1910, as the new player-manager. Though the Cardinals were never a profitable franchise, it did leap, in 1914, from last place, where it had finished the previous year, to third—the highest standing that any St. Louis franchise in the National League had achieved since the 1876 club finished second. In Mrs. B.'s first year as owner of the Cardinals, the team actually made a profit, and she was delighted. The honeymoon was a brief one. The following season, the Cardinals again sank back into the second division.

In 1914, the year Mrs. B. inherited the Cardinals, St. Louis also became the scene of one of professional baseball's turf wars when an independent new league, called the Federal, was created to compete with the American and National Leagues. With its relatively small metropolitan-area population, compared to such cities as New York, Chicago, Philadelphia, and Detroit, St. Louis could scarcely support the two baseball teams it already had. The new team was called the St. Louis Terriers, or more colloquially the Sloufeds, and its backers were two wealthy St. Louisans, Otto Stifel, a brewer, and Philip DeCatesby Ball, who had made his fortune from ice machines sold to breweries and to such companies as Armour and Swift for their meatpacking plants. Born poor, he was a rag-to-riches millionaire with an aggressive, obnoxious personality. After the Federal League collapsed, Ball purchased the Browns in 1916 from Hedges, folded the two teams into one, and moved the franchise to an antiquated ballpark in North St. Louis called Sportsman's Park.

Soon after he acquired the Browns, Ball appeared in the team's offices and asked to see Rickey. When Rickey appeared, he said, "I am Mr. Rickey, sir. Branch Rickey, field manager and general manager of the Browns. And you, sir, who are you?"

"So you're the goddamned prohibitionist," Ball sneered. "I'm Ball."

Ball had wanted to install Fielder Jones, formerly with the Chicago White Sox, as his new manager and planned to dismiss Rickey. But several of Ball's knowledgeable American League friends persuaded him to retain Rickey, whom they described as a valuable asset who had, after all, brought George Sisler to the Browns in 1915. Hedges had also provided Rickey, his protégé, with a contract for the 1916 season, and Ball had no choice but to honor it. As they faced one another, Ball bluntly informed the man he was saddled with, "Rickey, you're out as manager and Jones is in. You'll be my business manager."

He then immediately proceeded to demand to hear from Rickey what plans he, as the new business manager, had in mind for the team. Flummoxed, Rickey could only stutter a few meaningless phrases. Impatiently, Ball finally shouted, "Well, goddamnit, do it. You're the boss. You're the boss." Grabbing his hat and coat, he walked out of the office.

Not only had Ball left Rickey speechless, but the two men had also taken an instant dislike to one another. According to Rickey's biographer, Murray Polner, "Rickey's endless talk and large vocabulary made [Ball] uncomfortable. Rickey was, in turn, uncomfortable with Ball's crudeness; he considered Ball uncouth and, in matters of baseball, virtually illiterate."

Around this same time, the marriage between Schuyler and Helene Britton was foundering. After they were divorced, Mrs. B. succeeded him as president of the Cardinals. By 1916, the Cardinals were playing to almost empty bleachers. Late that year, she summoned James C. Jones, her legal adviser, and manager Huggins to her mansion. With America's entry into the war in Europe almost a certainty, and the divorce having taken a personal toll, Mrs. B. announced that she wanted to sell the club. The Cardinals had performed unremarkably for most of her stewardship, and she had lost interest in owning the team.

That season, the St. Louis Cardinals ended up in last place and declared bankruptcy. A gleeful Ball declared that such a fate could never befall the Browns.

Mrs. Britton was asking $375,000 for the franchise, with a down payment of $75,000. Though it was a bargain price, the city's wealthy individuals were skittish about investing such a large sum of money in a lackluster club at such an uncertain time. When no buyer came forward, rumors began circulating that Mrs. Britton might sell the Cardinals to another city. To prevent this blow to civic pride, the Mercantile Club, whose membership consisted of local merchants, held a gala dinner to raise enough capital to purchase the team, with shares priced at $25 apiece. An insurance executive came up with the idea of the Knot Hole Gang. Each investor who bought $50 worth of stock also received one Knot Hole ticket, good for one kid during the season. An entire section of bleachers was to be set aside for the Knot Hole Gang. The sales campaign included figures on juvenile delinquency, a stirring appeal to the businessmen's sense of civic duty in keeping troubled young boys off the streets, and a plan for each investor to "adopt" a boy through a network of cooperating agencies, including the YMCA, the Juvenile Court, and other organizations. Although the drive netted only $50,000, Mrs. Britton agreed to sell the team to the local businessmen at the reduced down payment.

Among the most urgent orders of business for the new ownership was to find a club president. The group was satisfied with Huggins as manager, and the Knot Hole Gang could be depended on as a steady source of income. But none of the officers knew anything about baseball from the inside. Jones, the lawyer who had negotiated on behalf of Mrs. Britton, obligingly assembled seven local sportswriters and editors in his office and asked each of them to write down on a slip of paper the name of an individual he would recommend as a candidate for the job. After he passed around the hat, he read the names—or name, rather, for all seven had written the same one: Branch Rickey, the business manager of the St. Louis Browns.

When Jones approached Rickey and invited him to take over the presidency of the Cardinals, the overjoyed Rickey immediately accepted. According to Rickey, he then informed Ball of the offer, and the Browns owner instantly approved of the new arrangement and wished Rickey well. But after discussing the matter with one of his advisers, Ball changed his mind. Rickey took the job with the Cardinals, Ball sued him, and Rickey countersued. The matter was eventually settled in the courts, though not to Ball's liking, and Rickey began his long association with the Cardinals and the National League. "It was a historic moment," baseball historian Frederick Lieb has noted, for no man in that era of baseball, "with the possible exception of Judge Landis and Babe Ruth, has left so deep an impress on the game as Branch Rickey."

Even though the Browns were the laughingstock of baseball, consistently outlosing even the Washington Senators, connoisseurs of the great American game—sports journalists, team owners, managers, and players—recognized that their losing ways had not been the fault of their industrious business manager. Even back then, burdened with an inept ball club that, with almost diabolical perversity, thwarted his genius at every turn, Branch Rickey was regarded by almost everybody—including, finally, Ball himself—as one of the most brilliant minds in baseball.

When Rickey took over as president and general manager of the Cardinals, Huggins was still field manager. A graduate of the University of Cincinnati Law School, he claimed that Mrs.

Britton had promised him and his partner, yeast magnate Julius Fleischmann of Cincinnati, an opportunity to buy the team. After learning that Mrs. B. had sold the team to a syndicate instead, the disgruntled Huggins remained with the Cardinals only one year, leading them to third place, and then took a job as manager of the New York Yankees. In 1918, Rickey hired Jack Hendricks as his replacement, and that season the Cardinals returned to the cellar.

Rickey's chief scout was Charley Barrett. Like Rickey, Barrett had a well-deserved reputation for recognizing promising young players. All too often, though, when a scout for another team heard that Barrett was interested in signing someone up, a wealthier club suddenly intervened with a higher offer. With bitter frequency, Barrett returned from his bargain-hunting expeditions empty-handed.

Further compounding the Cardinals' tribulations was the very nature of the minor league system. Often, when a Major League club optioned a player, it sent him to a minor league team, where theoretically he could mature and develop his talent until he was ready for prime time. In reality, that practice also amounted to a free loan of a player to a club that was not affiliated with the lending Major League team. Frequently, neither the proprietary team nor the player benefited from the time he spent at some baseball boot camp in the boondocks. Overzealous minor league managers often overworked pitchers and ignored the other players. Also these minor league teams earned a significant portion of their profit by selling players they had already acquired on their own, and the teams concentrated on developing them at the expense of those merely on loan.

———————

Then came that day in the summer of 1917 when Rickey sat down to dinner with three other baseball executives at a restaurant on Upper Broadway in Manhattan. The man who had invited Rickey to dinner was Charles A. Stoneham, the new owner of the New York Giants, and he had brought with him his manager, John McGraw, and a Giants stockholder named Francis C. McQuade.

Stoneham knew that the Cardinals organization was all but bankrupt, and in fact $150,000 in debt. He had come to make a deal that, in his opinion, would easily solve Rickey's problem.

It so happened that, back in 1915, before Rickey had joined the Cardinals organization, it had acquired an eighteen-year-old phenomenon from the Texas-Oklahoma League named Rogers Hornsby. A surly loner who did not drink, smoke, or even watch movies because he thought that might damage his eyesight, Hornsby had batted .313 in his first season in the Major Leagues, in 1916, and the next year hit .327, the second highest in the National League.

Stoneham offered to buy Hornsby for $150,000—the exact amount of the Cardinals' debt. Rickey, though, as Peter Golenbock has observed, "had seen what happened to teams that had sold their best players for cash. Connie Mack had sold his stars following the 1914 season and was doomed to years in the second division. Meanwhile, Boston [Red Sox] and Chicago [White Sox], the teams that had paid him the money for Eddie Collins, Jack Barry, and Herb Penock, had become powerhouses." Similarly, after the Boston Red Sox sold off their stars to New York, the Yankees had begun their rise to dominance.

Rickey declined the offer.

"Your board of directors will hang you for betraying their trust," Stoneham chastised him. "You must have a price. What is it?"

"Half a million dollars," Rickey replied.

When Stoneham upped his offer to $200,000, Rickey turned it down as well. Eventually, the Giants owner raised his bid to

$300,000, but the Cardinals general manager still said no. Though he worried that the board of directors might take a dim view of his refusal to trade Hornsby for such a considerable amount of money, Rickey knew that his star shortstop was literally invaluable. Hornsby was indispensable if the Cardinals were ever to become a pennant contender and a World Series champion. Without Hornsby, the team was doomed to be mired in mediocrity, and that could only mean it would wallow in debt and the second division indefinitely. Nobody wanted to pay good money to watch a bad team.

The very next afternoon, though, the unforeseen happened—and it was both a near tragedy and a blessing. After collecting a grounder during that day's game, Cardinals shortstop Johnny Lavan threw to second without looking, hit Hornsby in the head, and knocked him out cold.

Hornsby recovered, and Rickey began to ponder. He realized, first of all, just how vulnerable the Cardinals were, even with a star like Hornsby in their ranks. Second, he factored into his problem the likely reality that the St. Louis Cardinals would never have the deep pockets of a team such as the New York Giants, who were able to buy proven talent that other franchises could seldom afford. At the same time, Rickey was determined not to follow the example of other debt-ridden teams and sell off its best talent simply to play another day. Given the nature of his seemingly insoluble dilemma, he began to wonder whether there was not some other way the Cardinals could prosper as a business and excel as a baseball team.

The impossible dream that came to the Cardinals general manager shortly after his dinner with Stoneham, McGraw, and McQuade was both spectacularly simple and brilliantly audacious: "a chain of minor league teams of various classifications—a kindergarten, grade school, preparatory school, and a university of baseball—which eventually would graduate shin-

and cleaned. He even persuaded his parents to take out a mort-
gage on their farm and invest five thousand dollars in the Cardinals. His only assistant was a young man named Bill DeWitt,
who was later to become general manager and minority owner
of the St. Louis Browns. To save the cost of a salary for a field
manager, Rickey took on that position in addition to his duties
as general manager. Rickey now owned two hundred shares in
the St. Louis Cardinals, and he was thrilled when he heard that
a young automobile dealer named Sam Breadon had purchased
a similar number of shares. Then, in January 1920, Breadon
took control of the team. Like Rickey, he had a dream that the
St. Louis Cardinals could some day be more than just another
also-ran midwestern ball club.

Born on July 26, 1876, Breadon was the son of a Scottish immigrant father who had worked as a drayman and died of over-
work while still in his forties. His mother was Irish. Many years
later, among the photographs hanging on the walls of Breadon's
office of baseball stars, managers, and friends, was a group shot
of a football team, circa 1891, showing young Breadon wearing
the shoulder pads of a football player for a YMCA team in New
York. At the turn of the century, Breadon joined thousands of
others who were migrating westward in search of a better life,
and on arriving in St. Louis in 1902 he took a job at a mechanic's
shop. When his employer discovered that Breadon was plotting
to open his own garage, he fired him, forcing Breadon to live on
a food budget of fifteen cents a day.

Breadon's lucky break came during the St. Louis World's
Fair of 1904, when he got the idea of selling popcorn to visitors.
After obtaining credit, he purchased three thousand packages
of popcorn, hired a team of boys to hawk them, and wound up
with a profit of thirty-five dollars. Breadon was to call that time
the turning point in his life, because he had not given up in the
face of despair. Later he sold White Steamer automobiles with

a partner, Marion Lambert of the pharmaceutical company, and then bought a Ford dealership, the city's first. In due course, he also opened up one of the largest Pierce-Arrow dealerships in the country, based in the city's Central West End. A supersalesman, he reputedly sold 280 of the luxury motorcars in one year alone, at a cost of five thousand dollars and up each.

In 1917, Breadon became one of the original investors who purchased the St. Louis Cardinals from Mrs. Britton, buying eighty shares for two thousand dollars. Over the next few years, he continued to buy stock until he had financial control of the team. In January 1920, after putting another five thousand dollars into the club, he joined the board of directors and also took over Rickey's duties as president. Rickey, who had been president, became vice president. This new arrangement allowed Rickey to turn his full attention to managing the team.

Breadon was already a millionaire several times over when he and Rickey first encountered one another. A convivial man, Breadon was quickly dubbed "Singing Sam" by sportswriters, who noted his fondness for breaking into song at parties. Though Rickey and Breadon seldom socialized, the new owner "was in awe of Rickey's knowledge of the game," as Polner observed, "precisely the attribute he so sorely lacked."

Among Rickey's innovations were blackboard talks, pits where players could practice sliding, and plays to catch a runner off base. He was also a master statistician and kept his figures and other data in a large notebook in the dugout. He knew by how many feet each opposing batter had been thrown out at first on a grounder, and how far each pitcher's different kinds of pitches had been hit. He was able to predict, at least theoretically, how any given batter would perform against any given pitcher.

Breadon and Rickey had a few disagreements, most of them centered on Breadon's stinginess toward players when it came time to determine salaries. Yet he could also be generous, particularly toward Rickey, who was soon earning fifteen thousand dollars a year. Breadon also gave Rickey a free rein in developing the baseball talent that only a man with his long experience and unique aptitude could. He also did not try to keep his general manager behind closed doors, but allowed him to speak openly with reporters, both about baseball and about anything else on his mind. Once the outspoken Rickey was even offered seven thousand dollars by promoters to debate in public the antiprohibition lawyer Clarence Darrow, who had humiliated William Jennings Bryan in the famous Scopes "monkey trial." Rickey, the passionate, nonimbibing Methodist, was tempted to take up the challenge, but his wife, Jane, talked him out of it, telling him frankly that he would almost certainly lose.

During this period, in the early 1920s, Rickey also created the team's familiar logo of a pair of redbirds. While attending a dinner at a Presbyterian church hall in Ferguson, a St. Louis suburb, he had taken close notice of red paper cutouts of cardinals set up as decorations on the white tablecloths. Later he approached Edward H. Schmidt, a commercial artist, and asked him to design the logo: two cardinals perched opposite one another on a bat.

Breadon also provided Rickey with the funds to begin assembling a championship team when he cleverly persuaded Phil Ball, owner of the St. Louis Browns, to rent out Sportsman's Park to the Cardinals, for the bargain price of $20,000 per year, when the Browns were on the road. After the lease was signed, Breadon then sold the dilapidated Federal Park, a firetrap at Vandeventer Avenue and Natural Bridge Road where the Cardinals had been playing, to the city for $200,000, and another part of the plot to a streetcar company for $75,000. Finally, Rickey had the wherewithal to pursue his vision of a farm system for the St. Louis Cardinals.

As the idea gradually became known, sportswriters, team owners, ballplayers, and fans responded at first with derision, ridiculing the scheme as "chain-store baseball" or "Rickey's plantation," the latter clearly implying that players were no different from slaves. Some caricaturists drew sketches of young ballplayers wearing prison stripes and fettered with a ball and chain.

Yet Rickey was not dissuaded. Breadon shared Rickey's dream of building a baseball farm system for one simple reason: It would protect the team from poaching by wealthier clubs. The two men took their first step in February 1921, when the Cardinals purchased half the stock of a minor league team in Syracuse, New York, that played in the International League. Finally, the St. Louis club had a minor league team of its very own, where it could dispatch promising young talent for development.

In October of that year, the board of directors allocated an additional twenty-five thousand dollars for Breadon and Rickey to use at their discretion to purchase either players or another minor league holding. Around the same time, the pair discovered that owning only half of a minor league ball club had its own peculiar set of problems. A case in point involved Jim Bottomley, a prospect from Illinois who had been sent to Syracuse for grooming. When other Major League teams offered the Syracuse president good money for Bottomley, he wanted to accept. But Rickey, who had discovered Bottomley, demanded that the player be returned to the Cardinals—for significantly less money than other teams were tendering. The transaction left the Syracuse president considerably disgruntled.

That incident, and a somewhat similar one involving a partly owned minor league Houston team in the Texas League, now prompted Rickey and Breadon to purchase the other half of the Syracuse stock. After secretly increasing their holdings of the Houston team to 90 percent, the two men took control of that team as well.

In 1923, when Breadon made his final payment to Mrs. Britton, the Cardinals were out of debt, and by 1925 the franchise had acquired two other farm clubs—one in Sioux City, Iowa, and the other in Fort Smith, Arkansas.

This gradual acquisition of farm clubs and homegrown talent, along with shrewd trading by Rickey, had begun to pay off as early as 1922, when the Cardinals finished in the black. With the Browns providing little competition for the hearts of St. Louis fans, the Cardinals soon became the undisputed hometown favorites, drawing up to a half million spectators a year. Despite their popularity, however, they continued to flounder in the second division and were frequently in last place. Finally, on May 30, 1925, with the Cardinals stuck in the cellar, Breadon decided something had to be done. Taking a train to Pittsburgh, where the team was playing, he summoned Rickey to his room in the Hotel Schenley and told him that he was being dismissed as manager of the team. The new Cardinals manager, as of right then, was Rogers Hornsby.

In 1920, Hornsby had moved from shortstop to second base and then gone on to win six straight batting titles, beginning with a .370 average. Over the next five years he posted averages of .397, .401, .384, .424, and .403. Despite his mighty presence in the lineup, however, the Cardinals had still not been able to win a pennant.

When Rickey heard that he had been replaced as field manager, he protested to Breadon, "You can't do this to me, Sam. You're ruining me."

"I'm doing you the greatest favor one man ever did for another," Breadon calmly replied, explaining that he was promoting Rickey to the front office, where his real genius lay. Breadon knew his man. As a strategist and appraiser of talent, Rickey was literally without equal, but there were others who surpassed him in managerial ability on the field.

Later that morning, Hornsby was sitting in the hotel lobby when Rickey, looking quite dejected, approached and said he had just been fired and that Hornsby was the new field manager.

"Do you want the job?" Rickey asked his star player. Hornsby, only twenty-nine, shook his head to indicate that he did not.

"Good, then," Rickey prodded. "Then would you go upstairs to his room and tell Breadon to give me another chance?"

"I'll do my best," Hornsby said, and went off.

Breadon, when he heard Hornsby ask that Rickey be given a second chance, heatedly replied, "I won't have any goddamned Sunday School teacher running my team. You're going to run it!"

"No, I'm not," Hornsby adamantly replied.

When he repeated his conversation with Breadon to Rickey, the Cardinals ex-manager exploded in anger, saying, "Judas Priest! The man is stabbing me in the back."

Ultimately, Rickey agreed to the promotion—which he viewed as a demotion—only on condition that Breadon buy out his company stock, and he insisted on working as a salaried administrator only. If Rickey had held onto his holdings, his personal wealth in the years to come would have been considerably greater. He was still nurturing his resentment when an offer came from Northwestern University in Chicago to become its athletic director. He was greatly tempted to accept the offer, but his fifth and sixth children were still quite young, and the ever-sensible Jane Rickey talked him out of it.

Ultimately, Rickey was to become the highest-paid figure in baseball, on or off the field. By 1922, his annual salary plus bonus came to about $100,000. Over the next five-year contract period, that amount increased to $150,000, then soared to $250,000 for the 1932–1937 period. Before he departed for the Brooklyn Dodgers, his salary spiked at $350,000. To Rickey's and Breadon's credit, they also eventually raised the salaries of players as revenues increased. In time, during Rickey's stewardship, the Cardinals' payroll ranked second highest in the Major Leagues, after that of Connie Mack's Philadelphia Athletics.

After the repeal of prohibition in 1933, part of Rickey's salary was paid for from broadcasting contracts with breweries, from whiskey advertisements in Sportsman's Park, and from the sale of beer at home games. Breadon approved of and promoted that revenue stream, and Rickey opposed it, but during the hard times of the Depression Rickey had little chance of success. As the country gradually recovered its economic footing, though, the money that the Cardinals earned from such sources was to play a major role in Rickey's decision to leave the team.

2

ME 'N' PAUL

Albert Monroe Dean was born in the Ozark mountains of Missouri, spent his adolescent years in Oklahoma, and as a young man went to work in the sawmills of the Arkansas Ozarks near the town of Lucas. He was thirty-two years old when he met twenty-four-year-old Alma Nelson. They were married in 1904.

Monroe and Alma Dean were sharecroppers, owning no land of their own and living on a rent-free farm in return for tending the crops of their landlady, Mrs. Hattie Blair, and receiving a percentage of the profits. Alma and Monroe's first two children, Charles and Sarah May, died in infancy. Elmer was born in 1908, Jay Hanna on January 16, 1910, and Paul on August 15, 1913. All three of the surviving children were born in Mrs. Blair's house in Lucas. Jay Hanna was named after the Wall Street financier Jay Gould and Mark Hanna, a flamboyant political figure from the William McKinley era, as if, though Alma and Monroe could not give their son money, they could give him promise and personality.

In 1916, Jay entered the Pinelog School on Sand Ridge Mountain, Arkansas, and attended the first and second grades. His mother's illness interrupted his schooling; she had contracted tuberculosis and was soon so bedridden that she could no longer carry out her household chores. Alma died in March 1917, when Jay was seven and Paul four, and she was buried in the Pinelog cemetery near the school.

Sometime before 1920, Monroe remarried. His new wife was a widow, Cora Parham, and she had three children: Herman, Claude, and Carol. The family moved to Chickalah, Arkansas, forty-five miles to the east, at the southern end of the Ozark National Forest, and survived mostly by sharecropping cotton.

In 1925, the Deans were on the move again, resettling in Spaulding, Oklahoma, about two hundred miles due west. Jay and Paul attended school sporadically. The Deans' migratory existence was mostly to blame. During harvest time, Monroe and his family traveled as far south as the cotton fields of Mississippi, looking for work. In later life, Jay—then known to the world as Dizzy Dean—was to recall, "I never knew anyone who had it as tough as my father did."

Dizzy's own childhood was no less brutal. He first joined his father in the cotton fields when he was only four. By age ten, he was picking up to five hundred pounds a day—the work of a grown man—and his formal education all but ceased. "If I had finished the second grade in school," Dizzy once said, "I would have went a year longer than my old man." Some newspaper profiles or biographies claim that he ultimately made it as far as the fourth grade, despite frequent absences from class. According to one often-repeated and somewhat romanticized account of Dean's early life, he always managed to show up at school at least on Fridays, when he and the other children were divided into teams and played a game of baseball. Still other sources say that Dean's last year of school was the sixth grade in a one-room clapboard elementary school in Chickalah. In later years, Dean recalled how, when he was twelve, and Paul nine, the two of them also once helped the Spaulding, Oklahoma, high school team defeat Oklahoma City Teachers' College, with Dizzy pitching and Paul hitting in the winning run.

At some point in his early youth, Jay Hanna changed his name to Jerome Herman. As with his place and date of birth, and his elementary education, Dean himself, various relatives, and assorted biographers and journalists provided numerous accounts of when and why he changed his name, and few agree. Some biographies also report that, at times, Jerome called himself Jay Hanner. That variation may perhaps have been a result of sportswriters misunderstanding Dizzy's drawling pronunciation of *Hanna*. The most commonly accepted account of why Jay Hanna changed his name is that Jerome Herman was the name of a boyhood friend who had died. Jay allegedly asked his father if he could take his deceased friend's name as his own to please the dead youth's grieving mother, so that she might at least have a surrogate son. Monroe consented, though it took some getting used to.

What all of the stories of Dean's childhood tacitly agree on is that cotton picking and the game of baseball, played on countless sandlots in the South and Southwest, provided Jerome Herman Dean with the discipline, self-reliance, and training for life's future demands every bit as much as generations of privileged young Englishmen received, under entirely different circumstances, on the playing fields of Eton. With Paul at shortstop and Elmer in the outfield, the young Jerome soon earned a reputation as a local phenomenon wherever he went.

Dizzy also had an uncle, the Reverend Bland R. Dean, an itinerant country preacher. "I think I once took up the collection for him after a sermon in a tent," Dizzy Dean later remembered. "Well, anyway, it was either me or Paul. I was always solemn like after listenin' to him. He could make things sound awful real." One day, after being subjected to one of Preacher Dean's fire-and-brimstone sermons, Jerome had to pitch a game. "The Lord he had his arms around me all the time," Dizzy said. "Yes, he did. Like to have choked me, he held me so tight. Whenever I was gonna go wild, he just patted me on the head, and the next guy popped up."

Jerome's two stepbrothers, Herman and Claude, enlisted in the army. One day they tried to persuade Jerome to enlist as well, describing for him the good life that awaited him in the military. The army, they told him, would supply him with three meals a day, his first pair of new shoes, and regular hours. The impulsive Jerome might have joined up if he could, but there was one seemingly insurmountable problem: The army accepted only men who had reached their eighteenth birthday, and he was still years away from being eligible.

In the fall of 1925, Jerome Dean heard about the American and National Leagues for the first time. Until then, baseball had been nothing more than a pastime he had first played as a schoolboy, and now and then indulged in with friends and family when there was no work or they all had a day off. But on that October day he listened to announcer Graham McNamee describe on a crystal radio set the concluding game of the 1925 World Series, when the Pittsburgh Pirates defeated Walter Johnson and the Washington Senators in the rain. Only then did the adolescent Dean begin to understand that baseball was not just a game that men and boys played in the twilight hours after a long day in the fields, but *the* great American pastime— a sport in which the nation's finest athletes competed against one another for amounts of money almost beyond the comprehension of a sharecropper's son from the Ozarks whose only talents were picking cotton and throwing a ball.

The migrant Deans wandered from state to state in two Ford pickup trucks, with Monroe driving one and Elmer, the oldest Dean boy, or a field hand the other. As time and occasion warranted, they stopped to fish or to hunt for rabbits, squirrels, or deer. Though outwardly their vagabond existence might seem, from a century's distance, carefree and gypsylike, their lot was stressful and difficult. Going from county to county, and state to state, looking for work was hard, and picking cotton was hard. The family spent many nights in a bare sharecropper's cabin, and if none was available they slept in an open field.

When there was no work, Monroe and his three sons, and a few other sharecroppers, relaxed by playing a pickup game of baseball as best they could, insofar as they did not possess a bat, a baseball, or a glove. Instead they used the handle of a hoe or a whittled-down tree branch for a bat, and they wrapped strips of tape around an apple core, a hickory nut, a walnut, a rock, or some other object to make some semblance of a baseball. As their passion for the game increased, eventually they invested in a used real baseball. Occasionally, Monroe and his three sons played pickup games with other men and boys for money, usually about fifty cents or a dollar a game. The money they earned, or lost, in this way was the equivalent of a day's wages.

One day in November 1926, Monroe and his three sons were wandering through Texas, not far from San Antonio, during cotton-picking season. Earlier that day, they had cleared a cotton patch. Now they were in search of work at another field that needed picking. Elmer and a fellow field hand were in one jalopy, and Monroe, Jerome, and Paul in the second.

At a railroad crossing, with a freight train heading toward them, the first car crossed the tracks and continued on its way. But the second, carrying Monroe and his two younger sons, waited until the long string of boxcars had rumbled slowly past. When they were able to proceed again, the first car was long gone. The expectation that the pair of vehicles would quickly hook up again was somehow thwarted—perhaps by a turn that the first car took, but that the second did not; or by a misunderstood agreement on where to meet up. In those days, with no money to speak of in anyone's pocket and telephones a rarity, Monroe had little recourse in his frantic attempt to find his missing son. Complicating matters, and adding to the Deans' worry about Elmer's fate, was the fact that the oldest Dean boy was mildly retarded.

Around this same time, while they were simultaneously searching both for Elmer and more work, Monroe and his two sons drove down a dirt road that led past a high wire fence bearing signs that read "U.S. Government Military Reservation—Authorized Persons Only."

Remembering what his stepbrothers, Herman and Claude, had told him about the good life they were living in the army, Jerome Dean now felt inspired by the signs to follow their example. Surely, life in the army was better than picking cotton fourteen hours a day, or driving aimlessly down one dirt road after another, looking for work. Another enticement to the near-destitute Jerome was the nineteen-dollar monthly pay he would receive. Somehow, he persuaded his father to allow him to enlist in the military, and to vouch that he was eighteen—even though he was still a few months' shy of his seventeenth birthday.

After they arrived in San Antonio, Jerome enlisted at Fort Sam Houston. Monroe declared that his son was of age, that he had been born in Holdenville, Oklahoma, and that he had received an elementary school education. The boy signed up under his real name, Jay Hanna. Perhaps Monroe tendered Holdenville as his son's birthplace to ensure that his genuine birth record, confirming his being an underage adolescent, would not be found. In any case, the enlistment officer most likely had no interest in verifying that information; he had a new recruit.

In the army, Private Jay Hanna, serial number RA6233400, was attached to the 3rd Wagon Company of the Quartermaster

Corps and assigned the job of cleaning the stables, since the corps was mostly horse-drawn. He also washed out latrines, peeled potatoes while on KP duty, and slept at night on a bunk bed in the barracks. But he was happy because he had his first pair of new shoes and—another novelty—money in his pocket. His first time out on the qualification range, the boy who had learned to shoot while hunting for food in the Ozarks also won a sharpshooter's badge with a Springfield rifle.

Only after he had been at Fort Sam Houston for some months did Dean learn that enlisted men could play baseball. The athletic fields were a series of interlocking diamonds. One Sunday morning in the spring of 1927, Dean ambled down to one of the ball fields and stood behind the chicken wire backstop to watch a game and see if he could join in. He could not help but admire all the professional equipment: the new bats and balls and the gloves smelling of fresh leather. He had never seen the like.

Dean was invited to try out for the 3rd Wagon team and quickly gained a reputation as a hard-pitching mountain boy who wanted to throw barefoot, though his sergeant insisted that he wear spikes. In the first interleague game, the 3rd Wagon played against the 12th Field Artillery. Its captain was Master Sergeant James K. "Jimmie" Brought. The Fort Sam Houston team that Brought assembled each year in the playoffs usually dominated the army's South and Southwestern Leagues. Dean led the team to a 1-to-0 victory, while hitting a home run to account for the only score. He also allowed only two hits and struck out ten. This was the first real baseball game that Dean had ever played, using a real baseball, a real bat, and a real glove, and wearing an actual uniform with spiked shoes.

The canny Brought soon arranged for Dean to be transferred to the 12th Field Artillery. In August, the transfer came through. At the same time, he was also promoted to private first class. With Dean leading the way that fall, the team won the army's championship playoffs.

Word of the army's unusually gifted pitcher soon leaked out to semiprofessional teams in San Antonio. In the spring of 1928, Dean was approached and asked whether he would pitch a game for one of the teams. The man added that, of course, he would be paid for his services. The offer was perfectly legal. There was no army regulation at the time prohibiting a man on a day pass from earning extra money playing ball. But Brought was outraged anyway because he wanted to save his star player for his own team. Exhibiting the ornery independence that was to get him into so many future difficulties, Dean disobeyed Brought's direct order not to play, got a weekend pass, went to San Antonio, pitched, and won. The next day he pitched again, this time for the 12th Field Artillery, though he surrendered numerous hits and was saved only by his teammates' firepower.

The following Friday, during evening chow in the mess hall, two military policemen appeared and escorted Dean to the guardhouse, where he was locked in a cell. He had planned to ask for another weekend pass and to pitch another game for the San Antonio team on Saturday, and then, as usual, a Sunday game for his army teammates. When he asked why he had been arrested, the MPs said they were acting on orders from Sergeant Brought. On Sunday morning, the sergeant came to fetch his star pitcher, and a disheartened Dean again asked why he had been so mistreated, when he had never stinted in his efforts for the Brought team.

"Just call it a rap on the knuckles to teach you a lesson, like you was in school," Brought said, smiling. "I want you in condition to pitch your best on Sundays, and if this is how I gotta keep you from pitching in town, then it's the way it's going to be."

"I learned my lesson," Dean replied, pretending to be remorseful, while secretly wondering how to outwit Brought.

"And just to show you there's no hard feelings," he continued, "I'm gonna pitch extra good today."

"Your usual will do," Brought said.

True to his promise, Dean pitched a two-hit shutout over the Medical Section, striking out eleven and batting in two runs as he led the team to a 4-to-0 victory. Afterward, as Dean was changing back into his army fatigues, Brought came over and explained why he had been so hard on him.

"You see, kid, there was a Major League scout out there today. A scout from the St. Louis Cardinals. He came all the way down here just to see you pitch."

Brought said that the man was a "bird dog," or scout's scout, who sometimes recommended promising players to the man responsible for finding new baseball talent.

"So I told this scout—I told him you're the clumsiest kid I ever seen going into a windup, but you can throw hard and you got a good curve." After a pause, Brought added, "I also told him you were the dizziest kid I ever had in my outfit."

"Me? Dizzy?" Dean asked, with a grin.

"Yeah, you," Brought replied. "Dizzy."

The nickname stuck. At first, Dean's teammates had called him "Foggy," because his favorite pitch was the "fogger," a fastball he claimed was so fast that most batters could not even see it—just the wisp of fog it left in its wake. In many games, he threw only fastballs. But Brought's more appropriate nickname soon prevailed, and in time everybody was calling the young, hard-throwing Private Dean "Dizzy."

———

Sam Breadon's astute move to replace Branch Rickey as manager of the St. Louis Cardinals had reaped both immediate and long-term benefits for the team. Even though it had finished fourth in 1925, Rogers Hornsby, who had finally accepted the job of player-manager, won the Most Valuable Player award. The following year, he took the manpower that Rickey had recruited and turned it into a pennant winner—and then into world champions when the Cardinals defeated the New York Yankees in the World Series in seven games.

The Cardinals were able to defeat the Yankees in that memorable Series, thanks to the pitching arm of the great Grover Cleveland Alexander. Joe McCarthy, a career minor leaguer, had recently taken over the Chicago Cubs, and had run out of patience with Alexander, who often showed up drunk for a game. Alexander similarly held the new Cubs manager in low regard. Rickey was out of town when Alexander was placed on waivers, and Breadon, with Hornsby's blessing, instantly moved to sign him up.

The 1926 World Series that pitted St. Louis against New York featured such veteran Bronx Bombers as Babe Ruth and Bob Meusel, and such up-and-coming stars as Lou Gehrig, Leo Durocher, and Tony Lazzeri. Alexander repaid Hornsby's confidence by winning the second and sixth games. Then, in the climactic seventh game, Alexander relieved Jesse Haines in the seventh inning with the bases loaded, two out, and the Cardinals hanging onto a 3-to-2 lead. He struck out Lazzeri, then held the lead, and the Cardinals won the Series, though it was never known whether Alexander pitched that game drunk, hungover, or sober.

When the Cardinals won their first pennant, after thirty-eight years, they also demonstrated the soundness of the Breadon-Rickey farm system. Not a man on the team cost more than ten thousand dollars—tangible proof, in Stockton's words, "that players could be picked green, trained, polished, and developed into valuable major leaguers." Of the twenty-five players on the team, fifteen had spent their entire baseball career with the Cardinals organization.

Despite the Cardinals' victory march under Hornsby, the relationship between Breadon and his cantankerous new manager was tenuous. Late in the season, during the drive to the pennant, Hornsby had asked the Cardinals president to cancel an exhibition game so that his exhausted players could have an extra day of rest. Feeling bound to honor a contract he had made, Breadon visited Hornsby in the clubhouse and explained that he had to refuse the request.

"You're money hungry," the furious Hornsby shouted. "Get the hell out of here."

Even after the Cardinals won the Series, the relationship between owner and manager did not improve. Hornsby demanded a three-year contract calling for a salary of fifty thousand dollars a year. Breadon countered with a one-year contract for that amount, but in fact really wanted to trade him. "When Rickey tried to mediate," according to Polner, "Breadon told him he could never forget nor forgive the public humiliation of Hornsby's throwing him out of the clubhouse last season in full view of the players."

When Hornsby declined the one-year offer, the equally hard-nosed Breadon promptly traded him to the New York Giants in exchange for second baseman Frank Frisch and pitcher Jimmy Ring. The trade was the biggest and most flamboyant that the world of baseball had ever seen, and it left just about everybody—including the principals—stunned.

Understandably, both local sportswriters and Cardinal fans were outraged that Breadon and Rickey had traded away, with almost tragic willfulness, the great Rajah. But there were two factors involved that neither the fans nor the sports scribes fully understood. First, though Rickey was still smarting at being replaced as manager by Hornsby, he was above all the consummate professional who knew that his first duty was to the team, and that his own self-interest was secondary. The problem with

Hornsby lay not so much in his salary demands as in what he would do with so much money, for his gambling habits had become an increasing irritant and might easily lead to an embarrassment for the Cardinals, or worse. The 1919 Black Sox gambling scandal was, after all, still in the recent past.

Second, Rickey sensed an opportunity to make what would be the greatest trade of his career. As a fielder, Frisch was nearly peerless. In an era when switch-hitters were few, he could hit from both the left and the right sides of the plate with considerable power. He was also a fleet runner and an accomplished base stealer. It seemed to Rickey and Breadon that there was virtually nothing that Frisch could not do.

Risking the fans' ire, and then winning them over when a seemingly foolish trade proved practically clairvoyant, emboldened Rickey and Breadon to act with increasing decisiveness. Hornsby was replaced as manager by Bob O'Farrell, who was then replaced the following season by Bill McKechnie. He lasted as manager for a year, and then Billy Southworth took over. On second thought, Rickey and Breadon decided that perhaps McKechnie was not so bad after all, and brought him back partway into the 1929 season. But McKechnie had second thoughts of his own and bolted at season's end when the Boston Braves offered him a long-term contract for more money. Charley "Gabby" Street then took over.

A southerner from Huntsville, Alabama, Street, a salty, garrulous character also affectionately known as Old Sarge, had been Walter Johnson's battery mate in Washington. He once caught a ball dropped from the top of the Washington Monument, but was not much of a threat, either when he was crouching behind the plate or standing beside it as a batter. He had enlisted in the army in World War I, saw considerable action in the Argonne region of France, and was discharged with the rank of sergeant.

The Cardinals had hired Street as a pitching coach in 1929. When he took over as manager, his appointment marked the fifth year in a row that the team was starting a new season with a new man in charge. A reformed heavy drinker, Street was an old-style manager who relied more on hunches than tactics. Though he talked tough, like the army man he was, he was popular and well liked both by players and sportswriters. "I know all the words," he once commented. But he seldom used them on his starting lineup. Underperforming rookies, though, got the full treatment.

———

After the bird dog went to visit Fort Sam Houston to see Private Jerome Dean in action, word quickly spread. Throughout the summer of 1928, the scout returned several times, and Brought still refused to allow his star pitcher to play for the semipro team. Dean had become convinced that he was headed for the Major Leagues more-or-less immediately, and at the end of summer, when no summons to join the professional ranks had come, he grew morose.

Soon after New Year's Day 1929, Dean heard a voice on the loudspeaker attached to the orderly room roof ordering him to report to the company sergeant. A man was waiting to see him, and Dean now felt that this must be the long-awaited visit from the St. Louis Cardinals scout. But the visitor introduced himself as a representative of the San Antonio Public Service Corporation, and said apologetically that he knew Dean was hoping to get a visit from a scout for a Major League team. He also told Dean that he did not think Sergeant Brought's strategy for getting Dean a pro contract was going to work because professional clubs did not think army baseball talent was really worth their time. The bird dog had obviously been doing Brought a personal favor just by showing up. The only way to get into the Majors was by first playing in the minors—specifically, on the San Antonio team. The man further explained that the team was not, strictly speaking, minor league, but part of a company-team circuit that was just a notch below the minors—or semipro. Major League scouts, though, considered the semipro leagues about on a par with the minors for talent picking.

The visitor suggested that Dean quit the army and play for the San Antonio team. Dean had been in the service for two years at that point, which meant that he could legally buy his way out for a hundred dollars. If he agreed to take the job, he could read gas meters during the off-season and play ball during the summer. Dean asked for time to think the matter over, because first he wanted to discuss it with Brought and with his father.

When Dean asked his commanding officer for his opinion, Brought not only encouraged him to leave the army, admitting that the visitor had been right about barracks teams not really being taken seriously by the Majors. He also offered to loan Dean some money if he needed help in scraping together the hundred dollars required to buy his way out of the service. Dean declined Brought's generous offer, saying his father had found plenty of work in the fields and had agreed to give him the money. Dean then took the job with the San Antonio Public Service Corp., ostensibly as a reader of gas meters, for thirty dollars a week.

Dean never forgot his army days, though, nor did the army ever forget him. At the height of Dean's fame, a popular recruitment poster showed Dean's face over a bold caption that read: THE ARMY TRAINED HIM.

One day while Dean was pitching for the San Antonio Public Service team, he was observed by another bird dog—in this instance, an anonymous railroad conductor—who knew an unusually good pitcher when he saw one. He contacted Don Curtis, a Cardinals scout, who also worked for the Kansas-Texas

Railroad that ran into San Antonio. After watching Dean pitch a few games, Curtis and his semipro manager, Riley Harris, met with Dean at the Mailton Hotel in San Antonio on May 25, 1929, and Dean signed a contract to pitch for the Houston Buffaloes in the Texas League for one hundred dollars a month. He was to report for duty the following spring.

When Dean reported to Houston in March 1930, along with scores of other boys, he passed muster and was sent to the St. Joseph, Missouri, Saints, a Cardinals Class A farm team in the Western Association. He was so impoverished that he did not even possess a suitcase and owned only the clothes he was wearing. In his first professional game for the Saints, against the Denver Bears, he allowed four hits and three runs, and the Saints won, 4 to 3. Dean went on to win seventeen games for St. Joseph, while losing eight.

By now the Cardinals farm system extended to Greensboro, North Carolina, of the Piedmont League; St. Joseph; and Shawnee, Oklahoma, of the Western Association. At some point, Rickey read a report on Dean from a veteran catcher named Charles Abbott, who said, "I've been warming Dean up, and he has more stuff than any pitcher I've ever caught."

Though that kind of extravagant praise was commonplace back then, Dean was chosen to pitch for Houston in an exhibition game against the Chicago White Sox. The occasion also gave rise to another, probably spurious, version of how he acquired his nickname. Among the formidable battery of players he pitched to that afternoon were Bill Hunnefield, Chalmers Cissell, Carl Reynolds, Smead Jolley, and Willie Kamm. As Dean's fastball blazed past one batter after another, according to sportswriter Lee Allen, White Sox coach Mike Kelly remarked to his players, "That kid is making you look dizzy." Some of the players soon took up the refrain. Whether or not the anecdote is true, Dean was clearly a baseball legend in the making.

A few days later, Lloyd Gregory, who reported on the Houston club for the *Sporting News,* provided Dean with his first national notice when he wrote, "Two of the rookies showing exceptional promise are: Dizzy Dean, from San Antonio, and Roger Traweek from Mexia, both right handers. These young twirlers lack polish, but each has a lot of natural ability, and a season in Class D baseball would work wonders for them."

Traweek soon vanished into oblivion. Dean was scheduled to be transferred to the Cardinals team in Shawnee, in Class C. But the St. Joseph Saints, recently moved from Topeka, had a pressing need for pitchers, so the Cardinals decided instead to keep Dean in the Western Association, where he would continue to play Class A ball for St. Joseph.

While in St. Joseph, according to J. Roy Stockton, Dean got into the habit of borrowing cars, which he liked to drive "pell-mell against traffic in one-way streets." Once, while racing another young blood, he led Earl Matthews, the chief of police, on a five-block chase. Arrested, he spent the night in the town jail. "But Dizzy forgave everything," Stockton wrote. "The next time he saw the chief he slapped him on the back with a cheery 'Hello, Chieffy, old boy, how the how are you?'"

Dean also had a habit of registering at several hotels simultaneously. On one occasion, while living in St. Joseph, he was registered at the YMCA, the St. Francis Hotel, and the Hotel Robidoux, and slept at whichever one he was closest to when sleep overtook him.

Branch Rickey saw Dean pitch in four of the games he won. The first time occurred at the Saints' spring training camp in Shawnee. Peering at his future star while standing behind the screen and puffing on his ever-present cigar, Rickey was somewhat impressed by Dean's performance, but not overwhelmed. Dean had pitched two innings, giving up both a double and a single, without getting a single strikeout.

That evening, Dean was passing through the lobby of the Aldridge Hotel, where the team was staying, and saw the Cardinals potentate sitting in a chair, reading the evening newspaper.

"Hello, Branch," Dean said, extending his hand. "I'm Dizzy Dean, the fella who's gonna win you a lot of ball games."

"Hello, Mr. Dean," Rickey replied.

"Say, Branch," Dean told him, "don't waste your time sendin' me to St. Joe. Bring me right up to the Cardinals. If I can strike 'em out here, I can strike 'em out there. I can win you a flag."

No other ballplayer ever addressed Rickey as Branch. He was always "Mr. Rickey," even to old friends like George Sisler. But Dean was always to call him Branch, or refer to him as "my pal, Branch"—except, of course, when he was unhappy about a contract negotiation. Then Dean dismissively called him simply "Rickey." But those days were still in the future.

Rickey liked young Dean's outgoing manner and was eventually impressed by his first year with the Saints, but wanted to see him pitch against stronger batters. In August 1930, Dean was transferred to the Houston Buffaloes, a Triple A team in the Texas League—a major step up. He pitched his first game as an official member of the Buffs on the very night he arrived in Houston, defeating San Antonio by a score of 12 to 1, and striking out fourteen. He went on to win his next five games as well, including a season-ending 8-to-1 victory over Beaumont when he struck out sixteen batters.

"He was beginning to create a legend," Vince Staten noted, "but, as usual with Diz, the legend wasn't just for pitching. George Payne, his Houston roommate, told reporters that Diz would borrow his shirts and ties and then leave them in hotel room wastebaskets. He also recalled the time Diz started a road trip carrying a large suitcase containing only a pack of cigarettes."

In the waning days of the 1930 season, Dean seemed about to get his long-awaited big break. The St. Louis Cardinals summoned him to pitch in his first big-league game. Under rookie manager Gabby Street, the team was in a desperate fight for the pennant, with only three games separating the top four clubs—St. Louis, the Chicago Cubs, the New York Giants, and the Brooklyn Dodgers—in one of the National League's tightest races in fifteen years.

Rickey had strengthened the team's bullpen when he engineered a trade that brought Burleigh "Old Stubblebeard" Grimes, a brawny spitballer, from the Boston Braves. For most of the season, the Cardinals were running in fourth place, with Brooklyn holding the lead; but in August, the Redbirds caught fire. In mid-September, Street's club traveled east for a series of games with the Dodgers and Giants. Brooklyn now led the league by one game, with the Cardinals, Giants, and Cubs battling it out for second place, just a few percentage points separating them.

Dean was ordered to join the Cardinals in New York. When he showed up at the hotel, he was now carrying two suitcases, as Cardinal first baseman Rip Collins later recalled. "He and Tony Kaufman [another Houston pitcher who had also been called up with Dean] went to their room and Diz wanted one of Tony's shirts. He asked Tony what size he was and Tony said 15 1/2, and Diz said that might be a little too tight for him but he could leave the collar open. Then he asked to borrow one, and Tony says, 'Do you mean to say you haven't got a clean shirt in those two bags?' and Diz says, 'Nope, look for yourself.' Well, Tony opens them and you know what's in there? Wild West books! The only books he ever tried to read, I guess, and two bags full. And no clothes! Was the son of a bitch dizzy? You tell me."

The Cardinals were scheduled to play four more games against the Giants at the Polo Grounds when Dean arrived, and he begged Street to let him pitch, telling him, "I can beat those clowns." But Street wisely did not want to gamble with an unproven recruit, not yet twenty-one and just out of the minors. The Cardinals went on to win all four of those games.

After playing the Braves in Boston, when they took two of three games, the Cardinals returned to New York for a three-game series with the Dodgers. Dean soon learned that he had a team rival whose eccentric behavior and brilliant pitching threatened to overshadow his own talents on both fronts: Flint Rhem, a colorful South Carolinian who spoke with such a pronounced Dixie drawl that several players had difficulty understanding him. Rhem had the potential to be a great pitcher, but his athletic prowess was somewhat overshadowed by his even greater fondness for moonshine.

Rhem also had the distinction of having thrown a pitch to Babe Ruth, during the fourth game of the 1926 World Series, that the Sultan of Swat smacked for the longest recorded home run in the history of Sportsman's Park. Ruth had already hit two homers when, in the sixth inning, he sent the ball well over five hundred feet, high above the center-field bleachers and onto Grand Avenue.

Now, on the eve of the first game with Brooklyn, Rhem disappeared. The next morning, he showed up, "bleary-eyed and disheveled," in the words of Frederick G. Lieb, "with one of baseball's weirdest tales." Rhem claimed that he had been standing in front of the hotel where the Cardinals were staying when two armed men pushed him into a waiting cab, then took him to New Jersey, where they "compelled Rhem to guzzle cups of raw whiskey."

Rickey, the teetotaler, believed Rhem's story, and asked the police to investigate. New York's newspapers bannered the kidnapping on their front pages—a plot by gamblers to cripple the Cardinals' chances and give Brooklyn the edge. But the St. Louis team took the series with Brooklyn anyway.

When the team assembled to leave for Philadelphia for their next engagement, though, now it was Dean who was nowhere to be seen. He had wandered into New York's bright lights and got lost; he only managed to rejoin the team the next day.

St. Louis clinched the pennant on September 27, the next to last day of the season, when Jesse "Pop" Haines led the Cardinals to a 10-to-5 victory over the Pirates in a home game. The cautious Street then decided to put Dean into the lineup. On the morning that he was scheduled to pitch, Dean awoke with a bad stomachache, which he blamed on having eaten a rancid hotdog the evening before.

Fortunately, the Pirates were in even worse shape. The previous night, a group of Pirates had traipsed across the Mississippi to party at a supper club in East St. Louis, Illinois, owned by one of their own, pitcher Heine Meine. The Pittsburgh hurler, a native of St. Louis, lived in the off-season in Luxembourg, Missouri, and was known as the "Count of Luxembourg."

The next morning, several of the Pirates were so hungover that they were barely able to make it through the nine innings. Years later, remembering that time, slugger Paul Waner asked Dean, "What'd we get off you, Diz? Three hits? We were lucky to get three."

"Well, Paul," Dean replied, as only he could, "you was the greatest drunk ballplayer I ever struck out."

Prior to the game, Dean was chatting with a scout when Sam Breadon wandered by. Having misplaced his own cleats, Dean was wearing a pair borrowed from Burleigh Grimes.

"How do you feel today, Mr. Dean?" Breadon inquired.

"Fine," Dean replied.

"Well, you'd better be," Breadon said. "You're going to pitch today, and that Pittsburgh team is pretty tough—the Waner brothers and Pie Traynor. Good hitters."

"You might think they're tough," Dean replied, with his trademark grin, "but they won't look so tough when they have to face old Diz."

That afternoon, the brash twenty-year-old rookie went the full nine innings, pitching a three-hitter and subduing the Pirates 3 to 1. He also proved himself at bat. Once, when the Pirates closed in, expecting a bunt, Dizzy smacked the ball into shallow left field for a base hit.

Among the spectators at that last game of the season was Red Smith, at the time a second-string sportswriter for the *St. Louis Star-Times,* who reported, "If a single performance in a single meaningless game can be taken as a criterion, then Dean is destined for stardom. The youngster showed burning speed, a wide, sweeping curve, a clever change, and best of all, unusual control for a rookie. You should know this young man."

Unfortunately, because of his late call-up, Dean was ineligible to accompany the Cardinals when they journeyed to Philadelphia to challenge the Athletics for the championship.

Some time later, during the winter months, Dean showed up at Rickey's office in Sportsman's Park in St. Louis to talk salary. Dean insisted that his salary for the upcoming season should be more than the customary three thousand dollars, and for two hours he kept up a steady barrage of reasons why he needed a big increase in his salary. A rumpled, worn-out Rickey later emerged from the session and exclaimed, "Judas Priest! If there was another player like Dean in baseball, as God is my judge, I would most certainly get out of this game."

———— • ————

Dean arrived for spring training in Bradenton, Florida, in late January 1931 and took a room in the Dixie Grande Hotel, the team's headquarters. Not surprisingly, he had a difficult—or rather, impossible—time adhering to the regimen. He and man-ager Gabby Street, the former army sergeant, fought constantly.

Players did not receive salaries during the training season and were expected to have their own spending money, while the team picked up the cost of hotels, meals, and travel. Dean, though, did not have any money of his own. He solved that problem by cavalierly signing hotel, restaurant, and store receipts, and asking that the pieces of paper, so quickly forgotten when he walked out the door, be forwarded to the Cardinals' business office.

To pass the time before spring training began, he also took up golf, went to see wrestling matches at the local American Legion hall, wrote constant demands for advances on his salary to the front office, and treated himself to endless numbers of sodas, cigars, cigarettes, fountain pens, sunglasses, key chains, comic books, and assorted other goods and novelties.

By February 21, the Cardinals organization had had enough. In less than a month, Dean had run up personal debts and charges amounting to a staggering twenty-seven hundred dollars.

When Rickey confronted Dean about his debts, Dean told him, "I'm good for it. Take it outta my pay."

"What pay?" Rickey exclaimed, explaining that Dean had already used up nearly all of his 1931 salary.

"Nah," Dean replied. "But that's okay. You'll think of somethin'."

Rickey's solution was to create a deferred-repayment plan that would not significantly affect Dean's salary in either 1931 or 1932. But he also notified all shops, restaurants, and hotels in Bradenton that the Cardinals would no longer honor any of Dean's signed receipts. Henceforth, Dean's allowance was being drastically cut back to one dollar a day—literally, a single dollar each morning, and not seven dollars for the entire week, since Rickey already knew well enough that Dizzy would easily find a way to spend seven dollars in any given twenty-four-hour period.

On being informed of this new arrangement, a vexed Dean complained that there was no way he could survive on such a skimpy budget. He volunteered to become a professional wrestler, and later a daredevil parachuting from an airplane, but was turned down by promoters at both events. He also ordered a new Cardinals uniform, but a suspicious Rickey stopped the shipment, and later discovered that Dean had planned to use it as collateral for a thirteen-dollar loan.

Each morning thereafter, a humiliated Dean had to report to club secretary Clarence Lloyd and sign a receipt reading "Received today $1—Dizzy Dean." That was how Dean became the original "dollar-a-day" man of baseball legend. Rickey, though, still had a thing or two to learn about his unpredictable rookie. The first day that Dean received his dollar allotment, he dropped it into a slot machine before breakfast—and lost. The business manager refused to advance him the next day's dollar. Unrepentant, Dean spent his second day's dollar before noon.

Dean ultimately learned how to budget his dollar so that he had enough change in the evening to buy cigarettes and soda. But his attitude problem remained unchecked. Typical was the time when Street called for a morning workout. Dizzy remained in bed. When he was reprimanded for not joining his teammates, he replied, "Let some of the other clucks work out for the staff. Nobody can beat me."

In any case, manager Street was telling reporters that the key to the Cardinals' pennant drive was not Dean, but Flint Rhem— the very man who, only the year before, had claimed to have been kidnapped by Jersey mobsters. Rhem had blamed his throwing problems on his tonsils, not his drinking, and said those days were behind him now that he had had a tonsillectomy.

"A what?" Dean asked him.

"My tonsils," Rhem explained. "I had 'em taken out and my arm got well. I don't know how it happened or anything like that, but this flipper has never felt better."

Dean then requested permission from the Cardinals' physician for the same operation, claiming, "I ain't been swallowin' right lately." Though his teammates laughed, he was examined by an ear, nose, and throat specialist who, much to the team's amazement, recommended that Dean's tonsils come out. The operation was performed on March 3, 1931, in a room at the Dixie Grande. A half hour after the operation, according to John Kieran in the *New York Times*, Dean was relaxing with a nickel cigar and a mouthful of candy.

On March 31, Dean overslept, and Street thoroughly cussed him out, with most of the team listening. Dean gave back as good as he got and then added that he was leaving camp. Nobody talked to him like that, he said, as he packed his bag. He also turned in his No. 17 uniform and announced that he would be on the 8:38 night train bound for San Antonio, where a semipro team had offered him a contract to play for $250 a month.

Around six o'clock that evening, Rickey's chauffeured Buick pulled up in front of the Dixie Grande. Reporters were betting 100 to 1 that Dean had no intention of really leaving, and that his resignation from the Cardinals was only a ploy to get his dollar-a-day allowance raised. Dean got into the back seat of the car for a private conference with Rickey. The two men talked for a half hour. When a smiling Dean emerged, he brandished a five-dollar bill and told reporters, "I didn't have a chance. Branch did all the talkin', and I couldn't say a word. But I'm stayin', and I ain't got nothin' against the old Sarge."

Rickey had refused to up Dean's daily allowance, except when he had a "head cold" and required another twenty-five cents for cough syrup. "One of these days in St. Louis," Rickey prophesied to the reporters, "he'll be electrifying 40,000 spectators in Sportsman's Park. Mark my words."

The next morning, just to show Sarge who was boss, Dean went fishing and showed up late for practice. Again Dean was suspended, again Rickey intervened, and again Street gave his irksome rookie one more chance.

Dean also continued to splurge on countless candy bars and packs of cigarettes, despite Rickey's heroic efforts at curtailing his carefree spending, and to treat the girls hanging around at the local drugstore to milkshakes. Once he even signed a check in Rickey's name. Street, having run out of patience, suspended him for three days, and Dizzy promised to reform.

When the season began, Dean accompanied the team for their opening series of four games against Cincinnati. He was still with the Cardinals when they played four more games against Chicago, then returned home for a series of matches with the Pirates and Reds. But he did not play in any of those games and, on May 2, got word that he was being sent back to Houston for more seasoning. When the twenty-one-year-old Dean learned that he was heading back to Texas for another year, he replied, in genuine astonishment, "Don't you want to win the pennant *this* year?" Equally astonished was rookie shortstop Billy Myers, a teammate who wondered aloud whether anyone had ever heard of a team losing thirty games in one day. Asked what he meant, Myers replied, "Dizzy Dean just got sent down."

Dizzy Dean arrived in Houston on May 3, 1931, and that afternoon pitched a three-hit, 6-to-0 shutout against the Wichita Falls Spudders. Frustrated professionally, he proceeded that season to take out his anger on the batters in the Texas League, striking out 303 on his way to a 26–10 record.

On the road, he was highly popular with fans, with turnouts that normally averaged 350 to 450 a game, in those hard-pressed times, swelling up to five or six times that amount if Dean was pitching. In Houston, though, he came up almost dead last in the MVP poll when fans were asked to name the best player. Four teammates received more votes than he did, with future Cardinal Tex Carleton taking second place, and Dean beat out only one other player: Joe Medwick. Like Dean, the surly nineteen-year-old was not always easy to get along with.

A month after he returned to Houston, Dean also announced to his teammates that he was getting married. The bride-to-be was Patricia Nash, an attractive, twenty-four-year-old brunette with a reputation as a party girl. He had first met her back in 1929 in Houston while he was still in the army, and they had resumed dating when he returned to the city in 1930. Nash was a native of Denham, Mississippi, but had grown up in Bond, a small town just south of Hattiesburg on the Gulf coast. One of her two previous marriages had been annulled, and the other had ended in divorce. When Dean and Nash met again, she was working as a hosiery clerk at Paul's Shoe Store on Main Street. A frequent visitor to the ball grounds, Nash had also previously dated two of Dean's teammates, second baseman Carey Delph and third baseman Eddie Hock.

Dean wanted the wedding ceremony to be held at home plate, but club president Fred Ankenman vetoed the proposal. He also opposed the marriage, as did Rickey, and both men tried to talk Dean out of it. At the very least, they urged him to wait a few years. Not only was he just at the start of his professional career, with the need to concentrate all of his attention on playing ball, they told him, but Nash also seemed too mature and "experienced." Years later, Dean told Chicago columnist Irv Kupcinet that Ankenman and Rickey later dispatched another man with the Houston Buffaloes to ask Dean if he had heard the often-repeated rumor that "Patricia Nash has screwed half the men in town." Dean quoted himself as replying, "Sure, I heard it. I'm one of 'em. That's why I wanna marry her."

Dizzy Dean and Pat Nash were married on June 15, 1931, in the study of the Reverend Harry G. Knowles, minister of Houston's First Christian Church. None of the groom's or bride's relatives attended, only a few friends. Dean's best man was Andy Anderson, a sportswriter with the *Houston Press*. Anderson asked Dean how he felt.

"Like the bases are loaded in the bottom of the ninth," he answered, "and the cleanup batter's comin' in."

Before the ceremony, Dean paid Knowles the one-dollar fee, and tossed in as a bonus an autographed baseball.

Knowles asked the couple to join hands. Dean held Nash's hand with his fingers extended, telling the minister, "This here's how I hold a curve, Preacher."

The next day, Dean pitched against the Fort Worth Colts and was humbled by a late-inning home run.

"Boy," he told reporters, blaming exhaustion, "I didn't think marryin' would cost me a ballgame. I ain't sayin' my arm that's dead. It's my legs. They ain't got no life."

Dean and the new Mrs. Dean were to remain a devoted married couple for forty-three years. Despite her reputation before marriage, she became his "financial advisor and protector," in the words of Robert Gregory, "or, as she said later, 'I handle the money. What I say goes. No more of that crazy spending like he used to do. He depends on me. I'm his banker, bookkeeper, manager, and girlfriend.'"

Friends also noted that Pat Dean took the place of the mother Dizzy had lost in 1917. She bought his clothes, taught him table manners, and even made him read newspapers. "He's just a great big boy," she explained.

At the start of the 1932 season, a majority of the nation's sportswriters predicted that the St. Louis Cardinals would have little trouble capturing the pennant once again, just as they had in 1930 and 1931. Breadon, Rickey, and Street were equally optimistic, especially now that the team had one of the game's highest payrolls ever. During the off-season, though, the front office had traded away two of the team's pillars— Burleigh Grimes, who had helped lead the team to its two pennant wins, and left fielder Chick Hafey, who had won the batting championship with a .348 average. In Rickey's baseball creed, it was an article of faith to trade or sell high-salaried stars at the very moment their talent was about to wane, but when they still had some value to the club, and thereby not only to wring a maximum profit out of a player but to make room for up-and-coming players in the farm system. Rickey's contract also called for him to receive 10 percent of the sale of any Cardinals player.

In 1932, though, Rickey's policy of selling players in their prime appeared to backfire. After a strong start, the Redbirds began to slip in the standings, and by July they were skidding ever more deeply into the second division. Breadon and Rickey were roundly criticized for shipping off Grimes and Hafey, who had served so stoutly the year before. Yet Grimes managed to win only six games for the Cubs, though the team did win the pennant, and Hafey was sick for much of 1932. The Cardinals, though, plummeted by season's end to sixth place.

The collapse of the Cardinals, as it turned out, could not be blamed on the absence of Grimes and Hafey, but on the subpar performance of center fielder Pepper Martin. The same man who had been named "Athlete of the Year" by the Associated Press in 1931 hit only .235 in eighty-five games, and spent much of the season riding the bench. He also stole only nine bases. "The Oklahoman had a contagious personality," Lieb noted.

"When he was good, he could carry an entire team with his enthusiasm. But when Pepper Martin was low, the whole ball club suffered with him."

———— -

Dizzy Dean arrived in Bradenton during the winter of 1932, walked into the business office of the *Bradenton Herald,* pointed his two index fingers with cocked thumbs at the women sitting behind the desk, and announced, "Stick 'em up! This is a hold up!" If they found his practical joke merely juvenile, he thought it was uproarious and doubled over in laughter.

In an arrangement agreed on by Breadon and Brack Cheshire, the newspaper's sports editor, Dean had been told to report to the newspaper as soon as he got into town. Breadon wanted Cheshire to keep an eye on his unpredictable new pitcher.

Dean moved into the Dixie Grande Hotel, where his food and lodging, like that of his teammates, was picked up by the team. Dizzy, though, would go to the hotel barber every morning and have the man charge him double for a shave or haircut. Then, Dean would bill the club and split the difference with the barber. On another occasion, he called Cheshire to ask if he could borrow a few dollars because he had found a barnstorming stunt pilot who was willing to take Dean for a ride. Cheshire nearly choked when he heard Dean's request.

"Are you kidding?" he yelled. "You'll crash, and I'll get in trouble."

Dean also bought a yellow convertible and, on some mornings, drove his nephews, Loyd and Earl, to school. When they got out in the afternoon, Dean would be waiting to drive them home.

That spring, Dizzy earned a spot as a Cardinals regular, calling himself "the Great Dean" at the team's spring training camp. In an era of eccentric players, his oddball behavior only seemed to blossom. Dean liked to eat four or five meals a day, and still had no hesitation in telling a waitress to "put it on Mr. Breadon's tab."

Even in his rookie year, Dean's cockiness had become his official public trademark. He often mocked batters as they approached the plate, made funny faces at them, and laughed out loud after they struck out. He also had a temper. What particularly annoyed him was a batter who dug his back foot into the box before getting ready to hit. When this happened, Dean would sometimes walk halfway up to the plate, put his hands on his hips, and say, "Just keep on diggin', cause that's where they're gonna bury you."

Dean had become such a draw, though, that ironically he was much in demand on the exhibition circuit. Dean heartily disliked playing in exhibition games. In fact, few players took any pleasure in these games, which had no bearing on the standings of the team. If the majority of players meekly complied with these incursions on their free time, Dean took the opposite tack. He knew that the Cardinals were not so foolhardy as to swap him for someone else, since the chances of their coming out ahead in the bargain were virtually nonexistent. As a result, he played a constant game of mental arm wrestling with management—one that was to reach its headline-making apogee when he chose not to travel with the team to Detroit in August 1934. A remarkably similar prelude to that crisis occurred during the 1932 season.

While traveling from New York to Pittsburgh, the Cardinals had an off day, and Rickey filled it by scheduling an exhibition game in a Pennsylvania town. As usual, Street drew up a list of players available for the game, some of them regulars, and others substitutes. The list included Dean. The team was distributed among three Pullmans when the train pulled out of New York. At Harrisburg, Pennsylvania, one of the Pullmans switched off to go to the town where the exhibition game was being played, and the other two remained on the regular train for Pittsburgh.

Amazingly enough, when the train pulled into Pittsburgh, Dean and his wife were in one of those two Pullmans, and not, as they were supposed to be, elsewhere in Pennsylvania. Looking out the window, Dean asked in mock surprise, "What town is this?"

Told he was in Pittsburgh, he replied, "That can't be right. I ought to be in —."

Street was not persuaded by Dean's story that he had awakened in the wrong car, and fined him one hundred dollars. Dean resented being penalized and said he would not pay it. The Cardinals finally returned to St. Louis and were scheduled to open against the Brooklyn Dodgers.

"If I go in and shut out Brooklyn for you," Dean asked Street, "will you call off the fine?"

"I don't know," said Street. "I'll see."

Dean threw a shutout. Street sent word up to the press box: "That fine on Dean for missing the exhibition game is off."

In 1932, the consensus among many sportswriters was that the Cardinals, who had triumphed over the Philadelphia Athletics in the World Series, would repeat as National League champions. After the team lost five of their first seven games, many of the writers began to second-guess themselves. Dizzy Dean pitched his first game on April 23, going up against Pittsburgh. The Pirates took an early lead, but the Cardinals were able to rally from six runs behind to tie the score. At that point, Dean was sent in as a reliever. In the eighth inning, he struck out the first three batters he faced. But in the ninth, slugger Gussie Suhr hit a home run off him, and St. Louis lost.

"It was a shock to Dean," Stockton reported in the *Post-Dispatch*. "Dean stood there on the mound for several moments after the home run drive clattered among the empty seats. Then he saw the other Redbirds making for the clubhouse with their sweaters and paraphernalia, and he departed too, stunned and disappointed."

His first start came on May 3, and this time he shut out the Cincinnati Reds, 9 to 0. Later that month, on May 22, he lost his first big league game, when the Pirates pounded him for five runs, and a week later the Pirates beat him again, 8 to 6. By June, the Cardinals' record was 20–24, and their pennant hopes were fading.

That same month, Dean began to grouse aloud that he was not being treated fairly by the Cardinals. In particular, he grumbled about his low salary. Abruptly, on June 15, he walked out on the team, taking a train home to St. Louis from Philadelphia. When Street learned of his departure, he told reporters, "He'll be back with us. He's a hard proposition to handle."

Back in St. Louis, Dean announced that he was going to seek an unconditional release from his contract, on the grounds that he had been underage when he signed it. "I am not 21 yet," he said, "and therefore the contract has no value. I am entitled to my release."

Previously, "Judge" Kenesaw Mountain Landis had declared that several other players were free agents because they were underage and did not have their parents' countersignature on their contracts.

When Rickey, the lawyer, heard about Dean's intentions, he immediately called Frank Ankenman in Houston, who in his memoir later recounted what happened next: "Even in those days Diz would have brought several hundred thousand dollars in the open market. Mr. Rickey was frantic and wanted to know if I knew how old he was. I told him he must have been at least 21 when he signed the Cardinal contract. He wanted to know how I could prove it. I told him I would try and check."

Ankenman went to the Houston courthouse to check Dizzy's marriage license. The license showed Dean's true date of birth, and put the Cardinals in the clear. Yet, for decades afterward, his age continued to be reported inaccurately.

Even so, there was a hearing before Judge Landis. At one point, Rickey asked Dean if he had obtained a marriage license. "I did not have to have one," Dean calmly replied, "because everybody in Houston knew me." Rickey then asked, "Are you quite sure and positive?"

"I signed absolutely nothing," Dean insisted.

Rickey then pulled from his inside pocket a copy of the license, showed it to Dean, and asked, "Is that signature Jerome H. Dean yours or somebody else's, and also is the date correct?"

"You got me, Mr. Rickey," Dean admitted with a grin. "You got me."

Dean rejoined the Cardinals in New York. As part of the agreement, the St. Louis club refunded to Dean the sum of $225 that had been taken out of his paycheck over the past two years and sent in monthly installments to his father in Houston. Ankenman had worked out that arrangement with Monroe Dean, with Dizzy's consent, but Pat Dean was livid when she found out about it and insisted that the full amount be returned to her husband.

That year, Dean won eighteen games and lost fifteen. But he did lead the league in strikeouts, with 191—more than 54 over second-place Carl Hubbell. The champion Cardinals, though, slipped to a disappointing seventh place in the standings.

Breadon held manager Gabby Street responsible for the Cardinals' slide, and in July 1933 he called Frankie Frisch into his office to inform him that he was going to pay off Street for the season. He then asked his second baseman if he would accept the job as manager-player.

In his autobiography, Frisch recalled that moment:

> I guess every ballplayer occasionally has the idea that he'd like to be a manager someday. I probably often thought about what I'd do if I ever was put in charge of a ball club. But truthfully I didn't think I was ready to become a manager.
>
> I said, "Mr. Breadon, why don't you let Gabby finish out the season? We've only got about two months more and it wouldn't be such a blow to him if the change were made in the winter months."

But Breadon was resolute, and Frank Frisch became the new manager of the St. Louis Cardinals—the sixth in eight years. Rickey's philosophy as the Cardinals' business manager was to acquire the best baseball personnel he could get his hands on, and to give the field manager free rein to use those players with the best of his judgment. In 1934, Rickey was the strategist, and manager Frank Frisch, who also played second base, was his appointed tactician.

In his second season with the Cardinals, Dizzy Dean improved his record slightly, winning twenty games and losing eighteen, though he set a Major League record on July 30, 1933, when he struck out seventeen Cubs. He also led the league in strikeouts, with 199. Dean's rival was Cardinal newcomer Tex Carleton, who won seventeen games that year, losing eleven. Despite such exceptional performances by two of their star pitchers, and batting averages well over .300 by Frisch, Medwick, and Collins, the Cardinals finished in a disappointing fourth place.

Dean was also getting a reputation as one of the game's all-time eccentrics. As Frank Graham reported in the *New York Sun,* Dean had become "a flagrant offender against that commonly accepted rule that there shall be no fraternization between rival players before a game. Dizzy except when he is pitching is a friend of every other player in the league and observes all the amenities when he meets up with them."

During a game against Brooklyn at Ebbets Field during the 1933 season, Graham was later to report, Dean decided to visit the Brooklyn clubhouse before the game. He strolled in "just as [manager] Max Carey was calling a meeting to go over the Cardinal hitters. . . . He sat down and listened to every word Carey had to say. When Max was through talking, he turned to Dizzy. 'Was I right about how to pitch to you fellows?' he asked, with a smile. 'Yep,' said Dizzy. 'And now I'll tell you how I'm going to pitch to these mugs.' To the astonishment of the Brooklyn players, he went right down the batting order, telling each what his weakness was, and being so accurate about it his listeners knew they weren't being kidded. 'Now that I've told you what I'm going to pitch,' he said, 'come on out and let's see you hit it.' He picked up his glove, stalked from the clubhouse, and shut the Dodgers out."

Dizzy Dean also had a knack for making news inadvertently. One summer evening in 1933, he wandered into a St. Louis drugstore just as two robbers were holding it up. Ever the practical joker himself, he assumed that someone was merely playing a trick on the pharmacist, until "a pistol shoved into his ribs emphasized the serious nature of the occasion," according to Lee Allen. "When he was ordered to join other herded customers in a stockade, he promptly obeyed." For once in his life, he managed to keep his mouth shut.

The next day's newspapers reported Dean's presence at the scene of the crime. That evening, he received a telephone call from one of the robbers, who repentantly told him, "I didn't know you wuz in the store. I want you to know that I don't hold nothing against you personally, and to prove it I'm going to send you a bunch of neckties." A few days later, the ties arrived, as promised, and Dean shared them with his teammates.

Dizzy Dean now lived in Bradenton in the winter months, when he was not on the road earning extra money on the barnstorming circuit, or making guest appearances in vaudeville. In January 1934, noting that his rookie brother, Paul, was joining the team, Dean told a reporter from the *St. Louis Star-Times* that the Cardinals were sure to win the pennant.

"How are they going to stop us?" he asked. "Paul's going to be a sensation. He'll win 18 or 20 games. I'll count 20 or 25 myself. I won 20 last season, and I know I'll pass that figure."

For once, the boastful Dean was underestimating himself. He had no idea he was going to make baseball history and establish a pitching record that would remain unmatched for more than three decades.

———————

At their annual winter meeting in Chicago in December 1933, the owners of the National League teams came up with a novel suggestion to introduce a tenth man into the lineup—a so-called designated batter. In that golden age of great pitchers, the offensive power of many teams seemed not as potent as it could be. This tenth batter, the proposal went, would bat for the pitcher. But the American League nixed the idea—though, of course, it would introduce the designated hitter to professional baseball in 1973.

The owners also pondered once again whether to introduce night baseball—a blasphemous notion in the minds of many of the game's most ardent fans. With the incomes of wage earners at an all-time low, however, the owners realized that they could not just sit back and wait for the economy to catch up. Rather, they had to take measures to entice customers to go to the ball-park not just occasionally, but regularly.

The owners did agree on at least one strategy to boost attendance, and that was to begin using the "New Deal" baseball in 1934—the name borrowed, of course, from President Roosevelt's Depression-era social policies. The new, livelier baseball was wound tighter to make it harder. In turn, it would carry farther than a softer or "dead" ball when solidly hit with a bat. More offensive power, the theory went, would translate into a more exciting game. The new ball did, in fact, perform just as expected. By July the overall National League batting average was up more than 20 percent over that of the previous season.

Though some ball clubs continued to find themselves in financial straits, particularly the Boston Braves, the Philadelphia Athletics, and even the Chicago Cubs, who had won the pennant in 1932, the worst was over for the St. Louis Cardinals.

Another team in the black, as 1934 dawned, was the New York Giants, who had won the World Series the previous year. Player-manager Bill Terry, in an expansive mood, met with reporters on January 24 and predicted that the livelier new ball being introduced into the game that year would add 15 percentage points to his batting average. Terry was wrong. The new ball added 32 points. He also predicted that the Giants would finish in the top three in the league.

"I'll start with the same team that won the pennant," he told the sportswriters.

"You mean," one of them good-naturedly asked, "the team we picked for sixth place last year?"

Terry laughed and said, "The same team. Anybody want to bet a hat that we don't win?"

None of the writers took his bet.

"Pittsburgh, St. Louis, and Chicago will be the teams to beat," he said.

"How about the Dodgers, Bill?" asked a reporter for the *New York Sun.* "How will they do?"

"The Dodgers?" Terry joked. "Is Brooklyn still in the league?"

Most of the reporters took the remark as nothing more than a good-natured wisecrack. Neither the Associated Press nor the *New York Times* even mentioned it. But Tommy Holmes of the *Brooklyn Eagle* noted what he regarded as a slight. "It would be a good idea for Mr. Terry to insult the Dodgers at regular intervals hereafter," he wrote, "and especially just before the Giants and Dodgers are due to meet in a series. If I know my Brooklyn fan, he will go to the ballgame if he has to hammer down the gate."

An even more clairvoyant Harry Nash, writing in the *New York Post,* seconded Holmes: "Because of his unkind cut at the Dodgers, William Harold Terry is in for a ride. When those Brooklyn jockeys get through with Memphis Bill, he'll feel like a spavined nag that has hauled one load too many. It is amusing how quickly a Brooklynite can be aroused by a slur against the Dodgers. And if Bill Terry is thin-skinned as some say he is, he is due for a miserable season so far as Giant-Dodger games are concerned."

Nash and Holmes well understood the resentment that Terry's remark had instilled in both Dodger players and Dodger fans. In the final days of the season, Casey Stengel's Dodgers were to exact a terrible revenge.

Dizzy Dean, meanwhile, was heading off to Hot Springs, Arkansas, where, along with Rogers Hornsby, Lon Warneke, and George Sisler, he was being paid $250 to be a "professor" of baseball at Ray Doan's All-Star Baseball School—one of the first of its kind. The school attracted boys who aspired to play professional baseball, though few truly had any chance of making it even into the minors.

In November, Dean also appeared on the stage of the field house of Washington University in St. Louis at a cooking school sponsored by the *St. Louis Globe-Democrat*. As the audience looked on, Dean played the role of star student of Miss Jessie DeBoth, the instructor.

"Just separate those eggs, Dizzy," Miss DeBoth told Dean. He meekly did as she told him, breaking a few eggs and allowing them to plop into a bowl.

Then he picked up a few more eggs, but instead of breaking them, he segued into his famous windup and lobbed the eggs into the audience. Everyone ducked, then howled. The "eggs" were made of rubber.

During spring training in Bradenton in early March 1934, Paul Dean joined the St. Louis ball club. Dizzy was by now both a bona fide star and a certified oddball personality who was always good for at least a quote, and almost as often a story concerning his troublesome relations with the front office, and he wasted no time providing reporters with plenty of material.

"Paul is even greater than I am, if that's possible," he humbly opined—a remark that none of the reporters gathered around believed, nor did either Paul or Dizzy, though the brotherly affection was genuine. "And they're offerin' him the same salary they offered the other young pitchers. But he ain't no ordinary pitcher. He's a Dean. So we're askin' for $1,500 more to make it $4,500, and boys, if Paul don't get it, he's goin' back to Houston and work in a mill for some real money."

Paul remained silent, as usual when his loquacious brother was around, and one newspaper wasted no time the next day dubbing him "Harpo" after the Marx brother who never said a word but only tooted on his horn.

Rickey countered with a typical bold gambit. "Paul Dean has one foot in Columbus," he tersely observed. The threat was clear: Paul had just completed a 22–7 record for the Cardinals' top farm team, in Columbus, Ohio, but he had not yet played a single game in the big leagues and already he was demanding more money. Rickey was quite prepared to send him back to the minors if he did not sign a contract on the terms that the Cardinals were offering. Rickey was also no fool. He knew that he was really negotiating not with Paul, but with Dizzy.

"That Rickey's bluffin'," Dizzy claimed.

"No, he ain't," said Paul.

The two parties continued to negotiate in the press over the next several days. Dizzy blinked first, suggesting a compromise offer: $3,750 total. When Rickey ignored him, Paul, who dreaded the prospect of another year in the minors, told his brother, "There ain't no way they're gonna give me more money, so I'm signin', Diz."

On March 11, a Sunday, Paul Dean met with Rickey, signed the contract, and officially became a St. Louis Cardinal. After the two men shook hands, Dizzy made a pronouncement that was to become among the most widely quoted down the ages in the Dean anthology: "Me 'n' Paul are gonna have a family contest. If I win more games than he does, I'll lead the league. And if Paul wins more games than me, I'll run second. I don't see how anybody can beat us Redbirds with two Deans on the ballclub."

He then famously predicted, "We'll be sure to win 45 games between us, and if we have six more pitchers who can win about 50 other games, that will put us in the World Series. It ought to be a breeze from here on."

"That's right, Diz," echoed Paul.

Paul was as colorless as his brother Jerome was colorful. Unlike Dizzy, who ignored the advice of pitching coaches and just about everybody else, Paul was an eager learner. Yet in many ways the brothers were remarkably alike. They shared the same family features, were about the same size, and had identical tastes and habits—Jean Harlow and Mae West movies, hillbilly music, playing golf in Florida, wrestling with friends at a moment's notice, drinking cold milk (neither cared much for beer or hard liquor), smoking Lucky Strike and Camel cigarettes, hunting for quail, and listening to comedian Eddie Cantor on the radio. They also socialized with the same teammates, especially Pepper Martin, Burgess Whitehead, and rookie catcher Bill DeLancey. In St. Louis, they both maintained apartments at the modestly luxurious Forest Park Hotel in the city's Central West End, had rooms on the same floor, shared the same barber and shoeshine boy, and went to and from the ballpark together.

Dizzy also no longer dressed like a rube but wore hand-tailored suits, clean white shirts, and wing tips every day. "He looked like a New Deal farm official in charge of plowing under crops and killing every excess hog in the Ozarks," Robert Gregory remarked. "His table manners had improved, too, but his appetite usually refused to be swayed by alternatives to cornbread and beans, although he had just discovered Lea & Perrins steak sauce and liked to pour it on scrambled eggs."

Pat Dean, who now wore a 1.5-carat diamond ring, decided to take Paul in hand, just as she had Dizzy, advising him on clothes, food, an automobile, health, contracts, and occasionally even his pitching style. Paul, who had a temper when pushed too far, never complained, though only for the sake of keeping peace with his brother. But for the rest of his life, he could not abide being anywhere near Pat.

Perhaps only in one area were the brothers different. Dizzy unabashedly believed he was the world's greatest pitcher.

"I ain't no Dizzy," Paul once admitted. "But no one else is either."

"Yeah, but you ain't as far behind me as them other fellas, Paul," Dizzy graciously conceded.

Dizzy also had a nickname, and Paul did not. Dizzy not only liked the name but also frequently referred to himself as Dizzy in the third person. Paul, though, despised the attempt by sportswriters to dub him "Harpo"—or, later, "Daffy." He hated both names, and no one in his family or on the team ever used them, nor did the St. Louis newspapers. It was an era when sportswriters, often for the sake of fitting a name into a headline, rebaptized virtually every player with a colorful handle. The Cardinals' starting lineup included such noms de guerre as Ripper, Pepper, Ducky, the Fordham Flash, the Lip, Showboat, Kayo, Pop, Tex, Wild Bill, Dazzy, and Dizzy. In reserve were Spud, Chick, and Whitey. Paul had the distinction among his fellow teammates of actually being called by his real name. Perhaps also to show that he had a special relationship with the great Dizzy Dean that no one else had, he made a point of always calling his brother Jerome.

Paul Dean pitched his first game as a Cardinal on March 20 in an exhibition match against the Philadelphia Phillies, allowing five hits and no walks in three innings. The consensus was that he looked pretty good, and Paul uncharacteristically bragged, "I'm gonna win 25 games this year just to prove I got more stuff than Dizzy."

A few weeks later, Dizzy incited a brawl at a Bradenton sports arena. Accompanied by DeLancey and Reuben Stowe, a barber, he went to see a middleweight wrestling match between Cyclone Burns and Bulldog Mallory. The trio were sitting ringside when Burns sent Mallory crashing through the ropes. Landing right in front of Dean, he stumbled to his feet. Feigning angry desperation, Mallory grabbed a soda bottle and started to climb back into the ring.

"That ain't fair!" Dean cried out, as Mallory turned to look at him in astonishment. Shocked that a professional wrestler would behave in so unsportsmanlike a manner, Dean shouted, "Get that thing from him, Reuben!" The pint-sized barber managed to snatch the bottle away but hurt his finger in the process.

"You all right, Reuben?" Dean inquired. Then he looked up at Mallory and growled, "You ain't no wrestler, Bulldog. I could whup your ass."

After feigning a punch at Dean, Mallory rolled into the ring and allowed himself to be immediately pinned by Burns.

"You got peaches for balls!" a thoroughly disillusioned Dean bellowed.

Rising to his feet, the defeated wrestler motioned for Dean to climb into the ring and prove his case. Tossing off his coat, Dean leaped up, followed by DeLancey and Stowe. They were immediately accompanied by three or four dozen fans, all by this time whipped into a frenzy, who had no intention of seeing their young hero, the Great Dean, come to harm. As the crowd held Mallory captive, Dean meted out the wrestler's punishment, pummeling his stomach with a flurry of lefts and rights. Finally, several sheriff's deputies arrived and broke up the melee, though not before several of Mallory's supporters had also managed to get into the ring. One had torn off Dean's sleeve, and another had ripped off the back of his shirt.

The next day, the *Bradenton Herald* reported that one-time world welterweight wrestling champion George Jordan had challenged Dean to a match.

"I ain't got no time for this here, Georgie," Dean was quoted as responding. "I gotta go win them Redbirds a pennant, and you tell the old Bulldog, no hard feelin's."

3

THE GANG'S
ALL HERE

According to the 1930 census, the population of the United States was 122,775,046, or less than half of what it would be by the end of the century. The American and National Leagues each consisted of eight teams that played a 154-game schedule, meeting each other 22 times in a season—11 at home and 11 in the opponent's home city. Most franchises were owned individually or in partnerships, though few were profitable. Mostly, they were a source of civic pride. A majority of teams played in ballparks named after the men who had financed their construction or subsequent renovation, as in Detroit's Navin Field, Chicago's Wrigley Field and Comiskey Park, Shibe Park in Philadelphia, and Ebbets Field in Brooklyn.

Seating capacities varied greatly, but most were relatively small by modern-day standards, ranging from about 28,000 to 42,000. The oldest and smallest facility in the majors, Baker Bowl where the Phillies played, seated only 18,500. Most ballparks were also situated along major bus or subway lines in commercial areas, and admission averaged from $1.50 to $1.75. As the Depression worsened, the Yankees sharply reduced the price on 20,000 general admission seats, where fans could still buy hot dogs, peanuts, and soda. In January 1920, passage of the Volstead Act implemented the Eighteenth Amendment to the U.S. Constitution, which prohibited the sale of alcoholic beverages in the United States, and not until the amendment's repeal in 1933 was beer to become widely available again as a ballpark concession.

Cigarettes in the thirties were also being shrewdly marketed as symbols of sophisticated living and a sign of manliness. Many ballplayers appeared in advertisements for Camels, Chesterfields, and other popular brands. Smoking was a rite of passage for many young men, as well as an acceptable extravagance for sophisticated young women. Athletes smoked not only before and after games, but even during games, though Organized Baseball frowned on them smoking in uniform. At one later point, the Yankees' Joe DiMaggio was to duck into the passage behind the dugout nearly every half-inning for a smoke and a half cup of coffee. Many players, especially those from rural areas, also heavily used chewing tobacco.

Ballparks were rarely filled to capacity after 1930. "While the prosperous times most Americans had enjoyed for the past several years were clearly over by mid-1930," Charles C. Alexander wrote in *Breaking the Slump: Baseball in the Depression Era*, "and many minor leagues were in financial trouble, the Great Depression worked a delayed reaction on big-league baseball." Attendance in 1930 reached an all-time peak of about 10.1 million, but then hard times brought sparser crowds. The crowds were to return again in 1934 and 1935, mostly as a result of the acceptance of nighttime baseball; the minors also experienced a comeback. But baseball as a business continued to struggle throughout the rest of the decade.

The talent pool for professional baseball in the 1930s was probably also much larger than it is now, Alexander noted:

"One should keep in mind the immense baseball universe that used to exist outside Organized Baseball. Once upon a time, baseball was king, for both spectators and participants." It was the game everyone played, including middle-aged men, far into middle age in organized "semipro" leagues and in "loosely structured competition between small towns and rural communities. So not only relatively but in absolute numbers more Americans were probably playing baseball in the 1930s than at any time since."

Ballplayers, of course, were also noticeably smaller back then, though then as now, pitchers were bigger than other players on average. An average Yankee pitcher in 1936 stood six feet and weighed 186 pounds, and an average catcher stood at five feet eleven and weighed 180 pounds. In 2000, the average Yankee was six feet two inches and weighed 200 pounds. In the age of steroids, even those players seem puny by comparison.

Starting players, including pitchers, were expected to play the whole game. In those days, pitching coaches were a rarity, and on most teams nonexistent. Only in the late thirties did managers routinely begin to use late-inning relievers. An average game lasted about one-and-three-quarters hours.

Even during the Depression, though, and as always, ballplayers were better paid than wage earners in the general population. In 1932, a player earning only $3,000 was still earning more than twice as much as a typical industrial worker. Sportswriters and fans had little sympathy for players demanding raises. Although they earned meager salaries themselves, most journalists tended to take the owners' side in salary disputes. The two most publicized in the early 1930s involved its two greatest players, one a veteran and the other a relative newcomer. In 1934, Babe Ruth had to settle for $35,000 after having his salary cut from $80,000 in 1931 to $75,000 in 1932, and to $52,000 in 1933. Dizzy Dean, at the very height of his powers, took the radical and completely unheard-of step of walking out on his team at high noon in a Cardinals' pennant drive. A few other players tried to bargain with owners and general managers, but the overwhelming majority quietly accepted the terms of a contract. The typical ballplayer also seldom let an injury keep him out of a lineup.

Sports medicine was still in its infancy. Most teams employed professional trainers to keep their men in shape, but "such men possessed little knowledge of physical conditioning or the treatment of players' ailments beyond massage and Mercurochrome." Players were expected to play through their pain. After their professional careers ended, the majority of ballplayers had few options for making a living outside baseball.

The game was also rougher, at a time when batting helmets and forearm guards did not exist. Fistfights were common between players, or even between players and umpires. Umpires rarely issued a warning to pitchers who were throwing high and tight pitches. Brushbacks were considered a fair part of a pitcher's repertoire, a necessary tool to keep the batter from crowding the plate. Most fights on the field were triggered not by knockdown pitches but by spikings on the base path, or by what one player yelled at another.

Some high-salaried players, managers, and owners were also known to have lost heavily in the stock market crash of October 1929, as well as in succeeding years. Perhaps the two most notorious examples were Mickey Cochrane, the catcher for the Philadelphia Athletics, and the team's owner and manager, Connie Mack. In the fall of 1931 Cochrane also lost an astounding eighty thousand dollars in a Philadelphia bank failure.

The biggest draw in baseball was, of course, the New York Yankees, who carried an annual payroll of between $300,000 and $350,000 and attracted more than a million fans into Yankee Stadium each year. They also drew big crowds on the road and took their entitled 25 percent of ticket sales. In the National League, the two most financially sound franchises were the New York Giants and the Chicago Cubs. Since the arrival in 1902 of John McGraw, the Giants had won eleven pennants and four World Series as of 1933. The Giants were owned by a syndicate headed by New York stockbroker Charles Stoneham, and the proprietor of the Cubs was William Wrigley, Jr., a native of Germantown, Pennsylvania, whose gum business had made him one of the wealthiest men in the country. In addition to the Cubs, he also owned steamboats, tugs, yachts, hotels, and estates in Wisconsin and Arizona, as well as the Los Angeles Angels of the Pacific League. In addition, he owned nearby Catalina Island, where the Cubs held their spring training.

The poorest teams were the National League's Philadelphia Phillies and Boston Braves, and the American League's Boston Red Sox, Chicago White Sox, and St. Louis Browns. A Pennsylvania law dating to the eighteenth century forbade the Phillies, as well as the Athletics and the Pittsburgh Pirates, from playing home dates on Sundays, when typically they would draw the largest crowds. Finally, in a referendum in November 1933, voters in Philadelphia and Pittsburgh overwhelming approved a measure to allow local officials to license baseball and football games on Sundays. Until then, the Keystone State's strictly enforced blue law was an economic burden that required all three teams to schedule one-day jumps to New York, Chicago, or Cincinnati for Sunday games. The elimination of those jumps now translated into a significant savings for team owners, as well as wear and tear on the players.

The Baker Bowl where the Phillies played not only had the smallest seating capacity in the Majors but was also prized by sluggers for its right-field fence, covered in tin, which was only 280 feet from home plate. As a result, the team featured left-handed power hitters, notably Chuck Klein, who in 1929 hit forty-three home runs, mostly over that fence—not to mention another forty-five doubles that mostly bounced off it.

Attendance at Sportsman's Park was so poor that, in February 1934, both the Cardinals and the Browns discontinued local radio broadcasts, which had been aired since 1926, though only on weekdays for the past two years. The front office of both teams made the move because they believed that the broadcasts were keeping fans at home.

In 1934, Sportsman's Park was also one of the few remaining big-league ballparks that continued to operate without a public-address system. "It is very bush league nowadays," complained Sid Keener in the *St. Louis Star-Times*, "to have an announcer strut around the park in a futile attempt to inform fans of the numerous changes through an old battered megaphone." But the park was to remain without such a system until 1936. Until then, an announcer named Jim Kelley would march to the first-base side of the stands, hoist his megaphone, and begin to shout, "B-a-t-t-r-e-e-z-e f-e-r t-u-h-d-a-y's g-a-m-e," and then read the names of the battery and the rest of the players. He then repeated that routine on the third-base side, and when he was finished he retired to his stool near the grandstand screen. Each time a substitute batter, runner, or relief pitcher appeared, he rose to announce the change, and as often as not, the play was finished before he had completed trumpeting the appearance of the new player to the fans on both baselines.

During this period, finding and then signing the best baseball talent was much like horse-trading. As a result of the terms of the National Agreement of 1921, the three top-level minor leagues and two lesser leagues had exempted themselves from the annual player draft and could therefore hold onto any player they wanted to for as long as they wished—or rather, until they got the price they wanted for that player.

As part of his plan, Branch Rickey hired more scouts than any other team, and kept close tabs on how they had done in the Cardinals' growing network of farm clubs. One of his many axioms was "Out of quantity comes quality." The farm system revolutionized minor league baseball in the thirties, even though the baseball commissioner, most team owners, and most sportswriters still had strong reservations about it. Judge Landis, the commissioner, objected for two reasons: He believed, first, that the foundation of the minor leagues was local franchise ownership and, second, that the Cardinals' farm system prevented deserving players from reaching the Majors as quickly as they should, because the Cardinals had the power to hold them back at will. Dizzy Dean, in fact, was a case in point.

Against those arguments, Rickey noted that most minor league teams were in serious financial trouble and could use the support of a big-league team and vital cash assistance. "Rickey would go to his grave convinced that the expansion of farm systems—especially his own—had saved the minors in the worst of the Depression." He also noted that the Cardinals traded away or sold many players who had matured in their farm system.

Just before the start of 1934 spring training at the Cardinals camp in Bradenton, Florida, manager Frank Frisch arrived in St. Louis on March 1 after attending the funeral of his old mentor, John McGraw. When he took over from the popular and easygoing Gabby Street in late July 1933, he had clamped down hard, forbidding any heavy drinking or gambling, and strictly enforcing a midnight curfew. Already there was discontent among some of the players, who bridled under Frisch's disciplinarian rule. He also refused to compliment his players on making a good play, insisting that they were well-paid professionals who were expected to meet a standard of excellence on the field at all times.

Frisch held no one to a higher standard than himself, in fact. As a second baseman, his philosophy was simple: Do whatever was necessary to stop the ball. If he was unable to catch a grounder with his glove, he let the ball ricochet off his knees, chest, or even face, then chased after it, snatched it up, and, if it was the right play, fired the ball off to the first baseman. Once, when someone suggested he work on his technique, Frisch angrily replied, "My motto is the hell with technique. Get the ball!"

One testament to his brutal determination to let no ball pass came from outfielder Ross Young, a former Giants teammate. Back when Frisch played with New York, the team was traveling aboard a Pullman when a fan came back to chat with the players. It turned out that he was not only a baseball enthusiast, but an expert on snakes as well—as proved by the reptiles he was carrying in a burlap sack. Naturally, the players were curious to see this hobbyist's novel collection and gathered around. Obligingly, the man pulled out a snake for their admiration. "This one," he said, holding up a writhing three-foot snake, "is the North American coach whip. It is the fastest snake on this continent. I know you are all famous athletes, but if I were to throw this snake out into a field, not one of you could catch him."

"Frank Frisch could," Young replied.

Frisch was born in 1898. His father, a lace importer, had immigrated from Germany. At Fordham University in the Bronx, New York, young Frank's speed as a halfback earned him the nickname he would carry for his lifetime: the Fordham Flash. He also played basketball and baseball at the university's Rose Hill campus, where his coach was Artie Devlin, a former third baseman for the Giants. One day in May 1919, Devlin visited Giants manager John McGraw at the team's plush downtown office.

"John," Devlin told him, "I have a ballplayer for you. You know I wouldn't talk about a kid this way unless I sincerely believed it. But this kid is a Major League ballplayer. Right now, I mean."

"What's his name?" McGraw asked.

"Frisch. Frank Frisch. He knows he's a ballplayer, too. I don't mean he's swellheaded. He isn't. But he knows he's a ballplayer and nobody is going to talk him out of it. I could bring him down to the Polo Grounds and show him to you, but I'd rather you'd have somebody look at him in a regular game."

McGraw accommodatingly sent a scout to the campus to watch Frisch play. Frisch's performance proved so impressive that, three days later, McGraw signed him up. Frisch never spent a day in the minors. Not pleased by his son's choice of a vocation, his father roared, "Laces and linens. That's a business. Hitting a baseball is a game for little boys."

In his first few weeks as a pro, Frisch sat on the bench, or occasionally was sent in as a pinch runner. But after a few weeks, he started his first game, playing first base. The first batter up smashed a blistering grounder right at him. Unable to snare it in his glove, Frisch let the ball hammer into his chest, then ran after the ball and threw out the runner.

"That was all I had to see," McGraw later recalled. "The average youngster, nervous anyway, starting his first game in a spot like that, would have lost the ball. Frisch proved to me right there that he was the ballplayer I thought he was from the beginning."

The crusty McGraw and the campus hero soon developed a father-son-like relationship. McGraw enjoyed teasing Frisch, that rarity with a bachelor's degree, as "college boy." (McGraw had also doted on another "college boy," Christy Mathewson.)

In his first four years as a professional, Frisch left no doubt that beneath his flashy demeanor, he was an athlete of tremendous ability and drive. Not only did the Giants win the pennant in 1921, but Frisch hit .341. He also led the National League in stolen bases. In successive years, he hit .327, .348, and .328. In recognition of his prowess McGraw had named him team captain soon after he joined the club.

By 1926, Frisch was on top of the world. He also traveled extensively, had become something of a wine connoisseur, enjoyed going to the theater, and counted reading and gardening among his pastimes. As befitting a man who knew how to use his leisure time well, he also collected pipes.

Then one day his world fell apart when, while on a road trip in 1926, he made the mistake of getting into a row with his iron-willed mentor. McGraw was brutal in his criticism of any player who made a mistake, and he also had no use for anyone on his roster who claimed to be ill or have an injury. Midway through the season, Frisch was troubled by such agonizing charley horses that he worried whether his career might be affected if he continued to play despite the pain. Yet even more, he feared being called a cement head, and worse, by McGraw.

In Cincinnati, Frisch failed to field a ball that McGraw thought he should have caught. The Giants manager chastised his young protégé so mercilessly that afterward Frisch quickly took a shower and, in defiance of protocol, left the clubhouse before McGraw did.

Then, on a sweltering August day in St. Louis, a man at first broke for second on a hit-and-run play. As Frisch moved to cover the base, the batter hit a grounder that, Frisch later claimed in his autobiography, he could not have stopped "if I had a net on a long pole. McGraw called me a dumb Dutchman, with a lot of profane trimming, a concrete-head, and asked me what I was doing—trying to give away the ball game? I said, 'Mr. Mack, you don't mean that.' But he got on me harder than ever, and kept it up in the clubhouse after the game, which we lost."

That night, Frisch joined some of the other players for a few beers, but he did not reveal his intentions. As he sat brooding, he knew that he was going to part ways with the Giants and McGraw. That night, looking out over Forest Park from his hotel room in the Chase Hotel, he asked himself whether he was doing the right thing, and concluded that he no longer had a choice. Going down to the lobby, he gave a porter some cash and instructed him to buy a ticket for the noon train to New York, to collect his luggage at 10 A.M., to put it in a waiting cab, and not to tell anyone what he was doing. The porter knew who Frisch was, and he also knew who McGraw was, but he did as Frisch requested.

When Frisch reached New York, he read in the newspapers that McGraw had fined him five hundred dollars for leaving the club without authorization. Once Frisch got home, the phone began to ring constantly, but he refused to answer it. "I was angry, disgusted, down-in-the-dumps," he later wrote. "I was worried about the bad legs. I knew I shouldn't have been playing. If I kept on playing with the legs in that shape, it might mean the end of baseball for me. I went to a doctor and he advised me to take a rest."

Frisch later rejoined the team, and McGraw told him that the fine was going to stick. Though Frisch was soon playing again, he knew that his days as a Giant were numbered. He was traded to the Cardinals at the end of the season, and for many years the two men remained estranged. At first, Frisch was distraught when he learned where he would be playing, and he announced to one and all that there was no way he would ever move to the Midwest. Like many native New Yorkers, he regarded any city or town west of the Hudson River as a burg.

Soon, though, like the ferocious competitor that he was, he changed his mind and resolved that he would not only play for the Cardinals but also give them more than their money's worth. That winter he and his wife traveled to Saranac Lake in Upstate New York, where Branch Rickey had once gone to contemplate his destiny as he recovered from consumption, and for three months Frisch worked out until it was time to report for spring training. His hustle impressed a delighted Sam Breadon, who was later to remark, "In all the years I have had the Cardinals, no player ever played ball for me as Frank Frisch did in 1927."

The Cardinals won the pennant again in 1928, but lost the Series to the Yankees. In 1930, the Cardinals again won the pennant, but this time they lost the Series to Connie Mack's Philadelphia Athletics. The following year, Frisch hit .311, the Cardinals again won the pennant, and this time they defeated the A's for the world championship. That same year, Frisch also again led the National League in stolen bases and won the National League's Most Valuable Player award.

As Robert Hood observed, "When Frankie Frisch took over as manager of the Cardinals, he had ranked as one of baseball's greatest second basemen, in a class with Eddie Collins, Napoleon Lajoie, and Rogers Hornsby." Though no longer the exceptional fielder he had once been, he was still a powerful switch-hitter. When he arrived in Bradenton on March 5, 1934, his train was three hours late, but he still called for a 12:30 P.M. workout. A few players were not due to show up until the next day, or were holding out for more money, including rookie Paul Dean.

Years after the Giants traded Frisch, he and McGraw ran into each other at a party thrown on Travers Island, the New York Athletic Club's summer home on Long Island Sound. The two men were sitting at separate tables, but at the urging of their respective wives, Frisch ambled over to greet his old boss. "It was a gay party," Frisch remembered, "and before it was over McGraw and I not only were shaking hands, we had our arms around each other, and we were fast friends through the rest of his life. I had a deep respect and affection for him."

During McGraw's funeral, the pallbearers were standing around the casket, and Giants manager Bill Terry articulated what everyone, including Frisch, was thinking. "After all," said Terry, "he was a pretty good guy."

Even before the start of spring training in Bradenton, some of the Cardinal regulars were impatient for the season to begin. One of them was left fielder Joe Medwick, who had arrived in St. Louis weeks earlier to undergo daily treatments for a charley horse from the club physician, Dr. Robert Hyland.

The Cardinals organization had discovered its stalwart left fielder in 1930. Medwick was the son of immigrants from the part of the Austro-Hungarian Empire that is now Hungary. After the family settled in Carteret, New Jersey, Joe had excelled in football, basketball, and baseball in his freshman year in high school, earning four letters. A muscular young man with bulging forearms and biceps, piercing black eyes, and a hair-trigger temper, Medwick was also virtually unbeatable in two other highly competitive games: handball and Ping-Pong.

In his sophomore year, Medwick dropped out of school to help the family financially, going to work at a copper factory. It was not only a dangerous workplace, but also a dead end. Medwick's alarmed high school coach, recognizing the young athlete's potential, soon convinced his parents to insist that he return to school.

Medwick continued to play baseball with his school team, and with other teams as well, including one sponsored by the American Legion, and in September 1929 he took a trolley with a friend to Newark to try out for the Newark Bears, a farm team of the New York Yankees. The Newark manager was Tris Speaker, one of the game's greatest players in the first decade of the century, who had been told beforehand of Medwick's potential and said to him, when they met, "I've been looking for you, my boy." But the tryout did not go well, and afterward Speaker told Medwick that he was too young to play professional ball. He also privately thought that Medwick was a bad-ball hitter and would never reach the majors. "I would advise you to finish your education," he gently told the youngster, "before you enter professional baseball." As a consolation prize, he gave Medwick a bat signed by John J. McGraw.

Rejection only motivated Medwick all the more. In his last year in high school, he played both quarterback and fullback on the football team, scoring 145 points in nine games. In the fall of 1929, the family's financial situation became even more precarious after the stock market crash. His father lost a poolroom that he owned. Yet several alumni of the University of Notre Dame had heard of Medwick's reputation as an athlete and suggested that he consider accepting a football scholarship to the school. That offer was followed by two dozen other scholarship invitations, including ones from Princeton and Duke. Medwick also knew that scouts from the Yankees and Philadelphia Athletics were keeping an eye on him.

So also, as a matter of fact, were the St. Louis Cardinals. One day in mid-June 1930, Medwick was playing in a game in Island Heights, New Jersey. In five times at bat, he hit four doubles. After the game, a man approached and said to him, "I'm Pop Kelchner, scout for the Cards, and if you got a minute, kid, we might be able to work something out you'd like."

Kelchner offered Medwick a contract to sign with the St. Louis team, and Medwick asked for time to discuss the matter with his family. He was well aware of Branch Rickey's idea of a baseball "chain gang," and also of the team's reputation for having a high turnover among managers and players. In addition, Medwick had a high opinion of his own talents—an attitude that became part of his reputation as a surly individualist in future years. As he pondered his fate, Rickey himself showed up in Carteret and agreed to give Medwick a five-hundred-dollar signing bonus. Medwick accepted the terms and, later that same month, boarded a train for Scottsdale, Pennsylvania, to play with a Cardinals farm team. In a curious appendage to his contract, Medwick had insisted that he play under the name of Michael King so that he might preserve his amateur status as a potential football player named Joe Medwick if he decided to accept a football scholarship from Notre Dame.

During his year in Scottsdale, Medwick/King hit .428. Both the Yankees and the Tigers tried to buy him, but Rickey refused to sell.

In the spring of 1931, Medwick was sent to Houston to play for the Buffaloes. At the end of training, on March 31, he heard that Knute Rockne, the football coach of the Fighting Irish, had died in a plane crash. Tragic as that news was, it confirmed Medwick, who by now had dropped his pseudonym, in his decision to pursue baseball, not football, as his career. He was not yet twenty.

Two of Medwick's Houston teammates were also future members of the Gashouse Gang: Dizzy Dean and Tex Carleton. Medwick started out in a slump, but by mid-July had raised his average to .297. He and Dean had also been paired as roommates on a road trip, but the voluble southerner proved too much for the taciturn Jersey boy, who was something of a loner with an attitude problem. Medwick requested a different roommate, and his wish was granted.

That same month, a female baseball fan wrote a letter to the sports editor of the *Houston Post-Dispatch,* who printed it in his column called "Looking 'Em Over." The letter read, "Please tell me about Medwick. I have heard he was an Italian and can hardly speak English. Was this true? Joe Medwick was my favorite player, and I have nicknamed him 'Duckie' because he walks just like a duck. I understand he lives here with Eddie Hock. Was it true that Joe was so young he had to have Sheriff Hock look after him?"

In answering the letter, the columnist remarked that "come to think of it, Joe does walk with a sort of duck-like walk."

A nickname was born, and Duckie (or more commonly, Ducky) Medwick, in that era when a colorful handle was de rigueur, joined a list that included such other similarly dubbed players as Ducky Hale, Ducky Davenport, and Ducky Jones. Medwick was also to be known as Ducky Wucky, and, on occasion, as the Mad Hungarian, though he personally preferred Muscles. By now he was a powerfully built young man, who regularly worked out with barbells. His imposing strength and brooding personality added up to a reputation as a man who was not to be trifled with.

In 1932, Medwick hit .354 and drove in 111 runs, for a slugging average of .610. All the fans knew that this would be the Houston star's last season in Texas. At the end of August, he finally got the call—and a train ticket—to join the Cardinals. The team was playing in Chicago, and he was to meet them there. The year before, the Cardinals had won the World Series, but now they were stuck near the bottom of the standings. On September 1, Medwick met his new teammates in the clubhouse; but when they tried to fasten the Ducky Wucky label on him, he glowered. Manager Street told him that he would be batting second and went over the various signals for "steal," "bunt," and so on. In his first time at bat in the big leagues, Medwick hit into a force play at second. But after Frisch doubled, he rounded third and slid into home to score the game's first run. Though the Cardinals lost, sportswriter J. Roy Stockton was clearly impressed by Medwick's performance, even though he did not get a single hit:

> Medwick is a right-handed batter who steps into the bucket, much after the fashion of Al Simmons [the Philadelphia Athletics outfielder nicknamed "Bucketfoot" Al, who was to hit thirty-five home runs in 1932]. . . . He steps backward with his left foot as he swings, but he has so much power that he hits left- and right-field fences, despite what is generally considered a handicap to a batter. Medwick is only 20 years old, but he looks much older; and when you see him on the field, you would never classify him as a juvenile. He has the physique, the power, the speed and skill of a much older athlete.

Almost immediately, bad blood began to develop between Medwick and many of the other players. Even in his first weeks with the team, he criticized any teammate who, in his opinion, made a foolish error. Instead of buying his own newspaper each morning, he also usually found a used one in the clubhouse and read it. One day in Philadelphia he opened his locker to discover that it was stuffed with used newspapers. Yet none of the players confronted Medwick to his face. He was clearly a man no one wanted to get into a fistfight with. Despite his tough-guy reputation, Medwick was devoted to his family back home in Carteret. Every two weeks, when he received his paycheck, he mailed most of it to his mother.

In 1933, Medwick was the youngest player to report to spring training in Bradenton. At twenty-one, he was two years younger than the next youngest, Burgess Whitehead. In his rookie year, Medwick batted .349 and ranked in the top five in seven categories: runs scored, doubles, runs batted in, runs produced, slugging percentage, total bases, and home runs.

Also that year, Medwick formed a close relationship with Frisch. Their bond was not unlike that between Frisch and his old mentor, John J. McGraw. "Frankie was a great manager," Medwick recalled in later years. "He never gave up. He was a good teacher. He never bothered you. When you made a mistake, he'd take you aside and talk to you. He never showed you up, which was a great thing. And the way I always felt was: When I made a mistake I wanted the manager to tell me, not the other players. A player's got enough to take care of his own position and his own job. And I would not allow anybody to tell me . . . that I had made a mistake. Frankie Frisch, my manager, would tell me."

Of course, what Medwick did not want done unto him by his teammates, he did unto them so frequently that his criticisms were a considerable cause of friction on the team.

Medwick was also friendly with Leo Durocher, another East Coaster like himself, who later became his roommate on road trips. Neither had much use for the hillbilly clique centered on Dizzy Dean and Pepper Martin.

Like Medwick, Pepper Martin was another Cardinal so eager to start spring training that he had gone to St. Louis first, before heading down south to Bradenton. But Martin had no other agenda than to hang out at the clubhouse with trainers and assorted team officials, though in his enthusiasm he had arrived in the brutally cold city wearing only a light summer suit. The irrepressible third baseman had spent the winter hunting in his native Oklahoma.

Martin was born Johnny Leonard Roosevelt Martin, in honor of President Teddy Roosevelt, on February 29, 1904, the last of seven children of Celia Spears Martin and George Washington Martin, in what was still designated the Oklahoma Territory.

Martin's family were Mormons, of Irish extraction; some sports-writers later tried to disseminate a story claiming he also had Cherokee blood, but there was no proof. Martin grew up in a sod house that his father had built for his family on a 40-acre plot. The family later moved to a 160-acre farm near Temple, Oklahoma, where the main crop was cotton. Like the Dean brothers, Martin picked cotton as a boy and tended the family's livestock.

After a drought erased the family's livelihood, Martin's father found work in Oklahoma as a carpenter. Martin fell in love with baseball as a schoolboy, though on several occasions he was forced to drop out of class and become a newsboy to contribute money to his hard-pressed family.

"When I was nine, I delivered morning newspapers in Oklahoma City," he once told an interviewer. "I knew by heart the average of near every big leaguer. I saved enough money out of my earnings as a newsboy to buy my first glove, and I had it stuck in my back pocket wherever I went and whatever I did. Not so many kids in my neighborhood had gloves and owning that mitten gave me almost as much happiness as would a couple of home runs in a World Series game."

Like many boys growing up in rural areas, Martin also developed a passion for hunting. He was fifteen when, because of his irregular attendance, he finally received his elementary school diploma. In high school he did not fare much better and dropped out after only two years.

Martin's real education took place on the sandlots of Oklahoma City, where he played with a team sponsored by the Second Presbyterian Church, while supporting himself with a job at a filling station. Briefly, he also worked as an apprentice for a local tinsmith. One day, while cutting through some galvanized tin, he sliced the tip of his middle finger on his left hand. The accident convinced him not only to quit his job, but also to try his luck at playing professional ball. At first, the closest he got was selling peanuts and soda in a local Oklahoma City ballpark. Later he was drafted as a pitcher for batting practice. That led to a job as a batboy, and before long he was shagging flies in the outfield before games.

Over the next few years, Martin continued to play, either as an infielder or a pitcher, for a number of local teams. His speed and hustle were impressive enough, but no Major League scout signed him up because he was considered too young and too small. Determined to break into professional sports, Martin even joined a Native American professional football team, the Hominy Indians, in the fall of 1922. In the summer of 1923, the Oklahoma Gas and Electric Company offered him a job as an assistant lineman.

Intermittently, Martin also doggedly pursued his education and, just as doggedly and intermittently, continued to play professional football, as if he were still not sure where his interests lay, and where best to apply his extraordinary speed and agility. Most of the time, though, he worked as a grunter. A grunter, or grunt man, was someone who literally wrapped his arms around a coworker for Oklahoma G&E and hoisted him off the ground so that he could perform his work, even on occasion during blizzards. What kept Martin going, in all that time working on Oklahoma's lonely back roads, was his dream of one day playing professional baseball, which by now he had decided was his destiny.

By the end of 1923, Martin was nineteen years old, still unsigned, and trapped in a dead-end job. Reluctantly, he decided to give up all hope of becoming a professional ballplayer and find some other way of supporting himself. Briefly, he worked for a city golf course, fishing golf balls out of muddy ponds, then repainting and selling them. He also put in long hours as a day laborer, laying pipe. But the lure of baseball proved irresistible. It was probably around this time, according to Thomas

Barthel, Martin's biographer, "probably in the winter of 1923–24, when he may have played for a team in the 'Tomato Belt' in Mississippi, an area south of Jackson." During this low point in his life, as Martin later confessed to a reporter, he was a virtual hobo, hitching rides on freight trains from town to town. On one occasion, he reported for baseball duty in a moth-eaten car with two bird dogs and a shotgun in the backseat. "There were many times," he remembered, "when my one shirt would get its only bath in the creek."

In the spring of 1924, Martin finally broke into professional ball when he signed on as a pitcher with the Guthrie team in the Oklahoma State League, earning $125 a month; his team-mates at the higher end of the pay scale earned up to four times that amount. Later he was installed at shortstop, though his in-experience as an infielder, combined with an overabundance of enthusiasm, soon made him as much of a hazard as an asset. As Martin later explained, "Often my throws to first base were so high I was endangering the lives of the fans in the grandstand."

By July, low attendance had forced the league to disband, and the Guthrie management sold Martin to a team in Greenville, Texas, in the East Texas League. He performed well enough that, for the 1925 season, he signed a contract call-ing for twenty-four hundred dollars for the season—the team's maximum salary. Yet his old problem of throwing wild to first continued to plague him, even after he was reassigned to sec-ond base. To compensate for his erratic fielding, he spurred himself to steal more bases and improve his hitting. His sheer love of the game also expressed itself in other ways. On arriving in a town for a game, Martin frequently toured the streets the next morning in a horse-drawn wagon that held a sign adver-tising the afternoon's contest. Always among the first to get to the stadium, he also enjoyed helping the groundskeeper smooth out the infield. His diligence and enthusiasm paid off.

That year he batted .340, hitting 18 home runs and stealing 38 bases. On the other hand, playing second base in 86 games, he made 33 errors. As a pitcher, he allowed 52 hits in 53 innings.

Martin clearly had good reason not to be impressed by his own performance. That opinion was shared by not a few others, including Branch Rickey's chief scout, Charley Barrett, who later remembered, "He was without a doubt the worst ballplayer I ever saw—but how he could run and how he could slug that ball!" Like his employer, Barrett had an almost unerring eye for raw talent, and he wrote to Rickey that Martin "has speed and power, he can hit, and he has a wonderful arm." That exceptional speed soon earned Martin a nickname that was to endure for the remainder of his professional life: "the Wild Horse of the Osage." Reputedly, he was so fast that he could chase down rabbits on foot.

That was all Rickey wanted to hear. Raw talent was something he could not instill. But how to field was a skill that could be taught a young ballplayer. After all, that was why he had created the farm system.

Years later, Martin recounted what occurred next: "I was not satisfied with my playing and I didn't think I was getting along so good. What happens one day is this: L. K. Wise, the owner of the club, calls me in and says, 'I just sold you to the St. Louis Cardinals.' Folks, that was the nearest I ever came to fainting."

The Cardinals sent him to their team in Fort Smith, Arkansas, where Martin's Major League education began in earnest. It was while playing for Fort Smith that he also acquired his other nickname, Pepper, compliments of Blake Harper, the team owner, after watching him hop around the bases and listening to him talk nonstop.

While playing shortstop, Martin continued to be bedeviled by his old problem: throwing the ball over the head of the first baseman and into the stands. "But every time the manager had made up his mind to shoot me dead because of bad fielding," Martin later recalled, "I would make a hit or steal a base, and that is how I saved my life from one day to the next."

In *Voices of Baseball* Bob Chieger describes Martin as resembling, around this time, "a chunky, unshaven hobo who ran bases like a berserk locomotive, slept in the raw, and swore at pitchers in his sleep."

In 1930, Martin batted .363 for the Rochester, New York, Red Wings, a Cardinals farm team in the International League. The following year, Rickey installed him as a backup center fielder on the Cardinals roster. Finally, in June, Martin decided it was do-or-die time. He had had enough of being shunted back and forth to the minors, and being asked to do utility and pinch-hitting chores. Going directly to the office of Branch Rickey, he confronted the general manager, saying, "I'm tired of riding that bench. I want to get into the game, or I want you to trade me to some club that will play me."

Rickey obliged Martin by making room for him in center field by trading Taylor Douthit, and Martin soon returned the favor by becoming one of the Cardinals stalwarts, and the most colorful player on the Gashouse Gang after Dizzy Dean. Even after he became a star, he continued to pursue his various hobbies with a passion. These included hunting for rattlesnakes, while armed only with a stick and a burlap bag, in the hills of his native Oklahoma. The snakes were often donated to the St. Louis and other zoos. Midget auto racing was another unorthodox pursuit. He often spent his mornings before a game tinkering with his car, and arrived at the ball field with his face, hair, and hands smeared with oil.

Like Dizzy Dean, Martin was a chronic practical joker. Favorite pranks included tossing sneezing powder into a hotel lobby's ventilation fans, and dropping water balloons on the heads of passersby from an upstairs window. Also like Dizzy, he was a master of deadpan humor—often at Frisch's expense. After one Cardinal loss, the manager was in a particularly foul mood, and was berating his players in the clubhouse in language that was equally foul, when Martin interrupted.

"Frank, can I ask you a question?" he asked.

"Yeah," Frisch replied, "what?"

"Frank," he said, "I was just wondering whether I ought to paint my midget auto racer red with white wheels or white with red wheels."

Frisch shook his head and gave up, and the meeting was over.

The stocky, barrel-chested, very fast Martin stole sixteen bases in 1931, in an era when base stealing was not considered an important offensive tactic, though Frisch led the National League with twenty-eight. During the World Series that year, with the Cardinals opposing the Philadelphia A's, Martin vaulted into national headlines and became a household name when he hit .500 and stole five bases against catcher Mickey Cochrane. Martin's headfirst, belly-flopping slide when stealing bases was a crowd pleaser, unlike the conventional feet-first, fallaway, or hook slide.

Both Martin and Dizzy Dean were gifts from the gods to sportswriters down in Florida to cover spring training. One day Frank Graham, at the time a freelance sports journalist, was in town to watch an exhibition game between the Cardinals and the Giants. As he walked past the Dixie Grande Hotel, he stopped and did a double take. The barber at the first chair, wearing a regulation green smock, looked just like Pepper Martin. In fact, it *was* Pepper Martin. Not only that, but the customer he was coolly shaving with a straight razor was Dizzy Dean. Graham went in to investigate.

"Hi," Dizzy said, grinning, when Graham entered.

"What's the gag?" Graham asked.

"Aw, nothin'," Dean replied. "Old Pepper here had a new razor he wanted to try out, so I said he could try it out on me. Boy, he is some barber!"

Finishing up with a flourish, Martin slapped Dean with a hot towel. He massaged the pitcher's face, dusted him off with talcum powder, and sat him up in the chair. Martin ran a comb through Dean's hair, flicked him again with the towel, and bowed him out of the chair.

"Next!" he cried, at Frank Graham, but the sportswriter declined the offer.

———

Among the malcontents on the Cardinals squad in 1934, Leo "the Lip" Durocher stood out. A former factory worker and pool shark from Springfield, Massachusetts, he had caught the attention of the Yankees in 1925 while playing shortstop for Hartford, Connecticut, in the Eastern League.

Durocher was a big spender. He loved to gamble, frequented nightclubs, and had his suits tailor-made, and by 1928 he had become the team's first-string shortstop. His roommate during his years with the Yankees was Babe Ruth. Allegedly, Ruth suspected Durocher of stealing money and jewelry from him, later caught him with previously marked bills, and beat him up. Adding to Durocher's somewhat tarnished reputation were the bad checks the shortstop had a habit of passing to finance his lifestyle. By the end of the 1929 season, he was $10,000 in debt. While negotiating with Ed Barrow, the general manager of the Yankees, for the next season, Durocher not only asked for a raise from $4,500 to $6,500, but he needed $1,000 of that amount in advance to pay off a hotel bill. Barrow declined, and Durocher cursed him out. Barrow then banished him from paradise, trading Durocher to the lowly Cincinnati

Reds, who had finished in seventh place in 1929, just ahead of the Boston Braves.

Then an even worse fate befell the Lip. In May 1933, he was traded to St. Louis, a town even more off the map, even further removed from his beloved New York, than Cincinnati. As a man chronically in debt, he especially did not like being traded to a team that had a reputation for being cheapskates.

Durocher arrived in St. Louis as the result of a tragic accident that struck down the man he was hired to replace. One of the club's most promising players was its outstanding young shortstop, Charley Gelbert. Following the end of the Cardinals' dismal 1932 season, the twenty-six-year-old Gelbert returned to his home in rural Pennsylvania. One day in November he went rabbit hunting. When his foot got caught in a vine, he stumbled against a rock outcropping and his shotgun went off, discharging a full load of No. 6 shot into his left calf and ankle. The instep was also blown away and several nerves were destroyed. After gangrene set in, doctors wanted to amputate, but Gelbert vigorously resisted. Though the leg was finally saved, and the former star shortstop was able to return to the team, he was clearly no longer the player he had once been. The Cardinals traded him, but a desperate Rickey still had not found a suitable replacement when the 1933 season opened. Finally, he reached an agreement with the Cincinnati Reds. Rickey traded two pitchers and an infielder for Durocher and two pitchers. One of the pitchers Rickey traded was Paul Derringer.

"The release of Derringer," Lieb noted, "later one of the great National League pitchers, has been criticized as one of Rickey's biggest mistakes, but Branch needed an experienced shortstop badly, and Leo filled the bill in fine style."

Rickey was in a hotel room, lying in bed with a cold and chewing on an unlit cigar, when the newly acquired Durocher barged in and began making insulting comments about the Cardinals organization.

Rickey listened patiently, admitted that some of the young man's remarks were true, and then leaned over, pointing his cigar, and said, "I made this trade because I think we can win a lot of pennants with you at shortstop. You can do it for us, you can be the spark. You can help us win pennants."

Durocher's ego was bigger than the hole in his pocket. That was all he needed to hear.

Like his teammates, Joe Medwick and Pepper Martin, Durocher had shown up in St. Louis even before the start of spring training in Florida, though, in his case, his arrival had nothing to do with an excess of zeal to play ball. The Cardinals shortstop and ex-pool hall hustler was scheduled to play an exhibition match of pocket billiards with former world champion Frank Taberski. He lost, 100 to 64.

———— ◆ ————

The Cardinals pitching staff was both the team's weakness and the reason for its stellar success. The third man in the rotation after the Dean boys was James Otto "Tex" Carleton, whose curveball, like Paul Dean's, was thrown sideways. A graduate of Texas Christian University, he was also the only other college graduate on the team besides Frank Frisch and Burgess Whitehead. Like Medwick, he had a truculent disposition and seemed always to be looking for trouble. He was particularly annoyed by Dizzy's boasting, and by Paul's mere presence on the team. "He won't last a month in the big leagues," he predicted, referring to Paul, in the spring of 1934. Like most of the other pitchers on the staff, he was deeply resentful of the Deans and felt insecure and threatened by their ascendancy.

Carleton did have one moment of glory, however. On July 2, 1933, at the Polo Grounds, he led the Cardinals in one of the hardest-fought and greatest games in their history. Carl Hubbell was pitching for the Giants, and the two men each threw for sixteen scoreless innings before Pat Crawford was sent in to pinch-hit for Carleton. The Giants finally scored in the eighteenth inning to win, 1 to 0, and that year Hubbell won the MVP with a league-low 1.66 ERA. Carleton won seventeen games that year and was third in strikeouts behind Hubbell and Dean.

Rounding out the four-man starting rotation were two left-handers, Bill Walker and "Wild Bill" Hallahan. Walker was a local boy, from East St. Louis, Illinois, and had spent six years with the Giants before returning home to play for the Cardinals. His thirty hand-tailored suits put him in a class with Durocher and Ernie Orsatti as one of the team's fashion plates. In 1934, his chronic sore shoulder would limit him to a 12–4 record and a 3.12 ERA, though he was to prove invaluable in the September pennant race. In May, though, Medwick had broken Walker's wrist with a hard-hit ball, and Walker was forced to sit out the early part of the season. He relaxed by sitting in a lounge chair, wearing a smoking jacket and reading detective novels.

Hallahan, who came from Upstate New York, was called "Wild Bill" for the simple reason that no one, including himself, could be quite certain where the ball would end up after he released it from the mound. In 1930, 1931, and 1933, he also led the league in walks, with one every 2.2 innings. In 1933, he had been the National League's starting pitcher in baseball's first All-Star Game, but in 1934 he was to achieve only an 8–12 record, with a 4.26 ERA.

The bullpen of the Cardinals was seldom capable of offering true relief. Some cynics referred to it as an old folks' home. It did consist of veterans of genuine ability, and on occasion they surprised everyone and pitched a few worthwhile innings. Yet their authority on the mound was so precarious that Frisch's confidence in them continued to erode as the season wore on, with the result that the starting rotation pitched a league-leading seventy-eight complete games in 1934.

The chief reliever was Dazzy Vance, whom the Cardinals had acquired in February 1933 from the Cincinnati Reds for the waiver price of seventy-five hundred dollars. The Redbirds bullpen still lacked depth, and Rickey hoped that Vance could supply some much-needed stability in that department. Vance had no trouble fitting in with the likes of Dizzy and Pepper. Back in the 1920s, when Vance had been playing for Brooklyn, the off-field misadventures of Dazzy and some of his Dodger pals had inspired some New York sportswriters to dub them "the Daffiness Boys."

Clarence "Dazzy" Vance had been in the big leagues since 1922, after failing in three earlier attempts to gain the Majors that had been hampered by a chronic inflamed elbow. By then, he was already thirty-one years old with ten years' worth of experience in the minors. But the fourth time was the charm. Playing for Brooklyn, he launched a career that in 1924 saw him win the National League's first Most Valuable Player award—beating out the Cardinals' own Rogers Hornsby, who batted an awesome .424 that year—when he compiled a 28–6 record. In that year, he won fifteen in a row in one stretch, posted a 2.16 ERA, and struck out an impressive 262 batters—the most strikeouts by a National League pitcher since Christy Mathewson.

A native of Orient, Iowa, Vance once explained how he got his unusual nickname: "Well, it has nothing to do with 'dazzling speed,' as most fans believe," he recalled. "Back in Nebraska I knew a cowboy who, when he saw a horse, a gun, or a dog that he liked, would say, 'Ain't that a daisy,' only he would pronounce 'daisy' as 'dazzy.' I got to saying, 'Ain't that a dazzy,' and before I was 11 years old, the nickname was tacked on me."

Vance's last great season was 1928, when he went 22–10 with a league-leading 2.09 ERA and posted 200 strikeouts. He was also the highest-paid pitcher in baseball, earning $20,000 in 1928 and $25,000 in 1929. But by then his glory days were behind him, and he had yet to appear in a World Series. In 1932, his last year with Brooklyn, he finished with a 12–11 record and a 4.20 ERA.

The Cardinals' other elderly reliever, Jesse Joseph "Pop" Haines, had been born in a small town near Dayton, Ohio, and broke into professional baseball in 1914 with the Fort Wayne, Indiana, team of the Central League. He later played for teams in Saginaw, Michigan; Topeka; Tulsa; and Kansas City and eventually won ninety-seven games in the minors. Conventional wisdom, though, was that he was not Major League material. Both Cincinnati and Detroit hired him, and then sent him back down to the minors. Haines's response was only to keep trying harder.

Finally, after a particularly brilliant season for Kansas City in 1919, with a record of 21–5 and an ERA of 2.11, the big right-hander came to the attention of the young Branch Rickey. Rickey actually watched Haines pitch only two innings before heading directly to the office of the team's owner and offering to buy the pitcher for ten thousand dollars. After the owner agreed, Rickey had to figure out how to raise that kind of money, since he certainly did not have anywhere near that much in the bank. Back then, the Cardinals were about as broke as Haines himself.

Haines's longevity in the Majors was primarily due to his knuckleball. By 1934, though, he had been relegated to relief for the first time in his career. Haines added to the team's general dishevelment by always wearing a tattered, long-sleeved white shirt under his jersey, which fluttered like a flag when he pitched—and, of course, distracted batters as well. The practice of wearing an inner garment was later banned.

The Cardinals' only left-hander in the bullpen was Jim Mooney, a twenty-seven-year-old ex-teacher from Mooresburg, Tennessee, who in 1934 managed to win only two games. The remaining members of the bullpen, Flint Rhem and Jim Lindsey, were virtually worthless. So ineffective was the bullpen, in fact, that Frisch was to call on starter Dizzy Dean as a reliever seventeen times, in addition to his thirty-three starts.

———

One day during spring training, Rickey cast a cold eye on his new infield—Rip Collins at first, Frisch at second, Durocher at shortstop, and Martin at third—and did not like what he saw. His player-manager was clearly too old to keep up with the youngsters flanking him on either side.

"You know, Gene," he said, talking aloud to his young manager of information, Gene Karst, "Frisch has really slowed down in the field. I'm afraid he's going to play himself at second too often. I don't think we can win the pennant with him playing second base. We ought to trade Frankie to Boston. We could get Al Spohrer for him. I really ought to fly to St. Louis and convince Sam Breadon to make a trade."

If Frisch were traded, of course, that meant that the Cardinals would need a new manager. But Rickey's philosophy was that the players made the manager, not vice versa. A player he also had his eye on was Burgess Whitehead, the skillful young second baseman just out of the University of North Carolina who was known as the Gazelle. The problem with Whitehead, though, was that he had none of Frisch's batting power. On second and third thought, Rickey decided not to fly up to St. Louis.

Another potential weak spot that bothered Rickey was further down the middle at center field. That post was held by the capable Ernie Orsatti, an accomplished outfielder and a left-handed hitter who batted above .300 year after year—in those seasons, that is, when his injuries did not bring his presence on the field to a premature halt. In the off-season, Orsatti worked in Hollywood as a movie double and prop man. As a precaution, Rickey acquired George Watkins from the Giants as a backup.

Rickey also somehow convinced Breadon to put Rogers Hornsby back on the payroll. The great slugger and former Cardinals shortstop had been let go by the Chicago Cubs as player-manager in August 1932, and the Cubs went on to win the National League pennant. The Cubs later voted to deprive Hornsby of a share in their World Series winnings. Rickey installed Hornsby at second base that season, and also used him as a pinch-hitter, and the grand old champion repaid their confidence by hitting .325 in forty-six games. The following year, Breadon released Hornsby from his contract so that he could take over in mid season as manager of the Browns.

If Rickey had any doubts about Frisch's managerial abilities, they were not shared by *St. Louis Post-Dispatch* sportswriter J. Roy Stockton, who, during spring training, reported to his readers back home:

> Frisch seemed in control of the situation. He was a tough hombre last year when he took over the reins. He had to be. He was moving up from the ranks and the club was out of hand. The club was demoralized. Drastic measures were necessary and he took them. He gained the nickname "John McGraw Jr." and there was grumbling and muttering. But Frisch has "softened up," in the language of the dugout. He is closer to his players, kinder to them, more sociable. And while he makes it plain that he is the boss, he is not unreasonable, and if there is any discussion or discord in the camp, this observer, with many friends in the ranks, has failed to see or hear it.

Of course, there was no way either Frisch, Stockton, or anyone else could have foreseen that, midway through the season, the new manager would have the biggest mutiny in the history of baseball on his hands. Like a feral cat, Dizzy Dean, the Ozark mountain boy, was a creature no amount of coaxing, bullying, or pampering could domesticate. Frisch may have been the manager of the 1934 St. Louis Cardinals, but Jerome Herman "Dizzy" Dean was the unofficial ringleader.

In a sense, there were two different Cardinals teams that year, each composed of the same group of players and each vying for dominance over the other under their respective leaders, the gruff disciplinarian versus the most brilliant and successful rebel that the national pastime has ever known. Both had their confederates. The amazing thing that happened that year, and put the Cardinals forever in baseball's pantheon, is that, late in the season, Frisch's team and Dizzy's crew miraculously merged their identities. The St. Louis Cardinals became the Gashouse Gang—as the club came to be known. It was not inevitable. In fact, it was against all odds and, on the face of it, downright impossible. But somehow it happened.

———

Four days before opening day, April 17, a divorce suit brought by Ruby Hartley Durocher, the shortstop's wife, was begun in the domestic relations court in Cincinnati. Durocher had filed a cross petition in which he alleged that his wife had been having an affair with Charles McDonald, a concessionaire at the city's ballpark, who in turn was also being sued for divorce by his wife.

Ruby Durocher, who now lived in Cincinnati, took the stand and testified that she had visited her husband the previous June at a St. Louis hotel and discovered a stash of love letters addressed to him, including one from a New York chorus girl named Marie. In its coverage of the trial, the Cincinnati

Enquirer reported, "One 'Marie' letter told of being lonesome because her only chance to go out was with 'old fossils' who were 'not like my loving Leo.'"

Ruby Durocher also testified that subsequently, in January, her husband had hit her in the jaw and tied her up with a sheet. She offered a photograph of herself in evidence that showed, said the newspaper, "a badly distorted jaw."

In his cross-examination, Durocher's attorney asked Ruby whether she sometimes drank "quite a bit." She answered, "I do, on occasion."

On April 17, opening day, the hearing was resumed. Durocher's attorney presented evidence that Ruby had once been in a Cincinnati hotel room with another man. Ruby testified that Durocher had physically abused her but denied that she had provoked him by coming home drunk and telling him that their child was not his. "I had one black eye a month after I was married to that man," she said.

Ruby denied having an affair with Charles McDonald or any other man.

When Durocher took the stand, he was asked about the night he struck his wife. He testified:

> I got home about 11 o'clock, and went to bed. About two o'clock my wife came in. She took off her coat and hat, then snatched the covers off the bed. She seemed intoxicated, and I smelled liquor on her breath. I took the covers back and she snatched them a second time, cursing me. I tried to quiet her by telling her she would wake the baby, and out of a clear sky she said, "The baby needn't concern you. It doesn't belong to you." I said, "What did you say?" She said, "You heard me. The baby doesn't belong to you." Then I struck her.

The next day, the judge granted the Durochers a divorce and gave Ruby custody of the couple's three-year-old daughter. Durocher was ordered to pay ten dollars in monthly child support.

———————

Just before the Cardinals broke spring training, Frisch told his players, "Don't let anybody push you around. You've got to win games, especially the close ones. Your nights are your own, but your bodies belong to the Cardinals during the daylight."

He ended his lecture with this warning: "Now, if you'd rather go back to the mines and dig coal, or ride around the country in Pullmans and live in the best hotels at the expense of the club, speak right up. We haven't any room for softies; no holds are barred. That's the way we are."

"You said more'n a mouthful, Frank," Dizzy Dean said, when Frisch ended his talk. "Going to play ball."

4

THE GASHOUSE FOLLIES

Sam Breadon in 1934 was a silver-haired, blue-eyed, ruddy-complexioned man in the prime of life. Each morning, after breakfast, he usually drove first to his automobile agency, where he spent a few hours attending to business. Then he drove to Sportsman's Park.

At the start of the 1934 season, Breadon owned nearly 75 percent of the stock. Opening-day crowds at the ball games were also bigger than they had been in recent years, and club owners installed brass bands in the seats to instill a sense that the economy had turned the corner and good times were on their way again.

Even so, Breadon, like millions of other businessmen, still scrimped where he could, cutting the salaries of his managers, players, and office staff. Some of his cost-saving measures seemed downright pathetic. He once ordered an electric wall clock to be disconnected so he could save a few more pennies.

In 1933, in the very depths of the Depression, Breadon and Rickey had announced a new rule: No player would earn more than $10,000 a year. The year before, Frisch's salary had been cut from $28,000 to $18,500, and in 1933 it was further reduced to conform to the new maximum salary.

Despite his reputation as a cheapskate, the Cardinals owner, like Rickey, was popular both with his players and with the local population. Since their partnership had begun, Breadon and Rickey had brought four pennants and two World Series titles to town.

At a meeting of the board of directors in January 1934, Breadon had also announced that the Cardinals had finished the previous season in the black, despite the Depression and the team's sixth-place finish. His and Rickey's ruthless budget cutting had brilliantly produced a farm-raised team that regularly won pennants and world championships with low- to medium-salaried players, and also turned a profit.

In 1934, the consensus of most sportswriters was that the National League pennant would be won by the New York Giants, the Chicago Cubs, or the Pittsburgh Pirates. In a poll of 97 journalists, 40 named the Giants, and 34 picked the Cubs. The Pirates garnered only 9 votes, even though they had finished in second place the year before, with considerable depth both in pitching (Heine Meine, Waite Hoyt, Red Lucas) and hitting (outfielders Paul and Lloyd Waner and infielders Pie Traynor and Arky Vaughan).

But the Giants were the obvious team to watch—and for other teams to fear. Manager and first baseman Bill Terry, a formidable batter in his own right, led a squad that included such heavy hitters as Mel Ott, Lefty O'Doul, and Jo-Jo Moore. Four Giants pitchers were among the finest in the game: Carl Hubbell, Hal Schumacher, Freddie Fitzsimmons, and Roy Parmelee. Rounding out a team that was "strong up the middle" were catcher Gus Mancuso, second baseman Hughie Critz, and shortstop Travis Jackson.

The Cardinals ended up in fourth place in the poll, with 13 first-place votes, but also 14 votes predicting that they would finish the season in the second division.

In 1934, many teams were also fitted with spanking-clean new uniforms and equipment, after enduring the indignity of playing with used balls, bats, and gloves while wearing patched jerseys during the worst years of the Depression. On April 17, when the season began, a crowd of 40,000 at the Polo Grounds in New York watched Hubbell defeat the Phillies with a four-hitter, 6 to 1. Over in Brooklyn, Van Lingle Mungo led the Dodgers to an 8-to-7 win over the Boston Braves before 28,000 fans. Even in Cincinnati, 30,000 showed up for the contest pitting the Reds against the Cubs at Crosley Field.

But at Sportsman's Park, just 7,500 fans came out on a warm spring afternoon to see Dizzy Dean pitch against the Pittsburgh Pirates on opening day. His opponent on the mound was Heine Meine. Paul Waner, whom Dean had struck out in his debut game back in 1930, when the Pittsburgh slugger was hungover after a night of partying, was to lead the league in batting that season with a .362 average. But Dean surrendered only six hits, and the Cardinals flexed their muscles and dispatched Meine after three innings. St. Louis scored two runs in the second inning, two in the third, and three more in the fifth off reliever Waite Hoyt to bring the final score to 7 to 1. Virtually the entire team turned in a classic performance. Medwick homered and whacked two singles, Pepper Martin blasted two doubles and thrilled the fans with his trademark headfirst slide, Frisch collected two singles, even Durocher got two hits, and Dean struck out four batters while walking only one.

"Yeah, I guess the old flipper ain't changed none," Dean told reporters after the game, "but wait'll you fellows see my brother Paul tomorrow. He'll show 'em what this family has for breakfast."

Unfortunately, Paul's professional debut the next day failed to live up to either of the brothers' expectations. Despite trumpeting in the press that "another magnificent Dean" would be seen on the mound for the first time, only 5,000 fans showed up. At 182 pounds and standing six feet three inches, Paul had nearly the same build as Dizzy, and was just twenty years old. He claimed later that he did not feel the least bit nervous, though it did seem to him that the crowd had suddenly ballooned to 100,000. After Paul ended his warm-up, Dizzy called out from the sidelines, "Fog one in there, boy."

Rearing back, Paul whistled a strike past Paul Waner. In two more pitches, he struck him out. He then struck out outfielder Freddie Lindstrom as well. But Lloyd Waner singled, Traynor homered, and the Pirates went ahead, 2 to 0. The Pirates scored two more runs in the second inning, and Paul was yanked. Later the Cardinals rallied to tie the score, but Cookie Lavagetto's homer in the eighth inning gave the Pirates a 7-to-6 victory. Pittsburgh won the next day as well, with Wild Bill Hallahan absorbing a 14-to-4 punishment. Conventional wisdom quickly concluded that the St. Louis club was probably destined to wind up somewhere at the top of the second division, as some journalists had predicted.

That conviction was deepened when the league-leading Chicago Cubs arrived to administer a 2-to-1 loss to Tex Carleton, who was complaining that, though he was a veteran, he had been ranked below rookie Paul Dean in the rotation. Cubs owner Philip K. Wrigley, who had inherited the team upon his father's death two years earlier, now had slugger Chuck Klein on his payroll, and Klein's $30,000 salary was the highest in the National League, topping even the Giants' Bill Terry, who earned $27,500. The previous year, while playing for the Philadelphia Phillies, Klein had won the Triple Crown in batting.

On April 22, the Chicagoans exacted their revenge on Dizzy Dean for a wisecrack he had made the previous July after striking out seventeen Cubs. Appearing on a Chicago radio station, he had singled out losing pitcher Guy Bush, drawling, "They had boys like him down in the Texas League takin' care of our bats. He ain't got nothin'."

Bush had heard the broadcast and told his teammates about Dean's insulting comments. Now came the payback. With Dean pitching his second game, the Chicago team walloped him for six hits and four runs in the first inning. As Frisch walked to the mound to have a chat, a Chicago player shouted out, "Leave the son of a bitch in, Frank. We're not through yet."

In the second inning, after the Cubs got two more hits, Frisch sent Dean to the showers, as Bush called out, "Tell them on the radio how good you were, squirt." Down in the clubhouse, Dean could only grouse, "Them Cubbies can kiss my ass."

Paul Dean relieved his brother, but he was able to last only to the fourth inning before he followed Dizzy into the clubhouse. The Cubs blasted two more pitchers and won the game by 15 to 2.

The Dean brothers continued to be less than impressive. The Cardinals lost seven of their first nine games, then won four in a row, though without any help from Dizzy, whose record was 1–2, or Paul, who not only had a 0–0 record but a bewildering earned run average of 7.50. Frisch had all but given up on Paul after he was sent in as a reliever in late April against the Cubs in Chicago and promptly allowed Klein to sail a towering home run into the stands. Frisch pulled his rookie pitcher after only two innings.

Paul finally won his first game on May 3 when he was sent in as a reliever against the lowly Philadelphia Phillies. Medwick helped, hitting a grand slam. The Phillies scored against Paul in three of the five innings that he was on the mound, however, and some of his teammates, notably Carleton, made no secret of their belief that Paul belonged in the minors and was being kept on only because he was Dizzy's brother. "The brother act may become a one-man show," said Dick Farrington in the *Sporting News*. "There is grave doubting about Junior Dean."

Soon enough, Frisch began to see what Paul's problem was. He was trying to imitate his brother instead of developing his own style. The younger Dean also lacked Dizzy's enormous self-confidence, which no number of defeats, no criticism from colleagues, no taunting from opponents could erode. One day Frisch invited Paul to share a double porterhouse with him in the dining car of the Pullman as the team headed back from Pittsburgh to St. Louis.

"We open with the Giants in about a week," Frisch told him, "and you're going to start the third game. Those Giants will be tough, but smart pitching can beat them. Let's analyze their batting form."

Then Frisch got into the aisle and struck a pose. Over the next two hours, the manager and his pitcher went over the entire Giants roster—and never once did Frisch mention Dizzy's name. He simply reiterated the message that Paul had what it took to beat New York. After Frisch paid the check, Paul's only words were "Thanks, Mr. Frisch."

On May 11, Paul Dean walked to the mound in St. Louis to meet his fate. After Frisch's pep talk in the Pullman, Paul now had begun to cast off his identity as Dizzy's little brother. He had to stop trying to pitch like Dizzy and become his own man. The timing, though, could not have been worse. The Cardinals' opponents that day were the rugged New York Giants, and Paul was going up against none other than the great left-handed screwball artist Carl Hubbell, the only man who rivaled Dizzy as the best pitcher in the National League. It was do-or-die time.

As if on cue, a gloomy omen had also appeared out of the skies the day before and still lingered in the atmosphere. On May 9, a great cloud of dust 1,500 miles long, 900 miles wide, and 2 miles high had swirled up from the Great Plains and smothered one-third of the United States. The Great Depression was already oppressive enough, taking away people's livelihoods and hope. Now came this darkness at noon to taint the very air they were breathing. An Associated Press reporter, Robert Geiger, had wryly suggested that the dust-blown lands of Oklahoma, Kansas, and Nebraska had been so scooped out by the furnacelike winds carrying all the farmers' topsoil away that nothing remained but a giant Dust Bowl. The name stuck and quickly became part of the American lexicon.

There had been previous dust storms. Back in the spring of 1932 and 1933, blizzardlike clouds had turned the sky black and sent people scurrying into their storm shelters. But not until 1934 did these atmospheric upheavals reach such a proportion that much of the rest of the country also experienced them at first hand. The storm that arrived in St. Louis on May 10 was laying a blanket of grit that extended from Montana to Wyoming, North and South Dakota, Nebraska, northern Colorado, Kansas, Minnesota, Iowa, Missouri, Wisconsin, Illinois, Michigan, Ohio, Kentucky, and parts of West Virginia and Pennsylvania. Weather experts later estimated that this storm and those before it had blown away 650,000 tons of topsoil. The storms were caused by months of drought and the poor condition of the soil after years of overproduction. Housewives used damp towels and rags to seal off doors and windows, but animals in the field had no refuge. Neither, that day, did the Cardinals and Giants, or their fans. Tom Meany, who was covering the contest for the *New York World Telegram*, reported that the great Dust Bowl storm had "swept southeastward from Nebraska and the Dakotas to envelop the town in a murky haze."

May 11 was also Ladies' Day, and as usual, some of the Cardinals' distaff fans brought cakes, pies, and cinnamon buns to their favorite players. When the team went onto the field, Dizzy saw Hubbell warming up and said to his brother, "Beatin' him is going to take another great pitcher, and that's you, boy, so go on out there and do it."

The Cardinals took an early lead in the bottom of the first as Martin doubled, Frisch tripled, and Collins singled to bring his manager home. The Giants scored one run each in the second and the sixth to tie the score, as both Dean and Hubbell pitched with comparable control and poise. In the tenth, with one out, Durocher doubled. Paul Dean then sent a pop fly to short right, but second baseman Blondy Ryan bobbled it. With runners now at first and third, Hubbell intentionally walked Martin to load the bases. On his second pitch to switch-hitter Jack Rothrock, the right fielder smacked the ball into the left-field wall. The Giants lost, 3 to 2, and Paul Dean had won his first full game. He and Hubbell had allowed nine hits each. Paul's fastball, particularly in the late innings, had dominated the Giants, and he had walked only three batters. After the game, Dizzy told a reporter, "Them Giants don't have a pig's chance in winter of beatin' me 'n' Paul." It was to become a familiar, even tiresome, refrain as the season wore on.

The Cardinals were then scheduled to play two games against Brooklyn. Dizzy Dean pitched and the Redbirds committed five errors. They won anyway, 12 to 7. After a day off, Casey Stengel's Dodgers took the second game. The St. Louis loss was possibly attributable to a demoralizing incident that occurred a few hours before the game. While the Cardinals were taking batting practice, Tex Carleton approached the cage. But Medwick suddenly cut in front of him.

"Wait your turn like everybody else," Carleton chastised him.

"I'm tired of taking your abuse," Medwick replied. He had been performing superlatively for the Cardinals and had already racked up six homers. More to the point, he was being paid by a magazine to pose for a photograph and did not want to waste an opportunity to earn extra income. When he motioned for the pitcher to throw him the ball, Carleton grabbed Medwick's arm. The temperamental Medwick dropped his bat, whirled around, and hit Carleton with a right that grazed his eye, knocking him backward. Carleton retaliated with a right hook that caught the outfielder on the chin. Medwick connected with a hard right, and Carleton missed an uppercut. After a few more wild swings, teammates quickly separated the two, Frisch demanded that they shake hands, and that was that—almost. In fact, though, the cat was out of the bag, and news of the fight, such as it had been, spread quickly.

Among the Cardinals, the consensus was that had the fight been allowed to continue, Medwick would have lost. "Joe was the meanest fellow we had," Burgess Whitehead later commented, "but Tex was the toughest."

Dizzy Dean got under Medwick's skin on a number of occasions—probably, in fact, all of the time. Temperamentally, they were opposite numbers, the Good Ol' Boy with his cornpone humor versus the Loner. There is no record or rumor of any brawl between them, but they once came close to a fistfight. Durocher's biographer Gerald Eskenazi noted how, "in one dugout confrontation with Medwick, who failed to run down a fly, Dizzy and Paul made a threatening move toward the outfielder. Medwick picked up a bat and challenged, 'Come on, I'll break up this brother act right now.' Later in the game, Medwick hit a home run, spat over [Dizzy] Dean's shoes, and snarled, 'Okay, let's see if you can hold that lead, gutless.'"

Medwick had also once picked a fight with Paul Dean and on that occasion learned a lesson—that a wiry young sharecropper's son can be a mighty tough customer. During spring training, Paul himself had threatened to punch both Rip Collins and coach Mike Gonzalez during an altercation. Like Medwick, he did not need much of an excuse to get into a scrap. One night while the team was traveling to a game in a Pullman, Medwick, Paul, and a few others were passing the hours playing poker. "I just happened to look over there at him playin' cards at the table," Paul later recalled, referring to Medwick, "and I was out of the pot, so I just looked at his hole card and he got mad. So I thought I'd get up from that table and stomp the hell outta him. When I was gettin' up, he hit me in the eye. He hit me. And then I was all over him. I was on him with my feet and everything else. They pulled me off and took me to the drawin' room and kept me there about an hour. But Medwick and me made up. We was good friends until the day he died."

Medwick's churlish responses to Carleton's legitimate objection and to Paul Dean's innocent peek were among the first seeds planted in the minds of sportswriters that later flowered into the legend of the rough-and-tumble Gashouse Gang.

Dizzy Dean's own not infrequent temper tantrums and sometimes intractable disposition, when he was not being utterly charming, certainly laid the groundwork. Adding to the mystique of athletes who occasionally acted in the most unorthodox ways were snake-hunting and midget-auto-racing Pepper Martin; Leo Durocher, the pool-shark dandy from New York; and the grizzled, no-nonsense street boss, Frankie Frisch. In the background, of course, was the gang's church-going gray eminence, Branch Rickey—a benign, fedora-wearing teetotaler who ruled his empire with ruthless efficiency. The 1934 Cardinals were not yet being called the Gashouse Gang, but they were already behaving like members of a rowdy street gang, each with his own personality and agenda.

On the other hand, sometimes they acted just like big kids having the greatest time of their lives. One day, for example, while the Cardinals were in Boston, Frisch and a friend were taking a stroll when a bag of water exploded within inches of their feet. Calmly surveying a third-floor window of the hotel, the manager explained, "That one was thrown by Rip Collins. He's the best bomber of the lot."

Collins also liked to say to a rookie, "Hey, kid. Go to the clubhouse and get me the key to the batter's box." The youth would be on his way before he heard the laughter and realized what was up.

At other times, Frisch was less tolerant of Gashouse antics. Pepper Martin, whose whereabouts and intentions were always a bit uncertain, severely strained the manager's patience with his odd hours, unkempt appearance, and unpredictable behavior both on and off the field. Martin often brought his midget auto with him when the team traveled, taking it to the banked racing tracks in cities where the Cardinals played. One day, according to Cardinals historian John Devaney, "Martin came running into the clubhouse late for batting practice, with engine grease smeared all the way to his elbows." When Frisch demanded an explanation, Martin replied, "I'm sorry, Frank. But I had a bet with a guy I could beat him in a two-mile race and he was late showing up."

"That's great," Frisch exploded. "We're trying to win a pennant and you're trying to win a racing bet."

As he stormed off, Frisch suddenly stopped, wheeled around, and asked, "How much was the bet?"

"Two quarts of ice cream," Martin replied. "And I won, too."

Shaking his head, Frisch slowly muttered to himself, "No, we're not crazy. We're perfectly sane, all of us."

Overhearing him, Dizzy Dean murmured to Martin, "The manager is going out of his mind."

In his early years with the Cardinals, Martin had also organized a band called the Mississippi Mudcats: Martin played a guitar given to him as a Christmas present by his wife; Lon Warneke also played guitar; Max Lanier played harmonica; Bill McGee played violin; Bob Weil blew on a jug; and French Bordagaray strummed on a washboard with thimbles. Two of the band's favorites were "Buffalo Gal" and "Possum Up a Gum Stump." Martin also did not like sleeping on soft beds in hotels, and he often pulled the mattress off the bed and slept on the floor. On hot summer nights, he also roosted on a fire escape.

The colorful Martin's chief publicist was Branch Rickey, who understood that newspaper stories about the eccentricities and flamboyance of his players could only help sell tickets. In almost every city where the team traveled, Frisch would observe the team's general manager seeking out a reporter and regaling him with the latest antics of Dizzy Dean, Joe Medwick, Pepper Martin, or Ernie Orsatti, among others. Rickey was particularly close to Bill Corum, a Missouri native working for the *New York Journal-American,* who "never tired of recording the deeds of his beloved Cardinals," according to Polner.

One of Rickey's plants involving Martin concerned the time he struck out swinging, returned to the dugout complaining so loudly about the umpire that all of the spectators within earshot could not help but hear him, then sat down and, with a wicked smile, turned to a teammate and said, "Someone has to give this team color."

Although many of Rickey's plants were true, or at least inspired by fact, others were patently apocryphal, such as the one about the time Martin's wife delivered their third child while Pepper was playing a game. As soon as it was over, Pepper allegedly rushed to the maternity ward, burst into Mrs. Martin's room, and shouted, "Darling, great news, we won a doubleheader."

Rickey once told a reporter, "Pepper Martin is the most genuine person I've ever met in my life. There was never an ounce of pretense in the man. He was 100 percent in everything he did. When he fell in love, he fell head over heels in love. If he wanted a new shotgun, he went out and bought it, whether he could afford it or not. He went all out in everything he did, and that was why he was such a great ballplayer."

So many of the Gashouse Gang were known for their eccentricities and sheer zaniness that, in that annus mirabilis of 1934, even Martin's behavior did not stand out as particularly unusual. Superstitions, in particular, were not uncommon. According to one adhered to by several of the players, any team member who found a woman's hairpin on the ground was virtually guaranteed to get a base hit during the next game he played. Several local sportswriters were quite aware of this peculiar conviction, and two of them, Ray Gillespie and J. Roy Stockton, decided one day to have some fun with it. Knowing that Martin was in a batting slump, Gillespie sprinkled a dozen or so hairpins on the floor of the Cardinals dugout where Martin was certain to find them. Then they retreated to a spot where they could watch unobserved as the ballplayer stumbled "accidentally" upon his pot of gold.

Instead, Medwick came strolling out, saw the hairpins, and greedily began to snatch them up.

"No, no," Gillespie shouted. "Those are for Pepper—to get him out of his slump."

"The hell with Martin," Medwick snarled. "Let him find his own base hits."

⸺ ∙ ⸺

After splitting a pair of games with Brooklyn, the Cardinals left St. Louis to embark on a three-week road trip. Having won fourteen of their last sixteen games, they now occupied third place behind the Pirates and the Cubs. Those two teams stood virtually tied, separated by only a few percentage points, and the Cardinals were one and a half games out. Just behind them were the Giants. Cincinnati dwelled in the cellar, though Philadelphia and Brooklyn, as usual, were prepared to tumble into that spot at a moment's notice.

Paul Dean had never been to New York before, and his brother, who had acquired a taste for nightclubs and Broadway shows, told a reporter, "I know that town like a chicken in a coop and I'm gonna show Paul around."

The day of the Cardinals' departure also marked the last day of Burleigh Grimes in a Redbirds uniform. Grimes was the last remaining legal spitball pitcher in the Major Leagues. When the spitball was outlawed in 1921, the playing days of seventeen pitchers were abruptly threatened, since that was the principal weapon in their arsenal. An exception was therefore made for those artistes as long as their careers lasted. Grimes had won two games and lost one that season before retiring.

The Cardinals' first stop was Boston, where they won two out of three. Paul Dean captured his third win in the opening game of the series, with the help of homers by Frisch and catcher Virgil "Spud" Davis. The Braves took the second behind the hitting of their big gun, Wally Burger, who had hit twenty-seven homers in 1933; he went two for four. In the third match-up, Carleton made his first appearance since his feud with Medwick and allowed just three hits. Medwick's game-winning triple helped secure the Cardinals' 2-to-1 victory. Then, on a Sunday, they returned to the Polo Grounds for another showdown with the Giants.

The batting lineup of the Cardinals had now gelled, with Martin, at age thirty, leading off. Though he was no longer the team's fastest runner, his sheer zest for the game and boundless energy were unmatched. The *Sporting News* even suggested tongue in cheek that he be given a week's vacation each month to recuperate from his exertions in the previous three. Martin was to rack up nineteen errors, more than any other third baseman that season. Nor was he ever able to completely tame his throw, which was still known to sail on occasion into the boxes along the first-base line. Yet his twenty-three stolen bases were to lead the league and amount to more than twice the number posted by the entire starting lineup of the Giants.

Right fielder John Huston Rothrock batted second. Rescued by the Cardinals from a minor league team in Columbus, Ohio, where he had been sent by the Boston Red Sox after breaking a leg, Rothrock was the team's quiet, polite, uncomplaining stalwart, now in his mid twenties. Rickey had recruited him to replace George Watkins, who had been traded to the Giants. Rothrock was to be the only player in the National League in 1934 who played in every one of his team's games, and his 647 at bats were just shy of the record of 649 set that year by Doc Cramer of the Philadelphia Athletics. Rothrock was also the Cardinals' best defensive outfielder, possessing both good speed and a powerful arm.

Frisch, at thirty-five, was not quite the team's grand old man. That distinction was shared by forty-three-year-old Dazzy Vance and forty-year-old Jesse Haines. But the old Fordham star, who batted third, was still the Cardinals' money player. "Nobody doubted that he was the 'hardest-boiled egg in the Redbird nest,'" Robert Gregory noted, "but two-thirds of the players didn't grade him high as a manager. They said he couldn't think ahead, called for too many curve balls to opposing hitters, and that Durocher, as much as they disliked to admit it, was a better tactician." Another complaint was that Frisch still tried too hard to be like his old mentor, John McGraw. On a positive note, though, Frisch—perhaps worn down by the likes of Dizzy Dean and Pepper Martin—had begun to relax his disciplinarian rule.

Medwick, by now also dubbed "His Duckiness" in the sports pages, batted cleanup. He and Durocher were rivals as the least liked members of the team. Medwick played ball to a different drummer, knowing that he wielded the Cardinals' most powerful bat, yet struggling with feelings of inferiority. As a result, he felt the need to assert and prove himself constantly. He was also not liked by players on other teams. Dizzy frequently taunted his opponents, but with such good humor that it was impossible not to laugh. Medwick, though, would often lean against a batting cage during the pregame warm-up and ridicule the other team's players—and no one laughed at his mean-spirited comments. Medwick was also an indifferent left fielder.

The fifth man in the lineup was Rip Collins, a one-time coal miner from Altoona, Pennsylvania, who had come to the Cardinals in 1931 and had fretted all during the winter of 1933 that he might be traded. Though he fielded well enough, he was criticized for being slow. But Rickey had wisely ignored Frisch's suggestion that he be traded, and in 1934 the Cardinals' switch-hitting first baseman was to lead the league in four hitting categories. Collins so relished his nickname that he listed himself in telephone directories as James Rip Collins. He also moonlighted as an amateur journalist, contributing small items to the sports pages of newspapers, and loved going to nightspots and, whenever the team traveled to New York, to Broadway theaters. Collins was also the team's resident practical joker. Years later, recalling his times with the Gashouse Gang, he remarked, "I would've played for nothing."

Virgil "Spud" Davis, the sixth man in the lineup, was the team's heftiest player at six feet one inch and two hundred pounds. Hailing from Birmingham, Alabama, he was the personification of a southern gentleman. "He does not strut into hotel lobbies, on main thoroughfares, or on the ball field," said Sid Keener in the *St. Louis Star-Times*. "The Spud does not poke his nose into an open conversation but is reserved and retiring. He does not hoard his money, dresses in the height of fashion, enjoys good shows, and is fond of movies." A solid right-handed batter and talented catcher, Davis had been purchased from the Phillies in spring training, after that team's dismal 60–92 record had left him yearning to be traded. Rickey acquired him in the spring of 1934 as a replacement for Jimmie Wilson, who was shipped to Philadelphia because of his lack of hitting and inability to get along with Frisch. Davis immediately expressed his gratitude by telling reporters, "Who wouldn't throw his arm off for this bunch after getting away from the Phillies?" Despite his modesty and reserve, he did have a few eccentricities. Often, he would ask pitcher Dazzy Vance to chant a Seminole prayer over his bat before he marched to the plate.

Like Davis and Durocher, center fielder Ernie Orsatti, who batted seventh, was—in the parlance of the times—a swell dresser. A native of Los Angeles, he bought his clothes at exclusive shops on Sunset Boulevard, which earned him such affectionate nicknames, in that politically incorrect era, as the "Dashing Dago" and the "Hollywood Wop." His flamboyant fielding style, as he recklessly raced toward the wall to snag a hard-hit fly, also earned him another nickname: "the Showboat." A ladies' man who called every woman "darling," Orsatti had first appeared as a Hollywood double for star Beatrice Joy, who in the film *The Man Who Saw Tomorrow* gets lost in a rowboat and drifts for five hours before the Pacific Fleet finds him. He also worked as a prop man for Buster Keaton, though Rickey often claimed that his player was a double for the comedian as well. Orsatti's brother, a casting agent, owned the popular Blue Bird restaurant in Los Angeles, where some Cardinals players often ate when they were in town, and the team's center fielder also had a reputation in his own right as a chef. A favorite of other players, he occasionally whipped up elaborate

Italian dinners for his teammates and their wives or girlfriends. If Davis was the biggest Cardinal of them all, Orsatti at five feet seven inches and only 146 pounds was the smallest.

The *Sporting News* called Durocher, the eighth batter in the lineup, "the most dangerous .250 hitter in either league." His former roommate, Babe Ruth, once described him, referring to his hitting abilities, as "the All-American Out."

Frisch shrugged off the Lip's lack of power at the plate, admitting, "Any hitting that Leo gives us is a bonus. He'd be a big help to any club if he couldn't hit a lick." Yet Durocher was so supremely confident of his ability both as a batter and as a shortstop that, at the start of the season, he bet Frisch an entire wardrobe of autumn clothes that he would hit .300 for the year. (He lost, ending up with .260, with thirty doubles. Frisch was thrilled—by Durocher's outstanding performance at the plate, not that he had a new set of clothes.) Durocher rivaled if not outshone Orsatti as the team's fashion dandy. "His knowledge of current affairs came from Walter Winchell's column," noted Robert Gregory, "and his personal style from George Raft movies."

Like Medwick, though, the unpopular Durocher, in his capacity as field captain, could be brash and in-your-face. He never flinched from criticizing a teammate if he felt that the player had not given his all, or had made a mistake. He also disliked any Cardinal pitcher who took too long a time between pitches, and often expressed his disapproval by impatiently kicking up dirt as the minutes slowly passed. "Show me a guy who takes his time on the mound," he once explained, "and I'll show you a damned loser."

Durocher was also baseball's premier bench jockey, which in the 1934 World Series was to become a potent Cardinals weapon.

In mid season, Frisch replaced catcher Spud Davis with Bill DeLancey, whose throwing arm was even more powerful and who was a considerable left-handed hitter. In only 253 at bats, he was to finish the season with a .316 batting average. A twenty-two-year-old from Greensboro, North Carolina, DeLancey was nicknamed Kayo, oozed country charm, and spoke with a lazy drawl. He also cussed more than anyone on the team, with the possible exception of Frisch. One time, when DeLancey hit a grounder, he refused to run it out and instead pounded the plate because he had expected to sail the ball into the bleachers. Frisch fined him fifty dollars.

"Goddamnit, I oughta be fined, Frankie," DeLancey concurred. "Yes, suh, I had it comin'."

At year's end, St. Louis sportswriter J. Roy Stockton was to write, "When the star rookies of the year are named, Bill should be near the head of the list."

Among the strongest players on the Cardinals bench was utility infielder Burgess Whitehead, who had the distinction of being the only Phi Beta Kappa scholar in baseball and a 1931 graduate of the University of North Carolina. "He probably could answer every question you asked him on philosophy, psychology, and astronomy," a reporter for the *Philadelphia Inquirer* once declared, "and then tie you in knots with a few questions of his own. If you seated him at a banquet table, he probably would not make one mistake if they put seven different forks in front of him." Soft-spoken and well bred, the twenty-four-year-old reserve player was also the team's fastest runner—faster even than Martin. He and Paul Dean had become good friends during their playing days in Columbus, and Whitehead was also to become one of Dizzy's closest pals.

On May 20, Carl Hubbell took to the mound before a near-capacity crowd of 38,782 fans at the Polo Grounds in New York to avenge the loss he had suffered at the hands of Paul Dean nine days earlier. This time the great Giants hurler would be opposing Dizzy. "The stage is set," wrote Tommy Holmes in the *Brooklyn Eagle,* for a duel in the sun between the two "fastest" sharpshooters in the league.

In the third inning, Dean was charged with an unearned run when Durocher collected a Gus Mancuso grounder and fired it ten rows behind the first base dugout. In the fourth, Collins's home run into deep left brought in Medwick, who had singled. In the fifth, the Cardinals scored again. With the bases loaded, Frisch tripled, and then Medwick hit a line drive homer. For the first time in ten games, Hubbell was sent to the showers. Dean easily went the distance, whipping a fastball that, in the words of Tom Meany of the *New York World-Telegram,* "embarrassed most of the Giant hitters no end." The Cardinals' 9-to-5 victory was more lopsided than it appeared and, combined with a 16-to-1 Pirate loss to the Phillies, advanced the Cardinals into second place, just one game behind the Cubs.

In the second game of the series, the Redbirds faltered, with Hallahan the losing pitcher. But in the third meeting, Paul Dean garnered his fourth victory, and once again Medwick's mighty bat provided the decisive firepower as he blasted a bases-loaded triple over the head of center fielder Jo-Jo Moore. Medwick was now batting at a ferocious .366 clip.

The hot pace that the Dean brothers were setting sparked a new round of sports page hyperbole and good-natured fun.

"Does anyone appreciate the resentment small town people hold for citizens of big cities?" asked Jimmy Powers of the *New York Daily News.* "This explains more than anything the success of the Dean brothers. When you hand Paul or Jerome a baseball and then they are to pitch a nine-inning contest, they more or less mechanically turn in an excellent job. If you tell them to pitch against the New York Giants, their eyes glow fanatically, they snatch the horsehide and stride to the mound, nostrils breathing fire."

The *World-Telegram* ran a story with the headline "Brother Dean Is No Rube: He's Been Here Before and Knows Everything." A photograph showed Dizzy and Paul in front of a No Parking sign. The accompanying article, under the byline of Tom Meany, purported to be an "unexpurgated" report on one of the Dean brothers' jaunts around the city:

DIZ: And over there lies Brooklyn.

PAUL: Have they got a subway like New York?

DIZ: Sure, it goes under the East River.

PAUL: C'mon now, Diz. You said you wasn't goin' to kid me. I'm no hick. I was in the American Association a whole year. Could we go to a nightclub?

DIZ: A nightclub? Didn't you get enough of them arc lights at Columbus?

PAUL: I mean like you see in the movies. I'd like to see one of 'em.

DIZ: Well, if we win the pennant, your share of the World Series oughta buy you a ham sandwich in one, if you still wanna go.

PAUL: What's that big building over there?

DIZ: That's the "Em-parr" State—they call New York the "Em-parr" state, you know.

PAUL: Why do they do that?

DIZ: Because the Giants get all the close calls.

PAUL: Gee, Diz, you know everything, don't you?

DIZ: Practically.

The Cardinals then played another pair of games with Brooklyn, this time on the Dodgers' home turf, and split the series.

Paul Dean's salary continued to be a sore point, though, at least so far as Dizzy was concerned. He never passed up an opportunity to pester the team's manager about the lowly $3,000 remuneration Paul was getting, while the worthless—in Dizzy's view—Hallahan was hauling in $12,000. At the very least, Dizzy felt, Paul ought to get a $2,000 raise.

"Morning, noon, and night," Frisch later recalled, "he would ask me, 'Have you talked to the bosses yet about poor Paul's wages, Frankie?' And I'd reply, 'Phone Mr. Rickey yourself, Diz. Just say what's on your mind.'"

What was on Dizzy's mind, and what he did not shrink from sharing with reporters, was the possibility that the Dean brothers just might go on strike if Rickey continued to ignore their case. The St. Louis papers—and primarily stories filed by J. Roy Stockton, the only reporter who traveled with the team—repeatedly echoed Dizzy's complaint that his brother was underpaid, even though Paul himself seemed happy just to be in a Cardinals uniform. But Paul obviously felt more loyalty to his brother than to the Cardinals management and never openly dissented from Dizzy's views.

Dizzy occasionally threatened everything from the two of them going back to Arkansas to live on a farm, to playing semi-pro ball for five hundred dollars an appearance. In time, he also began to harp not only on Paul's humiliatingly low wage, but also on his own. He noted that other baseball stars, including Lou Gehrig, Jimmie Foxx, and Chuck Klein, were making three or four times as much as he was.

Despite the widespread poverty and unemployment gripping the nation, Dean's complaints struck a chord with the public. Even some sportswriters were initially sympathetic to Dizzy's point of view, casting him as the little guy standing up to his rich bosses. Rickey and Breadon were frequently portrayed as penny-pinchers. The press also reminded the public that the general manager was notorious for selling players before they reached their prime, so that he would get his hefty 10 percent commission on the sale. Joe Williams, in the *New York World-Telegram,* correctly noted that "a third-base coach in New York is likely to be paid more than a star in St. Louis or Cincinnati. Mr. Dizzy would be getting twice as much pitching for the Giants, and he would be worth it."

Three days later, a Philadelphia paper reported that the Dean brothers were pondering a strike.

"I don't know anything about a revolt," Frisch was reported as saying diplomatically. "Sure, everybody would like to have more money, but I have enough to do managing a ball club without taking a hand in the business of salaries."

When Dizzy was asked about the strike, he replied, "Let's forget it. Everything's going to be all right."

Stockton reported in the *St. Louis Post-Dispatch*, "Paul also was reluctant to discuss the strike, but intimated that he had reason to suppose that a new contract would be offered. Other players on the team do not take the strike threat seriously. Almost to a man they echo Frisch's thought that February is the time to engage in conversations about salary."

Despite his discontent, or to prove to the Cardinals just how valuable he was to the team, Dizzy was no slacker. The next day, he beat the Phillies, 5 to 2, in ten innings, and even started the winning rally with a home run.

At the end of May, Dizzy's record stood at 6–2. He had won five games in a row. After leading the Cardinals to a 9-to-6 victory over Cincinnati on May 30, Paul was now at an impressive 5–0. The Cardinals were closing in on Pittsburgh, which led the league by a half game, for first-place bragging rights. For the month, the St. Louis club had posted an extraordinary 21–6 record. Medwick and Collins were batting well over .300. The Durocher-Frisch combination was turning in more double plays than any other pair of infielders in the league. The long, long road trip was coming to an end, and the St. Louis Cardinals seemed primed to take the lead.

The team was in great spirits after the victory in Philadelphia, and they were even looking forward to a rare day off before the Memorial Day weekend. In the clubhouse after the game, Dizzy Dean was standing in front of his locker, Number 13—which he always insisted on having—searching for a missing lucky sock.

"Hey, who took that dirty sock out of my locker?" he called out. "I can't pitch unless I find it. I can't pitch unless I find it. Haven't worked a game this season without having it in my pocket."

A half dozen teammates joined Dean in the sock search, turning over piles of dirty laundry and ransacking other lockers for a frantic three minutes. If Dizzy Dean could pitch only with his lucky sock in his pocket, that sock was vitally important to the entire team.

"You've never had more than two socks in your entire life," Frisch finally growled. "You'll probably find it on your foot."

Dean glanced down at his right foot, and there it was. He had put the dirty lucky sock over his size 12 right foot. Sheepishly, he apologized for causing such an uproar.

———

After taking both games of a Memorial Day doubleheader in Cincinnati, and then a third game on the last day of the month, the Cardinals found themselves in first place. That was when the Dean brothers decided the time was ripe to go on strike. While the team was still in Cincinnati, Dizzy called on Frisch in his hotel room and again demanded a higher salary for his brother. Frisch replied that he would not ask Breadon to give

Paul Dean a raise. Dizzy continued to raise a stink, and Frisch finally told him, "If you don't want to pitch, go home."

In his own room afterward, an irritable Dizzy told reporters, "If Paul had my nerve, we'd both be back in St. Louis. I don't need a second invitation to leave when I'm not appreciated."

Paul, who was in the room, did announce, though, that his right arm was sore, and that he did not know when he might be able to pitch again.

"Paul must get $1,000 cash in the hand," Dizzy warned, "and there will be no compromising. When Paul and I went on strike in New York, Frisch promised he'd go to the office in St. Louis and plead our case. Now Frank has turned his back on us. Paul and I aren't running out on the other players—we'd do everything possible to help win the pennant and an extra $5,000 apiece, but we feel we're getting the run-around by the club, and if the management doesn't care about the extra money, why should we?"

He then noted, not for the first or last time, that his $7,500 salary, combined with Paul's $3,000, still did not equal the $12,500 given to Hallahan, even though the latter would be lucky to win just half as many games as Paul or Dizzy—in Dizzy's opinion.

"I'm satisfied with my own pay," he concluded, "which is what I got last year. But Paul must get $2,000 more, or the Cards won't win the pennant. Neither Paul nor I will pitch anymore under present circumstances."

Frisch declined to speak with reporters, but it was noted that he had met privately with Rickey, who was also in town. Later, Frisch conferred by telephone with Breadon, who assured his manager that he and Rickey fully supported him in handling the situation with the Dean brothers.

The Cardinals then arrived in Pittsburgh, with Dizzy scheduled to pitch in the first game of a doubleheader. In the morning, he cornered Frisch in the Cardinals' hotel and once again raised the matter of Paul's salary. When Frisch again replied that he did not have the authority to resolve the problem, Dean informed him that his arm was too sore to pitch that day. It had been hurting, in fact, ever since the team left St. Louis, Dean alleged, but he had played anyway, "in spite of the pain," for the good of the team. Now, though, said Dizzy, he had to think of himself. "I am not goin' to run the risk a ruinin' my pitchin' arm by workin' when it ain't right," he declared.

Frisch refused to believe that Dean's arm was sore and told Dizzy to get ready to pitch in the first game. Dean declined. Frisch then told both of the Deans to take off their uniforms and leave the team once and for all—he was sick of them. He also sent a telegram to Breadon, at his farm in Fenton, just outside of St. Louis, informing him of the latest development. Breadon had dispatched Rickey to Columbus, Ohio, the day before, to settle some matters involving the farm club in that city and chose not to issue a public statement until he could consult with his vice president.

The two Deans ignored Frisch's suggestion that they quit the club, but they did change into their sharkskin suits and watched the Pirates defeat the Cardinals in Forbes Field from behind the Cardinals dugout. Hallahan was the losing pitcher. The next day, a headline ran "Dizzy Walks Out to Help Brother."

The press reported Dizzy as saying, "Frisch promised me in New York he would see to it that Paul got some more money. But last night he tells me he ain't goin' to do nothin' of the sort. I'm satisfied with my contract, even if I am gettin' half of what I'm worth. But it ain't right to expect my brother to pitch the way he can pitch for what he's makin'."

Paul was also quoted: "What Dizzy says is right. I was told in New York I'd be fixed up, and I took that to mean a new contract. Now, they're tellin' us to take our suits off. Goddamn, it's hard to make a dollar nowadays."

Later that evening, Frisch summoned both Deans to his room, where he convened an arbitration board consisting of secretary Clarence Lloyd, coaches Mike Gonzalez and Buzzy Wares, and pitcher Jesse Haines. Dizzy and Paul reiterated their complaints, with Dizzy speaking for both of them.

Temporarily, the matter was resolved, though details of the meeting were not divulged. Perhaps the Cardinals promised Paul—and Dizzy, too—a bonus if they won a certain number of games, or perhaps they agreed to significantly higher salaries for each of them the following year. Neither the front office nor the Dean brothers later announced that any kind of agreement had been reached. Many observers inferred that Paul had received his $2,000 raise, but that was never confirmed—not then, nor later when the Dean brothers revealed that their combined salaries in 1934 totaled $10,500—the same as before the "strike." Dizzy only told reporters the next day that he was ready to pitch again.

"You know there must be something wrong with anybody who wouldn't pitch his arm off for old Frank," he said. "Show me a guy who says a word against old Frank, and I'll bash his face in."

A baseball strike was unheard of in 1934, and some sportswriters were sorry to see it end so anticlimactically. Dean may have gotten his inspiration from a surge in widespread labor strikes that year as both labor radicals and union activists seemed headed for a final showdown with big corporations. In May, striking San Francisco dockworkers faced down machine guns along the Embarcadero and effectively stopped all shipping from San Diego to Seattle. On so-called Bloody Thursday, July 5, a month before the Deans were to go on strike a third time, two strikers were killed by San Francisco police, and there was a mass funeral march by tens of thousands of strikers and sympathizers four days later. Hundreds of thousands of workers also struck that year in the textile, steel, automobile, and other industries as the demand for better wages and working conditions, in a struggle dating back two generations, came to a head. Given his background as a sharecropper's son, Dean's sympathies would have been with the rank and file. Breadon and Rickey were two of baseball's moneyed aristocrats. Rickey, in fact, now traveled in a plush-lined private railroad car when he visited a Cardinals farm club or traveled to one of the cities on the National League circuit to see the team play. Some sportswriters called Rickey "the Mahatma," because of his obvious piety, but an equally appropriate name would have been "the Maharajah."

To prove what a loyal company man he was, Dizzy demolished the Pirates in the first game of the doubleheader, 13 to 4. The game was also Frisch's two thousandth, in a fifteen-year career— a milestone that put him in the ranks of Ty Cobb, Tris Speaker, and Honus Wagner. The Cardinals amassed eighteen hits, as if to demonstrate that the walkout incident was over, and that they could now concentrate on winning the pennant. An exclamation point was added by Collins, who hit two homers and a triple to drive in seven runs.

By the time the Cardinals returned home, they sat atop the league standings by a fraction of a percentage point.

"I am glad the pitching Deans struck," Joe Williams opined in the *New York World-Telegram,* as he looked back on the brouhaha, "and I think this sort of striking in baseball ought to be encouraged. I see no reason why a young ballplayer should be expected to wait a full year for adequate recognition at the cashier's window once he has established his class."

Williams was not alone. John Lardner in the *New York Post* wrote that the Dean brothers' strike "was such a nice, clean, sentimental thing, no one but a magnate would have the heart to criticize it." He also presciently suggested that if players put on a united front and formed a players' union, they would be stronger "than either they or the magnates imagine."

———— • ————

St. Louis did have another team—the Browns. As of June 1, manager Rogers Hornsby had steered his players to thirteen victories in their last twenty contests, and they now ranked only three games behind the league-leading Yankees, and a half game ahead of the Senators, who had won the pennant the previous year. That year, though, St. Louis's "other team" was destined to end up in sixth place.

———— • ————

The Cardinals were now in town for a three-week stay—a welcome respite from the numbingly long hours spent on trains. In a superb, tightly played thirteen-inning game with Chicago, the Cardinals wrote another chapter in Gashouse lore. With Carleton on the mound opposing Pat Malone, a big, hard-drinking Irishman, the two teams traded runs, and by the twelfth inning they were tied, 6 to 6. Then Collins, with two out, lined a double into right field. Medwick, with a long lead off first, rounded third and charged toward home. As he slid into the plate, umpire Charles Rigler hoisted his thumb into the air to indicate that catcher Gabby Hartnett had tagged him out, even though Irving Vaughan of the *Chicago Tribune* conceded that "Medwick had one foot on the corner."

In a rage, Frisch dashed from the dugout and grabbed Rigler's arm to get his attention. Thinking he was being attacked, the umpire swung his mask, which crashed into Frisch's head with such force that the Cardinals manager stumbled back, almost losing consciousness. By this time, Hartnett and third-base coach Mike Gonzalez had reached the scene, with Medwick not far behind. The besieged Rigler swung his mask a second time, hitting Gonzalez on the shoulder and almost knocking him down. At the same time, a crowd of young boys and men rushed onto the field and formed a circle around the batter's box. Frisch was ejected, Rothrock took his place, and in the thirteenth inning the Cubs scored six runs. The loss dropped the Cardinals out of first place.

After the game, Frisch tried to defend himself.

"What am I supposed to do when I get a bad decision?" he asked. "Am I supposed to laugh it off?"

National League president John Heydler fined Rigler and Frisch one hundred dollars each for the altercation. Frisch had reason to be grateful that he had not been suspended. Rigler, as it turned out, reported the next day that he had a broken finger—not from the fight, but from when Pepper Martin's bat had caught the umpire's hand in the seventh inning.

After losing two more games to the Cubs on successive nights, the Cardinals fell to third place.

On June 8, a small footnote was added to baseball history when the Cincinnati Reds team flew to Chicago for a game. It marked the first time a nearly full roster had traveled from one city to another by air. According to the *New York Times,* "Larry MacPhail, general manager of the Reds, explained that flying from city to city gives the players opportunity for more rest." Six of the Reds players elected to go by train. The Cardinals were not to fly as a team until 1938, when they flew from Boston to Chicago.

In June, the weather in St. Louis often turns into a blast furnace that lasts until mid September. That year, on schedule, the grass in Sportsman's Park faded to a well-baked brown. Adding to the misery ushered in by the miles-long dust cloud in mid May, the Midwest was now caught in the grip of a heat wave that would last all summer and kill more than a thousand people. A two-year drought caused the Mississippi River to continue to drop and thus led to Missouri's worst farm crisis ever. St. Louis was also registering the highest temperatures since 1871. For thirty consecutive days, the thermometer reached 100 degrees or more.

On some days, Dizzy Dean attempted to provide comic relief for those fans who had braved the blistering sun with only a straw boater, a bottle of soda or beer, or a cardboard fan with an advertisement for a funeral parlor to protect themselves. On one occasion, Dizzy fried eggs atop the skillet-hot dugout roof, and another time he loudly demanded a cup of hot chocolate from a vendor.

In the month of June, the Cardinals barely managed to compile an unimpressive 13–14 record while allowing their formidable opponents, the Giants, to recapture first. In the process, the New Yorkers once again began to look like the champions nearly everyone assumed they would be. The Deans won eleven of the Cardinals' victories, Hallahan—whose record now stood at a miserable 0–4—did not win any, and three other pitchers (Mooney, Haines, and Lindsey) did not win any games that month either. Carleton won the two games that the Deans did not, but he also lost three. A major concern was that Dizzy Dean seemed to be tiring and, by August and September, might be worn out. On June 18, with no game scheduled, Dean had spent most of his off day having his arm worked on by trainer Doc Weaver.

On June 24, the temperature in St. Louis reached a humid 102, and umpires Bill Klem, George Barr, and Bill Stewart made more baseball history of a sort by removing their coats and calling the game in their shirtsleeves—a Major League first.

Just before the game, Dean appeared with a handful of sticks, used scorecards, and assorted other bits of scrap and started a fire in front of the Cardinals dugout.

"He fanned his little fire," Jimmy Powers reported in the *New York Daily News,* "rubbing his knuckles, encouraging and soberly inspecting it from every angle to make sure the little wigwam of sticks drew a good draft. When assured he had a respectable blaze, he procured two Cardinal blankets, and then stomped the earth, round and round, slapping his mouth in a series of yipping war cries."

Suddenly, Dean looked up at the skies, cupped his hand to an ear, and listened. Gazing at the cloudless sky, he extended his palm. Sure enough, he pantomimed, it was raining. His rain dance had worked! He lifted his beaming face to the heavens, letting the imaginary raindrops splash onto his face. Then he opened a make-believe umbrella and, to loud cheers and laughter, tiptoed into the dugout.

By now, Wild Bill Hallahan had all but vanished from public view, so ineffective had he become on the mound. Yet his poor record did not deter him from persistently criticizing Dizzy and Paul, whom he dismissed as "clods from the sticks." His lowest moment of public humiliation occurred on June 25 before a crowd of thirty-three hundred who had come out to see another duel between the two finest pitchers in the National League, Dizzy Dean and Carl Hubbell. Dean got sick that day and Frisch sent Hallahan in as his replacement. As announcer Jim Kelly went from one side of the field to the other to announce the switch through a megaphone, a chant went up among the fans of "We want Dean." Hallahan lasted only one and a third innings as the Giants scored seven runs. As he trudged to the dugout, he was booed by the crowd.

"Hallahan's toboggan slide has whittled Frisch's staff precisely down to the Dean brothers," Bill McCullough astutely— but inaccurately—observed in the *Brooklyn Times-Union* in June 1934, "and nowhere do the books show a team winning the pennant with two pitchers."

Nowhere, of course, except in legend, were the books to show two brothers, one of them a rookie, joining forces to compile an extraordinary total of forty-nine victories and ensuring a pennant for the Cardinals. The pitching staff's vulnerability and weakness became, in that one magnificent year only, the reason the two Dean brothers had such an unprecedented opportunity to step in and fill the void. If Carleton, Walker, or Hallahan had been able to perform at a level equal to their promise, and each win a minimum of fifteen games, Dizzy Dean would not have faced the challenge that fate set before him, and his greatest season would never have happened.

Also in June, Branch Rickey, like a field general desperately summoning reinforcements to bolster an overworked and exhausted front line, acquired Chick Fullis from Philadelphia as extra insurance in the outfield. In 1933, he had been the Phillies' regular center fielder, batting .309 in 151 games. His quality of play had not been as impressive in the early part of the 1934 season, though, and Breadon fretted that the Cardinals had not got the best of a trade that saw the team's spare outfielder, George "Kiddo" Davis, go to Philadelphia.

Two of Dizzy Dean's victories in June were controversial. During the 1930s, the official scorer had the authority to bestow the victory on whichever pitcher he felt was the most deserving. In a game against Brooklyn, a pinch-hitter was sent in for Hallahan, the starting pitcher, in the sixth inning. The Cardinals were losing, 4 to 0. Dean took over in the seventh, and the Cardinals rallied to win the game, 5 to 4. According to baseball's then-current guidelines, Dean would have been credited with a "save," and Hallahan would have been accorded the win. But the scorer gave the victory to Dean.

Four days later, the Cardinals and the Giants battled to a 7-to-7 tie at the end of eight innings, with the temperature on the field reaching a searing 115 degrees. In the top of the ninth,

Dean, the starting pitcher, loaded the bases on singles, and with two out he was replaced by Mooney, the big Tennessee southpaw. He retired the third out. When the Cardinals came to bat, DeLancey won the game with a home run. Again, the scorer handed the victory to Dean. Not only did sportswriters around the country raise their eyebrows at the decision, but there was grumbling in the Cardinals clubhouse as well.

After the game, Dean revealed that he had sustained a broken finger on his throwing hand during batting practice a few days earlier but had not told Frisch because he did not want to sit out the important series with the Giants.

Despite their antics, and their often-abrasive relationship with each other, the Gashouse Gang never lost its fierce desire to win. On July 2, Frisch, Dizzy Dean, and coach Mike Gonzalez were all banished from the field during a hard-fought game in Chicago. The contest pitted Paul Dean against Cubs ace Lon Warneke, who held the Cardinals to seven hits while gaining his eleventh victory of the season, and his third against St. Louis. In the bottom of the seventh, with the bases loaded, one out, and one run already home, Chuck Klein lofted a high pop-up in front of home plate. DeLancey tossed off his mask and got under the ball to make the out, but missed it. He then threw wildly to home plate, but missed, and Warneke scored from third.

Frisch protested to umpire Bill Klem. Dizzy Dean and Gonzalez quickly joined him, arguing that the ball should have been ruled an infield fly. In that case, Klein would have been automatically out, and Warneke most probably would have held at third. Klem responded by sending all three men to the showers; he later explained that DeLancey was not in a position to catch the ball, and therefore it could not have been called an infield fly. The game was continued under protest, Mooney replaced Paul Dean after the Cubs scored two more runs, and Chicago finally won by a score of 7 to 4. An Associated Press report blamed the Cardinals' bad mood on the "disastrous series" they had just played in Cincinnati.

It was not long, though, before Dizzy was back to his old tricks. During a game against the Braves, he went up to the Boston dugout before heading out to the mound at the top of the first inning, and announced, "I'm throwin' nothin' but fast balls at you today, sonnies. You don't have to worry none about havin' to try to hit the great Diz's curve ball."

True to his word, he threw only fastballs. The hapless Braves were able to get only three hits, and the Cardinals won. Dean knew that, when he was in peak form, he was unbeatable.

On July 4, every team in either league was scheduled to play a doubleheader. The collective attendance amounted to more than 200,000 and provided a financial windfall for every one of the franchises in those hard-pressed times. The largest crowd was in the Polo Grounds, where 40,000 fans watched the Giants take on the Braves. In the American League, another 40,000 saw the game in Detroit between the Tigers and the Cleveland Indians.

In St. Louis, a smaller crowd of 24,500 filled Sportsman's Park that day to see the Cardinals battle the Chicago Cubs. The two teams split the doubleheader, each time by a score of 6 to 2. Neither of the Deans pitched. Frisch had decided to give both brothers a well-deserved few days of rest. With good reason, Frisch wanted to avoid a collapse similar to that in 1933.

On July 8, just before the All-Star break, Dizzy Dean racked up his fourteenth win, and his sixth victory in a row, when he defeated Cincinnati, 6 to 1, in the first game of a doubleheader. Paul pitched the second game and struck out six batters in the first three innings. But in the fourth, the Reds pounded him for six runs, and the Cincinnati bench rode him mercilessly. Dizzy kept shouting for them to ease up on his kid brother, and they paid him no attention. Finally, a thoroughly riled Dizzy strode over to the Reds dugout and shouted, "Come on out and fight!" Some of the players just laughed.

"You're all just chicken," Dizzy spouted. Then, pointing at left fielder Harlin Pool, who had just belted a grand slam off Paul, he yelled, "You, you ain't no hitter. You're a banjo picker who's lucky."

Paul lost that game, and his record was now 10–4.

On July 10, the day of the All-Star Game, the Cardinals occupied third place, four games behind the Giants, and two games behind the Cubs.

———— • ————

Baseball's second All-Star Game was held at the Polo Grounds in Upper Manhattan before fifty thousand spectators, with another fifteen thousand turned away at the gate. The stadium sat on the west bank of the Harlem River; just a few hundred yards downriver, on the east bank in the Bronx, was Yankee Stadium. In the previous year, the inaugural contest had been played at Comiskey Park in Chicago. Babe Ruth won that game for the American League with a home run. The final score was 4 to 2.

For this second contest, the biggest vote getter on either team was Bill Terry, the player-manager of the Giants, with 121,110, and he was also wearing the cap of player-manager of the National League All-Stars because his Giants had won the 1933 World Series. Detroit second baseman Charlie Gehringer received the most votes in the American League balloting, with 120,781 tallies, and Gehrig placed second with 117,789 votes. Frisch's 120,141 votes put him third among players in both leagues, and ahead of Ruth, Joe Cronin of the Senators, and Gehrig.

Among National League pitchers, the Giants' Carl Hubbell received the most votes with 86,048. Dizzy Dean finished second with 62,201. Rounding out the top five were Lon Warneke of the Cubs, Van Lingle Mungo of the Dodgers, and Freddie Frankenhouse of the Braves.

Behind Hubbell was this starting lineup:

BILL TERRY, GIANTS	FIRST BASE
FRANK FRISCH, ST. LOUIS	SECOND BASE
TRAVIS JACKSON, NEW YORK	SHORTSTOP
PIE TRAYNOR, PITTSBURGH	THIRD BASE
JOE MEDWICK, ST. LOUIS	LEFT FIELD
KIKI CUYLER, CHICAGO	CENTER FIELD
WALLY BERGER, BOSTON	RIGHT FIELD
GABBY HARTNETT, CHICAGO	CATCHER

Sitting on the bench were these reserves:

ARKY VAUGHAN, PITTSBURGH	SHORTSTOP
PEPPER MARTIN, ST. LOUIS	THIRD BASE
MEL OTT, NEW YORK	CENTER FIELD
CHUCK KLEIN, CHICAGO	LEFT FIELD
PAUL WANER, PITTSBURGH	RIGHT FIELD
BABE HERMAN, CHICAGO	OUTFIELD
AL LOPEZ, BROOKLYN	CATCHER

Lefty Gomez of the Yankees had received the most votes for a pitcher in the American League with 84,712. The starting lineup for the American League, with Cronin at the helm, was:

LOU GEHRIG, YANKEES	FIRST BASE
CHARLIE GEHRINGER, DETROIT	SECOND BASE
JOE CRONIN, WASHINGTON	SHORTSTOP

PINKY HIGGINS, PHILADELPHIA	THIRD BASE
HEINIE MANUSH, WASHINGTON	LEFT FIELD
AL SIMMONS, CHICAGO	CENTER FIELD
BABE RUTH, NEW YORK	RIGHT FIELD
MICKEY COCHRANE, TIGERS	CATCHER

Other American League pitchers included Earl Whitehill of the Senators and Lefty Grove of the Red Sox, as well as Red Ruffing of the Yankees, Tommy Bridges of the Tigers, and Mel Harder of the Indians in reserve. Also sitting on the bench were these reserves:

WES FERRELL, BOSTON	CATCHER
JIMMIE FOXX, PHILADELPHIA	THIRD BASE
JIMMY DYKES, CHICAGO	THIRD BASE
BEN CHAPMAN, NEW YORK	OUTFIELD
EARL AVERILL, CLEVELAND	OUTFIELD
SAMMY WEST, ST. LOUIS	OUTFIELD

The Yankees placed six players on the All-Stars, the most of any team in either league, and the Giants and Cubs were each represented by five players. Four Cardinals made the National League's roster. An estimated sixty-thousand-dollar gate revenue, in addition to proceeds collected from CBS and NBC for the right to broadcast the game, was to be donated to the Players' Benevolent Fund, which had been established to help disabled former players.

That morning, Lou Gehrig had arrived at the ballpark late and absentmindedly locked his wife in the car as he hurried off to the clubhouse. Later, as he abashedly admitted to reporters, he wondered where she was, suddenly remembered, and sent a batboy with his car keys to get her. During batting practice, both Gehrig and Ruth socked several balls out of the park.

Pepper Martin entertained the crowd with a practice demonstration of the pitching technique he had perfected in the Texas League, "all waving arms and legs in his windup and facing first base at the finish of his follow through with his cheek full of an exaggerated chaw and his right hand wiggling, as if to cool off."

An astounding twenty-eight of the players on the field would later be elected to the National Baseball Hall of Fame. After the national anthem was played, sportswriter Frank Graham of the *New York Sun* presented Giants hurler Carl Hubbell with the 1933 Most Valuable Player award. Then it was game time. Dizzy Dean was disappointed that he had not been selected as the starting pitcher, but he made no secret of his admiration for Hubbell.

The game, nearly three hours long, was packed with "thrill upon thrill," said John Drebinger of the *New York Times,* and developed into "a titanic struggle of hitters, during which great names in the pitching industry were rudely jostled about."

Leading off the American League batting order, Gehringer whacked a single to center, then dashed to second when Wally Berger fumbled the ball. After Heine Manush walked, Hubbell appeared momentarily vulnerable, but he then struck out Babe Ruth with a screwball on the third strike; struck out Gehrig while ignoring a double steal by Gehringer and Manush; and closed the inning by striking out Jimmie Foxx.

Frisch, first up for the Nationals, lined a Gomez fastball into the upper right-field grandstand for a home run. But Gomez then readily retired the next three batters.

In the second inning, Hubbell struck out Simmons and Cronin—bringing to five the number of future Hall of Famers that he had struck out consecutively. After he retired the side in the third, Hubbell was greeted with a thunderous ovation as he walked to the clubhouse.

Gomez also appeared to have weathered his three innings relatively unscathed, except for the homer by Frisch. Then, with two out, Frisch walked, and Traynor, who was next up, singled as Frisch advanced to third. Medwick then sent the ball high into the upper left tier to give the Nationals a 4-to-0 lead.

"With the retirement of Hubbell, however," as Drebinger noted, "things suddenly took a turn for the worst for the Terry forces. The tall, angular Warneke came on, and the American Leaguers at once bristled with action."

The fourth started with the Cub right-hander Lon Warneke retiring Foxx. But Simmons then doubled to Medwick, and Cronin singled to Medwick, scoring Simmons. Dickey struck out, and Averill, batting for Gomez, tripled to Cuyler, scoring Cronin.

In the fifth inning, the Americans scored four more runs. Both Ruth and Gehrig walked. After conferring with Hartnett, Terry sent Warneke to the showers and called in Mungo, Casey Stengel's Brooklyn ace. Unimpressed, Foxx hammered a single to center, scoring Ruth. Simmons then cracked a sharp grounder toward left that Jackson was able to stop, but his hurried toss to second went wide, Foxx reached second safely, and Gehrig scored. Cronin then fouled out, but Dickey walked to fill the bases. Next up was Averill, who doubled down the right-field foul line to score two more.

Mungo then intentionally walked Gehringer in the hope of getting Ruffing, the American League pitcher, to hit into a double play. Instead, he knocked a single into left field, and two more runs crossed the plate. With Ruth and Gehrig the next two batters up, Mungo's predicament seemed hopeless, yet somehow he was able to retire the Babe on a grounder and strike out Lou. The Americans now led, 8 to 4.

In the bottom of the fifth, Terry sent in his firepower to even the score. Pepper Martin, batting for Mungo, walked.

Frisch, Taylor, and Klein all singled, the latter taking over from Medwick in center field. Harder took Ruffing's place on the mound. Waner batted for Berger, but in a double steal Traynor stole home.

In the last four innings, the Nationals were able to produce only one hit against Mel Harder, the Cleveland right-hander. Dizzy Dean took over as pitcher for the National League in the sixth, and surrendered a run when Frisch dropped a high fly by Simmons that went for a double. Simmons then scored when Cronin doubled to left. Frankenhouse pitched for the Nationals in the ninth. The American League won in nine innings, 9 to 7.

The day after the All-Star Game, the Cardinals traveled to Philadelphia to play the Phillies. Ahead of them was one of their longer road trips of the season, with games scheduled in Brooklyn, Boston, New York, Pittsburgh, and Chicago before they would return to Sportsman's Park on August 3. They lost the first game against the Phillies, then split a doubleheader, with Dizzy Dean the winning pitcher in the first contest.

In Brooklyn, the Cardinals won a doubleheader, with Dizzy again pitching the first game, 2 to 0; it was his fifth game in ten days. He also hit a home run. After the game, he tried to flag down a taxi at the players' gate at Ebbets Field, then hopped into one that was just pulling away from the curb. Inside was J. Roy Stockton of the *St. Louis Post-Dispatch.*

"It's all right," Dean good-naturedly told the journalist. "You can ride with me. I don't mind."

On the drive to the hotel in Manhattan, Dean talked and Stockton took notes.

"I love Brooklyn," Dean said, "the fans, Stengel, Mungo, and all of them writers who cover 'em." He mentioned three writers in particular: Tommy Holmes of the *Brooklyn Eagle,* Bill

McCullough of the *Brooklyn Times-Union,* and Roscoe McGowen of the *New York Times.*

"It's funny, but their bosses all came up with the same idea on the same day. They told 'em to get a piece on old Diz. Well, Tommy comes first and he wants to know where I was born and I tell him, Lucas, Arkansas, January 16, 1911. [As Dean well knew, he had been born the previous year.] Then it's not two minutes later after he leaves that McCullough comes along and doggone if he don't want the same piece. Now, I'm not gonna have their bosses bawl 'em out for gettin' the same story, so I tell Mac I was born in Bond, Mississippi—that's where my wife comes from—and I picked February 22, which is givin' George Washington a break. McGowen is next. Imagine a New York paper sendin' a man way over to Brooklyn every day. I guess me 'n' Paul has helped to get jobs for a lotta guys. Well, Roscoe, he's doin' the same story. So I give him a break too and I say Holdenville, Oklahoma, August 22. They do their stories and their bosses are all happy with 'em, see, because they got their scoops."

"But, Dizzy," Stockton interrupted, "when is your official birthday?"

"I swear I'm mixed up myself now," Dean, ever disingenuous, replied, "but I think I'll keep all three of 'em."

When the pair reached their destination, Dean said, "Well, here we are at the hotel. Take care of the cab, will you, Roy? I gotta see that secretary and get me some dough. Boy, did I put it on them Dodgers today."

Stockton duly reported his conversation to the readers of the *Post-Dispatch,* and later to the much bigger readership of the *Saturday Evening Post,* and the legend of Dizzy Dean's multiple birthdays was born. Stockton, perhaps because he was so pliable and willing to publicize Dean's fabrications, later became his ghostwriter as well.

Not to be outdone, other sportswriters soon joined in with their own "scoops." On July 26, the *New York World-Telegram* reported that Dean, though born Jay Hanna, "took the name Jerome Herman out of friendship for a battery mate in the San Antonio City league."

Dean toyed with sportswriters the same way he sometimes toyed with batters. Gradually, as the season wore on, he was becoming larger than life, a living legend, an outsize personality, a ballplayer possessed of almost mythic skill. Someone like Dizzy Dean came along only once in a generation, if that often, and he had begun to realize that he could tell people just about anything he wanted to, and they would believe it.

Though Dizzy was a braggart and a practical joker, and sometimes just plain obnoxious, the consensus among many of his teammates was that, at heart, he was a good fellow. Best of all, he just happened to be the best athlete in baseball in 1934, dominating the game as only a few players ever have. If he usually made good on his boasts to win games, he also had promises to keep that were made to those who were unable to see him pitch, as Stockton relates:

> Dizzy visited a children's hospital in St. Louis one day. He wrote his name in autograph books, told the youngsters how he threw his curve, and how he wound up to put the batter in the proper mental state. He told them much of his prowess, and when it was time to depart for the ballpark, to do on the field the great things he had been doing for them in story, he asked the children if there was any little thing he could do for them to make them happier.
>
> "Anything at all," he volunteered. "I don't bar nuthin' for you kids."
>
> One little fellow had a bright idea: "Strike out [Giants player-manager] Bill Terry for us this afternoon," and

soon it was a chorus: "Strike out Terry. Strike out Terry. We'll be listening over the radio. Do that for us."

"I'll do it," he reassured the youngsters. "And if I get a chance, I'll do it with the bases filled. I'll pitch this game for you."

"They would have to pick a guy like that," said Dizzy, as he told me about it in the dugout before the game. "Why didn't they say Vergez or Critz? That Terry is a tough bird."

In the ninth inning, with two out and the Cardinals leading, 2 to 1, a pinch hitter singled, Joe Moore hit safely, and Hughie Critz walked. Up came Terry. Dizzy edged toward the plate.

"I hate to do this, Bill," Dizzy grinned. "But I promised some kids in a hospital today that I'd strike you out with the bases loaded. That's why I walked little Hughie."

Terry struck out on three pitched balls.

At the height of his fame and ability in 1934, Dizzy Dean was a sinewy, slope-shouldered six feet three inches and weighed 189 pounds. His distinctive pitching style was recognizable anywhere: Rearing back, he kicked his left leg high in the air, and then fired the ball. If a batter managed to dribble a hit to third base or pop one into shallow left field, Dean could often be seen standing just off the mound, both hands on his hips, with a big grin on his face, enjoying every minute, as if he could not believe baseball could be so much fun.

"Dizzy had everything," Dean's teammate Leo Durocher once remarked. "Fastball, curve, and later, control. He gave it to them sidearm, overhand, three-quarters. The ball was always alive. He had a high hard one that came in around the shoulders, and just as the batter would swing at it, it would be up around his ears."

As of mid July, the conventional wisdom was that, despite Dizzy's presence on the mound, the National League race had settled into a spirited contest between the Giants, who led in the standings by two games, and the Chicago Cubs. The Cardinals were now five games out. Only eleven weeks remained in the season. An anonymous *Pittsburgh Post-Gazette* sportswriter spoke for many of his colleagues when he wrote, "Pitching and catching weaknesses have ruled out Frankie Frisch and his Redbirds as contenders."

One of the few dissenters to that opinion was Grantland Rice. In that era, many sportswriters were prone to try their hand at doggerel, and Rice was no exception. He was far better than most, however, as well as more percipient. As the teams continued to do combat in the torrid final days of July, he penned this verse in the *New York Sun*:

DIZZY GUNGA DEAN
(If Mr. Kipling Doesn't Mind)

You may talk of throwing arms that come up from Texas farms,
With a hope upon the fast one that is smoking;
But when it comes to pitching that will keep the batter twitching
I can slip you in a name that's past all joking;
For in old St. Louis town, where they called him once a clown,
There's a tall and gangling figure on the scene,
And of all that Redbird crew, there's one bloke that pulls 'em through,
Just a fellow by the name of Gunga Dean.
It is Dean—Dean—Dean—
You human coil of lasso—Dizzy Dean!
If it wasn't for old Dizzy
They'd be worse than fizzy-wizzy,
Come on and grab another—Gunga Dean.

5

DIZZY
IN THE
DOCK

Dizzy Dean and Frankie Frisch were one of baseball's all-time odd couples. Frisch was college-educated, someone who could appreciate fine wine, art, and literature. He was a company man, loyal to Branch Rickey and Sam Breadon to a fault, and he revered the memory of his late mentor, John McGraw. He played by the rules. The uneducated Dean seldom drank, liked to read pulp adventure tales about cowboys, preferred night-clubs to museums, and was forever harassing, pestering, and negotiating with the front office, which he loudly and publicly accused of being cheap and exploitative.

What they had in common was a genius for playing the game of baseball. Though they clashed and quarreled fre-quently, they mostly got along after learning how to tolerate what each perceived as the other's limitations, and to prize each other's unique abilities.

Frisch, of course, was by far the more mature man, but not the cleverer. It would perhaps be an exaggeration to say that theirs was a father-son kind of relationship, but certainly the Old Flash was Ol' Diz's most immediate authority figure, and Dizzy was Frisch's most troublesome problem child.

At bottom, Frisch admired and no doubt loved the boy wonder of the 1934 St. Louis Cardinals. The Gashouse Gang's manager was not quite the gruff, unyielding disciplinarian that his public image suggested. Though rigorous in an old-school way, he also knew when on occasion to bend the rules, look the other way, and enjoy a joke at his own expense.

In his autobiography, *Frank Frisch: The Fordham Flash,* written years after his retirement, Frisch named Dean to his hypothetical all-time All-Star roster drawn from teams between 1919 and 1945. In a list that included George Sisler at first, Ty Cobb in left field, Tris Speaker in center, and Babe Ruth in right, Frisch also numbered Dean among such other legendary pitchers as Walter Johnson, Lefty Grove, Grover Cleveland Alexander, and Dazzy Vance.

Dean was even better than his record indicated, Frisch also insisted. "I told him a thousand times," he recalled, "I meant it, and I still believe that if Dizzy had taken pitching really seriously," he could have won thirty games in a row, from 1933 to 1936 inclusive. "He shouldn't have lost more than a dozen in the four-year period. That's how good he was. But he loved to experiment, to fool around with the batter. He enjoyed getting a man out pitching to his strength and he did it many times. But naturally the good hitters surprised him now and then."

In the middle of the feverish 1934 pennant race, Frisch's relationship with Dean grew fractious and strained to the utmost, and culminated in one of the strangest episodes in all of baseball. In fact, so far as some of his teammates were concerned, Dean's erratic behavior had reached an intolerable point. People on both sides were fed up—Dizzy, and his brother Paul, with Breadon, Rickey, and Frisch; and those three strong-willed gentlemen with the two Dean boys.

As the pennant race steamed into August, the heat and the pressure to win made for a combustible mixture. Everyone's temper seemed to flare more often. Dizzy and Paul were now alternating, pitching almost every other day. On August 1, Paul beat the Cubs, 4 to 0. On August 3, Dizzy beat the Pirates, and the next day he relieved and saved against the Pirates. On August 5, the Pirates beat Paul. Then, on August 7, Dizzy beat the Reds. The next day, Dizzy relieved Paul and got the win against Cincinnati. In the twelfth inning of that game, Collins occupied second, with Durocher on deck. Chick Fullis hit a line drive into right field. Running down to the third-base line, Durocher shouted to Collins, as he rounded the base, "Slide! It's going to be close." But Collins crossed the plate standing up, and just barely missed being tagged out. Back in the dugout, a furious Durocher shouted at Collins, who was then in a tie for the league's home run title, "You ought to be fined for not sliding."

Collins angrily retorted, "You're trying to show me up," and questioned Durocher's authority to criticize him.

The two men almost got into a fight, but Frisch separated them, saying, "I give Leo my approval to criticize, Ripper, and he's right."

The next morning, Dizzy Dean was having breakfast with Stockton of the *Post-Dispatch*.

"This country may have needed a good five-cent cigar," Dean sagely observed, referring to the famous quip by Woodrow Wilson's vice president, Thomas Riley Marshall, "but what the Cardinals need is more Deans."

As he stirred his coffee, Dean already knew that another Dean just happened to be heading up to St. Louis at that very moment. On August 9, the Cardinals played an exhibition game in Terre Haute, Indiana, and afterward Dizzy and Paul Dean returned to St. Louis for a family reunion. Their older brother, Elmer, had just arrived in town by bus from Houston, where for the past year he had been scratching out a meager living as a peanut vendor at Buff Stadium.

Elmer had wound up in Houston in 1933 after Fred Ankenman, president of the Buffaloes farm team, heard that a third Dean brother was living in Arkansas. He had just signed Paul and reasoned that having the third Dean would be a tremendous attraction at the gate. But when Elmer tried out for the team, it quickly became apparent that he was not in the same league as his two brothers. When Elmer asked for a job anyway, Ankenman put him to work in the concession department.

Vince Staten wrote in *Ol' Diz*:

> Elmer was a sensation at first, thanks in large part to being a Dean brother. But soon his sales dropped off precipitously. Ankenman discovered the problem in a conversation with Houston fire commissioner Allie Anderson: "Allie said if I would just watch him for a while I could see the reason. Well, I did. In those days, cold drinks were sold in bottles, and the vendors would have a towel tied to the side of the trousers which they would use to wipe the tops of the bottles after removing the caps. I watched a sale being made by Elmer to a couple close by. He removed the caps, wiped the tops off with the towel, and then, using the same towel, he wiped the sweat off his face. We took him off selling cold drinks and changed him over to selling peanuts. He turned out to be the greatest peanut salesman you can imagine."

One day Rickey traveled to Houston to watch a double-header and observed Elmer entertaining the fans with the way he could fling bags of peanuts to customers across a half dozen aisles, and then catch their nickels in payment like a pro outfielder. It occurred to him that having Elmer selling peanuts in Sportsman's Park could only sell more tickets to the games. Losing Elmer suited Ankenman just fine, since Elmer, like Dizzy, had been complaining about his wages, and had been threatening to go on strike since June.

Dizzy and Paul had occasionally supplemented Elmer's income with small gifts of money. But Jerome knew that was not enough. Selling peanuts provided Elmer with summer employment, but the only way he could earn enough money to live on during the rest of the year was to do odd jobs, such as running errands for small businesses in the Houston neighborhood where he and his father shared a couple of rooms.

When they heard that he was heading for St. Louis, both Dizzy and Paul were hopeful that Rickey would reward them for their pitching efforts by giving Elmer a minor clerical job that would keep him busy and pay him a regular wage. Rickey, though, ever the showman, had other ideas. He wanted to establish Elmer as a headliner in the concession department, and he even ordered up a press release declaring that, when the Cardinals met the Cubs in a forthcoming game, Elmer, "with a big league delivery," would be pitching peanuts in the grandstand at Sportsman's Park.

The local papers immediately jumped at the opportunity to publicize yet another Dean story. One headline ran "Cards Buy a Third Dean Pitcher—And It's a Nutty Idea." Another read, "The Dean Brothers—Two Nuts and One Goober."

Dizzy and Paul were outraged by Rickey's decision to install Elmer as just another peanut vendor, and to exploit him into the bargain. Dizzy's wife, Pat, was the angriest of all. "That goddamned Rickey," she fumed. "He arranges for *his* brother to be a Cardinal scout, but it's peanuts for the Deans. He's trying to embarrass us when it's our pitching what's keeping us in the pennant race." She also advised Dizzy that it would not be in his best interests to have his brother selling peanuts in Sportsman's Park.

When Dizzy and Paul met Elmer at the bus station in St. Louis, Elmer was wearing an Eskimo Pie salesman's cap with his name stitched on it. He lasted three days as a peanut salesman. Then Pat Dean, in a fury, went to see Rickey and complained that it was humiliating and embarrassing for both her and her husband that Elmer was selling peanuts in the grandstand while Dizzy was pitching on the mound.

The tempest in a teapot soon ended. Only days after Elmer's arrival, the *St. Louis Star-Times* reported that "upholding the reputation and tradition of the Deans, the elder brother of Dizzy and Paul 'jumped' the club." He had returned to Houston to sell peanuts again at the Buffaloes games, telling the *St. Louis Globe-Democrat* that Major League baseball "ain't what it's cracked up to be." He added that he also did not "like the looks of St. Louis." Ankenman welcomed him back, saying, "We're glad to have him."

Elmer's arrival and precipitous departure seemed like just another colorful chapter in the Gashouse book of anecdotes. But Dizzy was as hot under the collar as the humid August weather.

Elmer's escapade provided a brief distraction from the Cardinals' lackluster performance on the field. "What's wrong with the Cardinals?" Sid Keener gloomily inquired in the *Star-Times*. He then went on to explain that erratic pitching and the rumors of team dissension were only part of the explanation. "I do not subscribe to the belief that the Cardinals have faded because of dissatisfaction among the players," he concluded. "It is just possible that the team's talent does not measure up to a championship standard, and that no amount of managerial masterminding can compensate for this."

By mid August, the Cardinals were five and a half games behind the Giants, and three and a half games behind the Chicago Cubs, and there seemed little chance that they would wind up in first place, much less go on to win the World Series, as the team had done in 1931 against Connie Mack's formidable Philadelphia Athletics.

That was the moment when Dizzy and Paul Dean decided to make matters much worse by launching the first players' strike in modern baseball history. In those difficult times, long before a players' union or high-powered agents, the majority of ball players were thankful just to have a job that paid far more than the average American could ever hope to earn. Once they signed a contract, they were set for another year, and never complained. After all, owners had a peremptory and chilling way of dealing with troublemakers who groused about their compensation: Trade 'em.

But when it came to money, Dizzy Dean was different from—and more courageous than—any other player in the history of baseball. It was only a two-person mutiny, but it was like nothing the game had ever seen. However, it was one thing to strike out a batter, or to send an opposing pitcher down in defeat. It was quite another to force Branch Rickey, who was every bit as shrewd and tough as Dizzy was, to give him more money.

After the Cardinals' three-game series in Cincinnati, where they had won two games and lost one, they headed home for a four-game series with the Chicago Cubs. St. Louis took the first two. Then, on August 12, a Sunday, an overflow crowd of 36,073 fans showed up because both Dizzy and Paul were scheduled to pitch in a doubleheader. But Paul lost the first game, 7 to 2, and the Cubs beat Dizzy in the second game, 6 to 4, bringing the Cardinals record at that point to sixty-two won and forty-six lost. It was the first time that both brothers had lost on the same day, and afterward everyone in the clubhouse was silent and dejected. With the season two-thirds over, the New York Giants, the pennant favorites, seemed unconquerable behind the pitching of the great Carl Hubbell and the fearsome batting prowess of Bill Terry, Mel Ott, and Jo-Jo Moore.

After the second game was over, the Cardinals were in a hurry to catch a train to Detroit to play an exhibition game the next day against the Tigers. "Dizzy didn't like exhibition games during the regular season," Cardinals manager Frankie Frisch later recalled. "None of us like them. In any pennant race a ball club welcomes a day off from the daily grind, and because baseball is an entertainment there aren't many days of rest. But the Cardinals, needing the money in those days, I'll admit, booked exhibition games regularly, especially in their farm club cities."

At Union Station, just before the train was scheduled to pull out of St. Louis, the club secretary, Clarence Lloyd, informed Frisch that everyone was on board except for Dizzy and Paul Dean.

"Talk to the conductor," Frisch told Lloyd. "They had a rough afternoon and may have been delayed. See if he can hold the train a few minutes."

The conductor obliged for a time, but when the Deans still did not appear, the train departed without them. When the Cardinals showed up the next morning at the Detroit ballpark, after the overnight journey in the Pullman, Tigers owner Frank Navin was livid when he learned that the Dean brothers would not be playing that afternoon. He had not only advertised them as one of the main attractions, but he had also given the Cardinals a three-thousand-dollar guarantee. Hundreds of kids, he added—not to mention the rest of the forty thousand fans crowded into every corner, including chairs set up behind the foul lines down to the bleachers—would be disappointed by not being able to see the great Dizzy Dean and his younger brother. The ho-hum game that followed saw fading veteran Bill Hallahan win his first game of any kind in twenty-eight days, and the Cardinals pummeled seldom-used pitcher Red Phillips for sixteen hits to win, 7 to 1. Until that moment, Wild Bill's record stood at 4–12, and he had not finished fourteen of the twenty-one games he had started.

The Deans' failure to make the trip did not go unnoticed by sportswriters and readers of the sports pages. An explanation was demanded. Unapologetic, Dean told Stockton of the *St. Louis Post-Dispatch,* "I did not see any reason to make the trip. Besides, I hurt my arm Sunday. That's why I lost my fastball. I pulled something loose in my right elbow in the fourth inning. I didn't have my stuff after that."

Paul seemed to equivocate, telling reporter Ray Gillespie of the rival *St. Louis Star-Times,* "I hurried out of the clubhouse Saturday after the game without reading the notice about the trip to Detroit. Then I went to the park Sunday morning without a coat or grip. I returned to the hotel for them after the doubleheader and waited around, thinking Jerome would pick me up. He did not show up, and when I called the station they told me the train had left. I'm not passing the buck to Jerome, 'cause I'm not sorry I stayed in St. Louis. I was really tired and needed a rest."

Frisch, of course, was furious when he discovered that the Dean brothers had unilaterally decided to skip the game in Detroit. An irate Sam Breadon, though he had always been tolerant of the Dean brothers' misbehavior, supported Frisch's decision to fine them.

Back in St. Louis on August 14, after another overnight train ride home, the Cardinals were getting suited up in the clubhouse to play a game against Philadelphia. Several of the players asked Dizzy where he had been. Dean made no excuses, admitting that he and Paul had missed the exhibition game on purpose. No doubt, he assumed that he would be forgiven and excused, just as he had been the previous year when Gabby Street was manager. Street had fined Dizzy one hundred dollars for missing a train. But when Dizzy threw a shutout against the Brooklyn Dodgers, old Gabby relented, and Dizzy never had to pay up. It was beyond his comprehension why Frisch, unlike Street, should take such a tough line. After all, Dizzy was leading the league not only in games won, but in strikeouts.

Approaching Frisch in the locker room, Dizzy asked, "Are we suspended?"

"I'm fining you $100, Dizzy," Frisch replied, "and Paul, $50. You boys shouldn't have run out on us."

"You can't fine me," Dizzy protested.

"I can't, huh?" Frisch replied. "It's $100, and it's going to stick."

Dumbfounded and insulted, Dizzy said, "If it does, me 'n' Paul are through with the Cardinals."

Walking over to the trainer's table, Dizzy lay down and told Doc Weaver, "Take a look at my arm. It's sore, and I think I'm comin' down with a cold. I ain't been feelin' right for days."

All of the other players had gathered around to watch. Ignoring Dizzy, Frisch said, "All right, it's time to go to the field. Let's go. Come on, Dizzy. Paul, let's go."

"We're not goin'," Dizzy said.

"You're not going? You're not going? Then take off those uniforms! You're suspended, both of you! Take 'em off, goddamnit, take 'em off!"

Dizzy leaped up from the table, shouting, "I'll show you what I think of this club!" Ripping off his shirt, he tore it to shreds, kicked over a stool and several benches, reached into his locker to grab his traveling grays, and tore that uniform up as well, yelling, "Nobody's gonna be wearin' this!"

Then he exclaimed, "This is a swell way to treat a fella who's been pitchin' his heart out for this no-good club. And just because I couldn't go to Detroit with a sore arm that's been killin' me, and stickin' me with a $100 fine. Me! Well, I ain't gonna pay it, you can bet yourself on that, and Paul ain't neither. I'm speakin' for him."

"We'll see," said Frisch.

The Deans got into their street clothes. As they headed for the exit, Frisch asked, "Where you going?"

"To get our pay," Dizzy replied. "We're quittin' this club and goin' to Florida to fish—I hear they're bitin'—and don't you dare try to stop us."

"That's all right with me," Frisch bellowed. "I don't care if you never come back!"

As Dizzy and Paul walked out the door, they were greeted by Gillespie of the *Star-Times,* who had heard the ruckus. The journalist asked Dizzy if he would mind tearing up his uniform again so that his photographer, who had just arrived, could take an action shot of the clubhouse fracas.

"Sure, Ray," Dean replied. "Let me find a piece around here somewhere."

Dizzy then tore a uniform a second time while the photographer snapped away. Paul also posed for a photograph showing him about to throw down his glove in disgust.

Then the Deans marched to the controller's office, where treasurer Bill DeWitt told them that he could not have their checks ready until the following day, August 15.

Dizzy, Paul, and Dizzy's wife, Pat, then watched the Cardinals play the Phillies in the grandstand behind the Philadelphia dugout. The Cardinal players, rallying behind their manager, beat the visitors that afternoon by a score of 5 to 1. Later Dizzy and Paul visited the press box and then signed autographs for fans. When a reporter said, "Dizzy, you'll be back in uniform and taking your turn by Thursday," Dizzy slapped down two five-dollar bills on a counter and said, "Here's 10 bucks that says I won't."

Finally, a disgruntled Pat Dean said, "Come on, Diz, let's go."

The three Deans got up to leave. When a reporter asked them where they were going, Dizzy again announced that they were going to take a fishing trip to Florida, "if we have enough money coming after they take those fines out of our pay."

There were many reasons for Dizzy's simmering rage, culminating in this sudden blowup. He had complained since spring training that both he and Paul were chronically underpaid. As the sons of a sharecropper who had themselves worked in the fields, they had bitter firsthand experience of feeling exploited, and they were sensitive about ever again being taken advantage of, even if their wages were now considerably higher than those of the average American worker.

Repeatedly, all that season, Dizzy had also complained about a soreness in his pitching arm. Some people believed him, and some did not. But no other pitcher in the Major Leagues in 1934 was being used nearly so frequently as Dizzy, both as a starter and as a reliever—often on alternate days. Having to pitch in a meaningless game up in Detroit was not only crass commercial exploitation, as Dizzy well knew, but it also meant having to throw one more time on a day when his right arm could have used the rest.

Then there was the matter of Elmer Dean, the most exploitable Dean of them all. At the very least, Dizzy had hoped that, as a gesture of appreciation for all that he had done for the Cardinals, Rickey and Breadon would thank him by providing Elmer with a modest clerical job in the Cardinals' front office. That certainly was not too much to expect, given all that Dean had done for the club so far and might be expected to contribute in the future. Moreover, there was precedent. Rickey had arranged for his own brother to be a baseball scout.

In sum, Dizzy and Paul Dean's walkout was the abrupt culmination of many things. The most important and volatile issue was a long-simmering argument over money that went back several years. Finally, the unpredictable Dizzy had had enough, and he just quit—and his quiet younger brother dutifully followed him out the door.

Rickey, when he heard about Dizzy's threat, called his bluff, offering to buy one-way train tickets to Florida for each brother. Breadon issued a statement saying that he was standing behind Frisch, and referring to the Deans as "rebels."

On August 15, Dizzy and Paul Dean received what they were told were their last paychecks—minus the fines and cost of the uniforms.

"I don't think that was nice," Dizzy lamely complained. "Them uniforms wuddn't destroyed. They coulda been mended. I was just mad and lost my temper."

When he encountered Frisch at the ballpark, Dean tried to minimize the brouhaha, saying, "Hi, Frankie, wanna win the pennant?"

"Of course, I do," Frisch replied.

"Then get us our money back and me 'n' Paul will be out there and help you along."

"Those fines stay," Frisch told him. "Take it or leave it. Go to Florida if you want to. I don't want you back unless it's on my terms."

Later, talking to reporters, Frisch said, "There are 10 million people out of work in this country, yet Dizzy Dean is willing to sacrifice the daily income of approximately $50 to fill the role of playboy." A sportswriter for a St. Louis paper noted, "The feeling of the Cardinal players toward the Deans has dropped from the freezing point to 10 degrees below zero since the latest rebellion."

Rickey, Breadon, and Frisch had decided that they could not lose face in this confrontation with their star player. Almost certainly, they were fully aware that the quiet, retiring Paul, despite his few public attempts at indignation, was merely following the lead of his brother.

"I appreciate the fine pitching the Deans have done," Frisch told reporters, "but that doesn't give them the privilege to do as they please. Even if it costs me my job, I'm standing pat. I won't give in because that would be unfair to others who have been fined and taken it like a man."

The day's game was postponed because of rain. With nothing to do, Dizzy and Paul holed up at the Forest Park Hotel. The brothers lay on Paul's bed, listening to a sports program on the radio in their undershirts, while Pat remained in the room she and Dizzy shared. Both brothers got a shock when the station broadcast a man-on-the-street reaction to the Dean brothers' walkout. Fans were describing them as "selfish," "spoiled," "brats," "ungrateful," and "great pitchers who thought they could get away with anything."

Chastened, Dizzy and Paul agreed that maybe it was time to end their revolt and rejoin the team.

It was on that day, August 15, that Paul was also first referred to as "Daffy"—in an unbylined article in the *Brooklyn Eagle*.

The next day, which also happened to be Paul's twenty-first birthday, Dizzy and Paul met with Breadon, Rickey, and Frisch to see if a solution to the standoff could be found. Dizzy and Paul stated that if the fines were rescinded and their full salaries restored, they would return to the club. The Cardinals refused to back down.

Dizzy, though, was optimistic that time was on his side. Referring to the uniforms he had destroyed, he told reporters, "I think I can get them patched up."

Frisch took a tougher line. "No player can be bigger than his club," he told reporters. "I've been playing ball 16 years in the National League, and I've done things I shouldn't have, and I've been fined and suspended. I had to take it. And that goes for everybody on this club—everybody. Something had to be done and I did it. There will be discipline on this club if we finish last, which of course we won't."

Frisch was alluding, of course, to the time when he himself had walked out on his manager, John McGraw—not over money, but a charley horse.

He also revealed that a straw vote among the players supported his actions, though there had been about a half dozen abstentions.

Meanwhile, Dizzy and Paul decided to remain in St. Louis at least until August 23, when the league-leading New York Giants were arriving in St. Louis for an important three-game series.

"Then we figure the Cards will ask us to rejoin the club," Dizzy told Gillespie of the *Star-Times*. "Now, while they are playing the Phillies, they don't have to worry about us. Anybody can beat the Phils. But it'll be different when the Giants come to town. It takes Diz and Paul to stop the Giants, and the Cards know it."

The loss of income now began to be a factor to the one person to whom it mattered most: Pat Dean. Hinting that the brothers would be back in uniform in a day or two, she gave reporters a calculatedly sentimental reason why the two brothers had not taken the train to Detroit: "Diz will never admit it, but the reason he did not go to Detroit was that he was heart-broken over that double-header Sunday. Dizzy was so disgusted that he simply didn't want to see anyone. He wouldn't even have a soda with me after the game. Diz hates to lose. It hurts his pride. If he had won, he could have gone to Detroit a hero, but losing, he felt he would be a heel."

She then appended another, starker reason why Dean and Paul might return to the fold, sooner rather than later: "The Dean family needs the money."

Dizzy also decided to take his case to the public, writing an open letter that had Pat Dean's fingerprints all over it, and that was printed in the August 17 *Post-Dispatch*:

> As a favor to me, I want you to print this letter. I want to present my side of this argument. I realize I made a mistake in not making the trip to Detroit. Had I known what the game was all about I would not have disappointed those kids for anything in the world. But I was so disgusted about losing that double-header Sunday that I didn't care if I never saw another game or not.
>
> You know how bad I hate to lose. And when Paul and I both lost before that crowd of loyal St. Louis people I was downhearted. It's bad enough to lose when I am away from home, but to go out there and pitch my heart out in that hot sun and still lose, well, you can imagine just how I felt.

Then, Tuesday, when the team came home I went to the park expecting a fine. I realized I had made a mistake. When I went into the clubhouse I expected Frank to call me over and tell me I was fined. But it seems as though everybody on the team had been told about it before I was. So when they all, from the bat boy on up, got through telling me I was fined I wasn't in any frame of mind to be jumped on. So I blew up. One thing brought on another, and when the storm was over I had torn up my uniforms.

The ball club announced I was suspended until I would accept the fines and that I could return when I was ready to. I wanted to return today, and I agreed to take the fines, suspension for two days without pay, and to pay for the two uniforms. But after I agreed to do that, the "powers that be" informed me that I would get another 10 days' suspension, because Paul does not care to return. Paul is 21 years old and a man with his own mind.

I have apologized and admitted I was wrong, and I want to go back to work now, and not 10 days from now. I leave it up to you and all the sports fans, what else can I do?

Sincerely,
"Dizzy" Dean

Abruptly changing his mind about remaining in St. Louis until the Giants arrived on August 23, a desperate Dizzy Dean then drove up to Chicago with his wife. The Cubs were playing the Boston Braves the next day, but Dizzy had other business besides watching the game. In the morning before game time, he visited Commissioner Landis, whose office was in the Windy City, and asked him to hold a hearing about the ten-day suspension, which Dizzy said was excessive. The commissioner agreed to hold a hearing on the following Monday in St.

Louis. Later an upbeat Dizzy signed dozens of scorecards for youngsters.

Then came yet another twist in the affair. While Dizzy was in Chicago, Paul abruptly returned to the fold, paying a fifty-dollar fine and accepting the loss of seventy dollars in salary for being off the payroll for three days. Not only had Paul repented, but Branch Rickey wanted him to be publicly humiliated, as an example to any other would-be rebels on the team. He drew up a document, which would have made even "a high school boy blush to autograph," in the words of the *Sporting News*, and insisted that Paul sign it. Paul meekly obliged. It read:

> I was wrong when I refused to go to Detroit and when I refused to go on the field when I was asked to do so. The Cardinals have been very good to me and I do not want manager Frisch to think I am unmindful of his considerations this spring when he continued to use me regularly after I looked bad in my first three or four games. He has always treated me kindly.
>
> I want to make up as much as I can for my mistake, and I also want to make more money next year. But above all, I want to help keep the Cardinals in the pennant race.

Later that day, Paul took over from Dazzy Vance in a game against the Philadelphia Phillies, pitching seven innings, allowing no runs, and giving up only four hits as the Cardinals won, 12 to 2. The win was Paul's thirteenth of the year.

The next day, August 18, Hallahan raised his record to 5–12 as he defeated the Boston Braves.

In yet another curious development, Rickey declined to announce who would be manager of the Cardinals in 1935. "That does not mean that Frisch will be replaced and it does not mean that he will be reappointed," he explained to reporters. "It merely means the club has adopted a policy to make no more announcements about managers during a season."

On the fifth day of his suspension, Dizzy drove back to St. Louis and went to see Breadon, saying he wanted to return to the fold—but on one condition. He expected to be reinstated with his pay to begin on the day he had offered to return, only to have his hands tied because Paul had refused to go along; but then, of course, Paul had paid his fine and rejoined, without telling Dizzy, who had been up in Chicago at the time, so it only seemed fair, to Dizzy at least, that he should receive the same treatment as Paul. Breadon vetoed Dizzy's request and informed him that his pay would resume as soon as his suspension was lifted.

On August 19, the Boston Braves pounded their way through six Cardinals pitchers, in the first game of a Sunday doubleheader played in St. Louis. Since there was now a shortage of Cardinals pitchers, Frisch announced that Pepper Martin, the third baseman, would be given a chance to work from the mound. "I've got a high hard one," Martin reassured his manager. "I think it will fool the batters."

By the seventh inning, the hard-hitting Braves had already dispatched Carleton, Haines, and Mooney. Frisch motioned to Martin to get ready to pitch.

"Frankie, I'm gonna put this fire out," Martin reassured his manager, "and you may be watchin' the new ace of your staff."

Knowing that Martin's knuckleball lacked much speed, Frisch dryly retorted, "Even if you bean somebody, it won't hurt them."

Martin threw for two innings before five thousand smiling fans, allowing only one hit.

Back in the dugout, Martin asked Frisch, "Frankie, from where you were standin', could you tell if my fast one had a hop on it? It looked to me like it was jumpin' like a jackrabbit and I think those Braves were scared of me."

In the eighth inning, the Boston Braves' pitching began to collapse, and the Cardinals managed to even the game at 8 to 8. In the ninth, Frisch sent Paul Dean to the mound, but the final score was 10 to 9, and Paul took the loss. In the second game, both Medwick and Collins homered, and Bill Walker limited the Braves to seven hits as the Cardinals won, 3 to 1. In the six days that Dizzy had been away from the team, they had played seven games, won six, and lost one. They were still in third place, however, and seven games out of first.

———

Then came the hearing, on Monday, August 20, the seventh day of Dizzy's suspension. The three-hour showdown was held behind closed doors in the forty-five-dollar-a-night suite of Judge Landis at the Park Plaza Hotel, but the proceedings were so loud and boisterous that reporters and others lingering in the hallway had no trouble hearing every word coming through the open transom.

The case of *J. H. Dean vs. the St. Louis National League Base-ball Club* got under way shortly after 10 A.M. Seated on one side of a long table were Dizzy and Paul Dean. Dizzy was acting as his own counsel. Aligned on the opposite side were Rickey the lawyer, Breadon, Frisch, the two coaches, traveling secretary Clarence Lloyd, trainer Doc Weaver, treasurer Bill DeWitt, Leo Durocher, Jesse Haines, and several administrative aides. Resting on the table was the evidence: two torn uniforms.

Rickey led for the prosecution, declaring that Dizzy Dean had been a problem player for the Cardinals organization beginning all the way back to the time when he was with the St. Joseph and Houston farm teams. Although acknowledging that Dizzy was a great pitcher, Rickey noted that he often gave in to "inexplicable" impulses, and the Cardinals had simply accepted his unpredictable behavior as the price they had to pay for keeping him happy.

"That ain't right, Judge," Dean protested, recalling that on one occasion he had been forced to stay in the home of a team official while recuperating from an illness.

"They charged me $80 or $100 to stay there while I was sick, and I coulda stayed at some other place for $35. That's what they did to me."

Glaring at Rickey, he declared, "You ain't fair with me. How did you treat my brother Elmer? You told me you'd give him a job at the ballpark, and what kind of job did you pick for him—sellin' peanuts in the stands."

"Yes," Rickey replied, in a musing tone, "but wasn't it at your invitation that the club brought Elmer from Texas? You knew he wasn't making much money in Houston, and you asked us to see what could be done for him. We tried and are still trying to help him with a job in Houston."

Rickey's question slyly suggested that, though he had come up with the idea of bringing Elmer to St. Louis after his conversation with Ankenman in Houston, he had only been doing Dizzy a favor. But Dizzy had other things on his mind.

"Don't you think you're takin' care of Elmer," Dizzy snapped. "Why, you ain't hardly keepin' care of us—me 'n' Paul."

"Hardly taking care of you, Dizzy?" Rickey rejoined. "Your salary is $7,500—a pretty good salary, I would say, for a young man your age, so you can't say we're not taking care of you."

When Dean did not reply, Rickey asked if he had ever criticized the Cardinals. In particular, had he called them cheap? Dean admitted that he had.

Rickey asked if Dean knew that the Cardinals had had the second highest payroll in the National League in 1933, and had the third highest that year, 1934.

Dean said that he did not know that. In response to a further question, he also acknowledged that he had ridiculed Rickey in the Cardinals clubhouse. Rickey then wanted to know whether, on the previous Thursday, Dean had said during a radio interview that he would never pitch for the Cardinals again.

"Yes," Dean said, "but I was all sore at the time and I'm sorry about it now. I did wrong by sayin' that."

Rickey asked if Dean had complained about having a sore arm when, in fact, his arm was not sore. Moreover, was it not true, the general manager demanded, that Dean's favorite excuse when he did not want to do something—for example, to play an exhibition game in Detroit—was to say that his arm was sore?

"No," Dean insisted. "I've had a sore arm for two months, and it's still sore."

During those two months, of course, he had won twenty-one games.

Rickey turned to one of his witnesses, Pop Haines, and asked him if Dizzy had ever complained about having a sore arm.

"Yes," Haines answered, "he told us once he could get a sore arm whenever he felt like it."

Rickey asked whether Haines could recall any time in particular when Dean made such an excuse.

"Yes," said Haines, "the night we were coming to New York from Boston, July 22 it was, and Dizzy said his arm hurt him so much he probably couldn't pitch for three or four weeks."

Then what happened? Rickey asked.

"He went out the next day and beat the Giants."

Did Haines see anything to indicate that Dean's arm was sore?

"I don't think you could beat those fellows if it was."

Rickey asked Haines why he thought Dean had said such a thing.

"I don't know, maybe for the fun of it, maybe to upset the manager."

Landis also interrogated Durocher, Lloyd, Weaver, and coaches Mike Gonzales and Clyde Ware. While Rickey was questioning a witness from the front office in support of his contentions, Dizzy interjected, "Sure, they'll say what you want. They'd be a fool if they didn't."

At one point, an angry Breadon yelled at Dizzy, "Don't you call me a liar, Dizzy."

"I ain't callin' you a liar," Dizzy shouted back, "but don't you call me one neither."

Frisch noted that Dizzy and Paul had disappointed hundreds of children who had shown up at the stadium in Detroit to watch them pitch. In his own defense, Dizzy said that Breadon still had not paid him some bonus money that was his due.

In his autobiography, Frisch characterized the hearing as "a long-winded affair." In his opinion, Landis did not appear as well disposed toward Rickey as he was to Breadon, "of whom he was very fond. Everybody got the idea the Judge was inclined to side with Dizzy, chiefly on the older Dean's contention that Breadon had no right to insist that Dizzy bring Paul back to the ranks with him. But finally the Commissioner decided that as manager I certainly had been within my rights in fining them for missing the exhibition game and in suspending them for failing to put on uniforms for a league game."

In his ruling, Commissioner Landis admonished Dizzy and Paul Dean in unequivocal terms, declaring:

> Ballplayers owe their public a certain obligation, and you two boys owed the city of Detroit, the management of the Tigers, and the management of the Cardinals something important in their lives. You should have done everything possible to accompany your team. But you didn't, did you?
>
> You were disgusted, Dizzy, you said, because you lost a game to the Cubs and you thought you might have a sore

arm. Paul, you said you were worried about your ankle and that you sat at your hotel waiting for Dizzy to pick you up and drive you to the station but that he never showed up. That's too deep for me and it's difficult for me to accept your statements.

You two boys owe it to your profession to show yourselves on the ball field at all times. People go out there, pay their money to see you, and you threw baseball down in this instance. Then when you were informed of your fines by the Cardinals, you got huffy and wanted to quit. You wouldn't go to the field. You were not going to do this, you were not going to do that.

I do not feel the Cardinals were unreasonable, either in their fine or their suspension of 10 days for you, Dizzy. I support them fully.

Landis also declared that it was up to Breadon whether Dean would be allowed to return before the ten-day suspension was up.

Rickey immediately suggested that the ten-day suspension be reduced to eight. Breadon had an even better idea, saying, "I don't want to be hard on Dizzy. I'll cut it to seven and make him eligible tomorrow—providing this meets with the manager's approval. What do you think, Frank?" The Cardinals were in a tight pennant race, after all, and Dizzy Dean's presence on the mound, despite the Cardinals' winning record in the past few games, was vital.

"It's all right with me," Frisch replied.

"What, the ten days?" an alarmed Breadon prodded.

"No, let's make it seven," Frisch said.

Dizzy asked for the fines to be revoked, but Landis ruled that they would stand.

After the hearing, Dizzy Dean declared, "I got a raw deal, but I'll be glad to be back out there on that mound."

He was still angry when photographers asked everyone at the hearing to gather together for a group shot. Dizzy, his brow creased, refused to smile, and he also declined to shake hands with Landis, Rickey, Breadon, or Frisch. In the end, the loss of salary, the fine, and the cost of two destroyed uniforms had cost him $486.

The ultimate result, though, was to strengthen the other players' respect for Frisch. Before the revolt, the Cardinals had ability; after the rebellion, team spirit and determination coalesced. Dizzy paid his fines and wrote a telegraphed apology to the fans in Detroit. Though sympathetic supporters from around the country sent him money to help him pay his fines, he sent back every dime.

Of course, it was not long before the two Deans were back in everyone's good graces. It was almost impossible to stay angry with those two fun-loving southern boys. Best of all, during the final stretch, the Dean brothers became virtually invincible.

Some of the credit for the Cardinals' newfound resolve and reenergized spirit also went to the voluble field captain, Leo Durocher, who during a clubhouse meeting said to his teammates, "Listen, you dumb clucks. Do you realize that while we are doing all this we are allowing a club to walk off with the pennant that has no more right to win than a flock of schoolboys in Peoria, not to mention blowing about 5,000 smacks apiece?"

According to John Drebinger in the *New York Times,* "Those words apparently had a magical effect. Overnight the Cards became a happy family. Frisch's word became absolute law. And today they are heading into the World Series."

On August 25, Elmer Dean was back in the news. Taking a page from his brothers' book, he had decided to walk away from baseball until management recognized his worth. "He's out on strike," the Associated Press quoted Walton Benson, the concession director in Houston, as saying. "He called me on the telephone. 'I want more money or I'll let your goobers go stale.' I told him, 'Nothing doing.' He said, 'I quit.'"

Many years later, when his autobiography was published in 1962, Frank Frisch finally revealed where exactly Dizzy and Paul Dean had gone that August day in 1934 when they decided to skip the exhibition game in Detroit. All the stories about Paul waiting in his hotel room for Dizzy to show up, or the two of them wanting to celebrate Paul's birthday just among themselves, or needing to rest their aching, weary arms—all were just, well, confabulations.

When the doubleheader was over and lost that day, Frisch wrote:

> [Dizzy] remembered that a friend of his with a big estate near Belleville, which was about 12 miles away in Illinois, was having an outdoor barbecue chicken dinner that evening. The friend, whom I will call Clarence, because that is his name, had expressed regrets about the exhibition game in Detroit. Otherwise, he told Dean, Dizzy and Paul could have had a nice evening at the Belleville party.
>
> And that's where Dizzy was while Clarence Lloyd was having the conductor hold the Detroit train for a few minutes. While we were on our way to Detroit, Dizzy and Paul were gnawing on fried chicken, enjoying it no end, and no doubt laughing heartily over the much better time they were having than were the rest of the Cardinals.

6

CASEY'S
REVENGE

The prodigal son returned to the Cardinals family on Friday, August 24, in a game at Sportsman's Park against the Giants. Dizzy Dean had missed nine games, and probably would have started in at least two of them, and possibly as many as four. Garry Schumacher, a reporter for the *New York Evening Journal,* described the moment Dean appeared in public for the first time since his suspension:

> He allowed his shoulders to slump and hung his head, focusing his eyes on the ground as though anxious to avoid the gaze of the crowd. Whenever manager Frisch offered a word of advice he listened with studied attention. The crowd got the impression he wanted them to get that here was a man sorry for his sins and anxious to make amends. As the game progressed, and his pitching won storms of approval, his attitude changed. He straightened his shoulders, became his old aggressive, assertive self. He began to talk to the Giant batters, taunt them as they came to the plate.

Dean gave up five hits as he shut out Terry's league-leading team, 5 to 0, for his twenty-second win.

"Yes, sir," Schumacher concluded, "it was Dizzy's day, his show. If St. Louis didn't kill the fatted calf in his honor last night, it is truly ungrateful."

Frisch sent Dizzy to the mound the very next day in another game against the Giants, but this time the Cardinals lost, after New York came from five runs behind to win, 7 to 6. "Back for a second time in as many days," remarked James P. Dawson in the *New York Times,* "it was asking too much of even the great Dizzy Dean to deliver."

After splitting a doubleheader with Brooklyn, and then losing a third game, the Cardinals were now seven games out of first place, with only thirty-six games left in the season. In August, as in May, the outlook wasn't brilliant. Diehard fans remembered, though, that in 1930 the Cardinals had been nine games out, on that same date, and had still managed to win the pennant.

Though the newspapers did not record any St. Louis fans slaughtering a fatted calf in Dean's honor upon his return, all was certainly forgiven. The very next day, in a game against the Dodgers, three thousand kids belonging to the Knot Hole Gang in the left-field bleachers began chanting, "We want Dean, we want Dean!" as first Tex Carleton, then Pop Haines, and then Jim Mooney went down in defeat.

On his triumphal return, Dean did not forget to bring along his braggadocio. In an interview with Bill McCullough of the *Brooklyn Times-Union*, he declared, "I know for a fact that the St. Louis club was offered $100,000 and a few good players for me, and several teams have been trying to buy Paul for $50,000. I don't care where I pitch, so long as I get the salary I'm entitled to. And that goes for Paul, too."

Dean may have been talking to a reporter, but his message was clearly addressed to Breadon and Rickey.

Around that time, Dizzy and Paul Dean were also offered a contract to appear in a postseason vaudeville act. The terms being offered were modest. But Dizzy, who usually made jokes at his own expense, was sly like a fox. Inserted into the vaudeville contract, at his insistence, was a clause that read, "If, by an act of God, St. Louis wins the pennant, this contract is null and void." Subsequently, the Dean brothers negotiated another contract on significantly better terms.

On Labor Day, Dizzy and Paul Dean lost another double-header, this time in Pittsburgh. The Cardinals and Chicago were now tied for second place, both teams five games behind the Giants. Gillespie of the *St. Louis Star-Times* asked Frisch if the team was ready to give up.

"Never, not until we're counted out officially," Frisch fired back. "No team of mine will give up. We're in this race until we're out of it, and, believe me, we'll fight to the last ditch. When I played under John McGraw, I was taught to fight to the finish, and you can bet your last dollar that every man playing for me will do the same."

No one better exemplified that never-give-up spirit than Dizzy Dean, the arch rebel himself. During a series in Pittsburgh, Frisch ordered him to catch a train for New York. But Dean disobeyed and remained behind in order to join some of his teammates in an exhibition game in Greensburg, Pennsylvania.

"That brings up the question," Gillespie noted, "if the Cardinals fined Dizzy $100 for failing to go to Detroit for an exhibition game, what will be the penalty—or bonus—for insisting on going to an exhibition game in Greensburg after the team management had excused him from so doing?"

True to form, Dizzy also continued to grumble about how difficult it was for him to win games with teammates who could neither hit nor field. None of them, he often complained, had the fighting spirit a team needed to take the pennant.

"I ought to whip the whole goddamned bunch of you—at the same time," Dizzy threatened one day, yelling at the entire team in the clubhouse after a game.

Spud Davis, the only Cardinal player physically bigger than Dean, listened patiently for a while, then said, "Shut the fuck up." Dean prudently did as he was told.

———

The New York Giants had led the National League for most of the season, and by September 5 they were seven games ahead of Frisch's Cardinals. The Cardinals had reigned atop the standings for only one brief twenty-four-hour period in June. But in the stretch, the Cardinals were to win an astounding twenty of their last twenty-five games. Still, some sportswriters were not impressed. After the Redbirds fell to the Phillies in one of their five losses, Cy Peterman of the *Philadelphia Evening Bulletin* dismissed the Cardinals as a "nine-day wonder," noting, "The St. Louis Cardinals, a two-pitcher outfit, is needlessly exciting the National League with a phony bid for the flag."

The hometown *St. Louis Post-Dispatch* was equally pessimistic, publishing on that same day an article with the headline "Seven Game Lead Too Big to Overcome, Redbirds Now Concede." They had conceded no such thing, however. That afternoon in the visitors' clubhouse in Ebbets Field, as Robert Gregory noted, Frank Frisch "was about to convene what he considered the most inspirational meeting of his playing and managerial career."

Frisch ordered all of his players to be at the clubhouse an hour earlier than usual. When they had assembled, as he later related to Sid Keener of the *St. Louis Star-Times*, "I burned them out like they had never been burned out before.

"'Are you fellows going to quit now?' I shouted. 'This race is just getting hot. It's not over yet and don't give up. We're going to fight to the finish, and, I'm telling you, we won't be beaten.'"

Frisch then reported that the change in his players' expressions astounded even him.

"They started kicking the bench around," he told Keener. "They grabbed their uniforms, and I saw them dressing with fires in their eyes—Diz and all the boys."

"We ain't givin' up, Frankie," Dizzy told Frisch. "I'm pitchin' today and I'll show you we ain't beat. Are we, boys?"

As Frisch later told Keener, "I can hardly describe the change in my ball club from then on."

That afternoon, Dean beat the Dodgers, 2 to 1.

By September 15, with about two weeks left in the season, the Cardinals had moved into undisputed second place. But the Giants were still five and a half games in front. The next day, a Sunday afternoon, the Cardinals visited the Polo Grounds to play a doubleheader against the Giants. The largest crowd in the stadium's history, 62,573, turned out for the occasion, with many patrons jamming the aisles or sitting two to a seat. Another 15,000 had been turned away, and the fire department had ordered all gates locked to prevent any more fans from entering. The Dean brothers led the Cardinals to two victories. In the second game, Paul Dean defeated Carl Hubbell, for his fourth defeat in five decisions against the Cardinals. Between them, Dizzy and Paul Dean had now won twelve games against the Giants.

"Ramblings of a fascinated onlooker at the Polo Grounds yesterday," Paul Gallico reported the next day in the *New York Daily News*:

> Dizzy Dean is a strange looking fellow. He has high Slavonic cheekbones and a large, big-lipped mouth, which is never quite closed. He never seems to change his

expression. He chews no gum or tobacco. He spits often. When he walks to the dugout after the inning is over, no one speaks to him on the way. He speaks to no one, but trudges with his eyes on the ground and his mouth open. Dizzy was interviewed before the game. He was asked what he thought of Frankie Frisch. He said, "I think Frisch is the most wonderful manager in the world."

The reporter asked, "Why, Diz?"

"Because," replied Dizzy, "he's the only man who could keep a club in a pennant fight with two pitchers."

"Who are the two pitchers, Dizzy?"

"Me 'n' Paul."

Three other Cardinal pitchers were standing beside him when he made this earnest statement. Maybe that is why he must pitch surrounded only by his own thoughts.

But the image of Dizzy Dean as the solitary hurler was only one side of his public persona. Another, equally estimable journalist, John Lardner, who wrote a syndicated sports column for the North American Newspaper Alliance, reported that same day on another side. Just before the weekend series with the Giants began, Dean had suddenly appeared in the Giants dugout, carrying a black cat. He then proceeded to point its nose at second baseman Hughie Critz,

an impressionable little fellow from Mississippi, and making all kinds of hex signs and mumbo passes in Hughie's direction.

"Cat, get Critz," said Mr. Dean. "Critz, get jinxed. Zmmmm."

Mr. Critz looked around for the nearest exit and vanished into the clubhouse. Mr. Dean seemed satisfied. "That got him," he said. "This will get 'em all."

Cardinals owner Sam
Breadon, a hard-nosed
businessman, also had a
soft side. Friends affec-
tionately called him
"Singing Sam" because
he enjoyed entertaining
his friends with a song.

A non-imbibing Methodist who refused to watch the Cardinals play on
a Sunday, Branch Rickey was also a visionary who created baseball's
farm system.

Frankie Frisch came to the Cardinals in the middle of the 1933 season in the most sensational trade in baseball history.

Frisch, who managed the Gashouse Gang to ninety-five victories in 1934, also fancied himself a wine connoisseur, and was an accomplished gardener.

In 1934, St. Louis's Sportsman's Park was one of the few Major League stadiums lacking a public-address system.

Dizzy Dean, the unpredictable ringleader of the Gashouse Gang, won thirty games in 1934 even though he went on strike at the height of the pennant race.

Despite their feuding, the scrappy Gashouse Gang managed to finish two games ahead of the favored New York Giants.

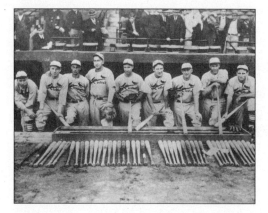

The Cardinals led the National League with a .288 batting average and were second in the league in pitching with a 3.69 ERA.

Dizzy Dean gets in the umpire's face, while Durocher pounds his glove in protest.

Speed merchant Pepper Martin excelled at stealing bases and also enjoyed driving his beloved midget auto racer around a racetrack before a game.

Moody slugger Joe Medwick, one of five in the St. Louis starting line-up to hit over .300, often picked fights with both teammates and opposing players.

Rookie catcher Bill DeLancey (left), a Southern boy, found a soul mate in Paul Dean.

It was impossible to call Dizzy by any other name. But Paul (left) refused to be called Harpo or Daffy.

Player-manager Mickey Cochrane, despite losing a fortune in the stock market, led the 1934 Detroit Tigers to a 101–53 record.

In his first year in Detroit, Cochrane batted .320, was named to the American League All-Star team, and won the Most Valuable Player Award.

Cardinals hurler Tex Carleton was often called "the third Dean" because he physically resembled Dizzy and Paul. But he lost to Detroit pitcher Elden Auker in Game 4 of the World Series.

After doubling with one out in the seventh inning of a 3–3 game, Leo Durocher scored the eventual winning run in Game 6 on a Paul Dean single.

Detroit fans—already angry that their team was losing Game 7 by a score of 9–0—took issue with a hard slide by the Cardinals' Joe Medwick and littered the field with bottles and other debris.

While pinch running at first base in Game 4, Dizzy Dean was beaned in the head by a would-be double-play throw from the Detroit second baseman. He was still able to start the next day.

The Giants won anyway.

St. Louis was then off for three days. During that period, the Giants won once and lost once. Then the Cardinals swept another doubleheader against the Boston Braves, this time with Tex Carleton and Bill Walker, who had returned to the lineup, doing the pitching. In his eagerness to overtake the Giants, Frisch proposed a tripleheader to make up for several lost games with Boston that had been rained out, but National League president John Heydler turned him down. A Boston sportswriter, although conceding that there was a "slim mathematical possibility" that the Cardinals could win the pennant, could not help but admire the team's "spirit and enthusiasm." At the same time, he reported that there had been a considerable amount of "popping off" among the Cardinals in the dugout during their two victorious games against the Braves, much of it by Dizzy Dean, and that Frisch had been ejected.

Unperturbed, Bill Terry of the Giants announced that same day that Carl Hubbell, who had just won his twenty-first game of the season, would be the starting pitcher in the first game of the World Series.

On September 21, just before the Dean brothers were to pitch a historic doubleheader against Brooklyn at Ebbets Field, Frisch held his customary meeting in the clubhouse. Dizzy was scheduled to pitch the first game, and Paul the second. Frisch's agenda that morning was to review the enemy's roster and tell the two pitchers how he wanted them to throw to each batter. At the same time, he also gave pointers to his infielders and outfielders on how he wanted them to position themselves when different batters stepped to the plate.

"Keep the ball high and outside for Leslie," Frisch advised the Dean brothers, referring to first baseman Sam Leslie. "He'll hit it over the fence if you get it inside."

"That ain't how I pitch to him," Dizzy protested. "I give him nothin' but low-and-inside stuff, and he ain't got a hit off me yet."

Frisch ignored Dizzy's comment and moved on to consider Tony Cuccinello, the second baseman.

"Nothing but curves for Tony," Frisch insisted. "He owns pitchers like Vance. Ask Dazzy. Tony'll slap a fast ball into the left-field lumber every time you give him one."

Keeping a straight face, Dizzy drawled, "That's mighty funny, I never have bothered to dish him up a curve yet, and he's still trying for his first loud foul off old Diz."

Nettled, but struggling to maintain his composure, Frisch continued to review each Dodger player—Joe Stripp, Johnny Frederick, Len Koenecke, and Al Lopez—giving pointers on how he wanted the Deans to pitch to each man. At every instance, Dizzy remarked that he liked to pitch to those men in the exact opposite way. With each interruption from Dizzy, Frisch's patience wore thinner, until he seemed ready to explode. Yet the last thing he needed during this red-hot pennant drive was another rupture with his star pitcher. Who knew what his temperamental hurler might do if he felt insulted? He had no idea, of course, that Dean was trying to aggravate him just for fun. Some of the other players, who knew what their teammate was up to, had to smother their laughter in a towel or hide behind a post.

"This is silly business, Frank," Dean finally explained to his fuming manager. "I've won 26 games already this season, and it don't look exactly right for an infielder like you to be tellin' a star like me how I should pitch."

Frisch's response was to tell Dizzy to go out, then, and pitch as he damn well pleased—though in much more colorful language.

For the first seven innings, Dean pitched exactly as he pleased—throwing fastballs to batters known to favor fastballs, among other taunts both to opposing batters and his own manager. Such was his mastery that the game, until that point, was a no-hitter.

With a no-hit game in sight, Frisch signaled for catcher Spud Davis to walk out to the mound and encourage Dizzy to bear down hard on the Brooklyn batters. But Durocher, the field captain, waved Davis back. In baseball superstition, any mention among the players that a no-hitter is in the works is a virtual guarantee that one of the next batters up will get a hit.

Dizzy went on to shut out the Dodgers, 1 to 0, while giving up only three hits—the first one in the eighth inning.

Dizzy later told St. Louis sportswriter J. Roy Stockton that the last thing on his mind was a no-hitter. "I didn't notice there wasn't any hits," Dizzy remarked after the game. "I sure was having a picnic with Frisch, though. You oughta seen the fellows in the clubhouse when I was puttin' him on. They was duckin' behind posts, trying to keep Frank from seein' how they was laughin', and I had a time keepin' a straight face myself. I hope Frisch manages the Cardinals forever. I sure love to drive that Dutchman nuts."

Paul then went on to pitch the first no-hitter in the National League since 1920, shutting out Brooklyn, 3 to 0.

"How would you feel?" Casey Stengel, the Dodgers manager, lamented at the end of the afternoon. "You get three itsy-bitsy hits off the big brother in the first game, and then you look around and there's the little brother with biscuits from the same table to throw at you."

"If'n I'd knowed Paul was gonna throw a no-hitter," Dizzy remarked after the second game, "well, I'd a throwed one, too."

In fact, though, Dizzy was never to pitch a no-hitter.

Dizzy's win broke the club record for victories in one season set by the great Cy Young, who in 1899 had won twenty-six and lost sixteen. The two victories also fulfilled Dizzy's boast at the start of the season that "me 'n' Paul" would win forty-five games between them. The win was his twenty-seventh, and Paul had now racked up his eighteenth—and the season was still not over.

The Giants, meanwhile, were having a collective nervous breakdown.

By September 24, they were leading the Cardinals by only two games. Just a few weeks earlier, St. Louis had been buried in third place. But the Giants had only four games left to play, whereas the Cardinals had six. Stanley Frank tried to reassure nervous Giant fans, writing in the *New York Post* that the New York team "cannot possibly blow the pennant no matter how hard they try." To prove it, the headline on the story read, "GIANTS REST UP FOR WORLD SERIES."

But after the Giants lost to the Phillies, and St. Louis defeated Pittsburgh, with Dizzy Dean posting his twenty-eighth victory, the Cardinals inched up to only one game behind. "The Giants are in a sea of trouble," Garry Schumacher admitted in the *New York Evening Journal*, "and their boat has sprung a leak!" He then went on to make a gloomy prediction: "Their collapse is a baseball story unlike anything in the annals of the game. No team in Major League history ever went into September with a seven-game lead and lost it. The Giants haven't done that yet, but it now appears inevitable."

On the very same day that the Cardinals defeated Pittsburgh, in the middle of baseball's greatest pennant drive, Leo Durocher, whose divorce had come through at the start of the season, got married again. Ernie Orsatti was best man at the ceremony, held in a judge's chambers in the Municipal Courts Building in St. Louis. Grace Dozier, the bride, wore a tailored black gown with a white ermine cape. Her divorce from her first husband had also come through that spring.

"Perhaps nothing shows better the spirit of the Gashouse Gang," observed Cardinals historian Frederick G. Lieb, "than the marriage of Leo Durocher, the club's aggressive shortstop, in the last week of that hectic season." The dapper ladies' man had fallen in love with the attractive Dozier, a fashion designer, Lieb reported, and had no intention of waiting until after the end of the season to marry her. Most other teams would have considered a player who dared to think about getting married in the tail end of a pennant race quite out of his mind, if not a slacker or a traitor to his club, and they would have resorted to all sorts of psychological and other pressure tactics to persuade him to postpone his wedding plans.

Branch Rickey, though, who was a friend of Dozier, thought otherwise. An ardent Cardinals fan, she herself had misgivings about marrying the star shortstop at such a critical time. After she made her feelings known to her fiancé, he appealed to Rickey, asking him to intervene on his behalf. Rickey telephoned the young woman and told her that if she really did want to marry Durocher, she should do it right away, so that he could free up his mind and concentrate only on baseball. They were married on the morning of September 26. The new Mrs. Durocher was also a woman with a considerable bank account, according to Durocher's biographer, Gerald Eskenazi, who noted, "The day after their marriage, Grace sat down and wrote out a dozen checks to clear up all [Durocher's] debts."

Later that same day, Durocher's old Yankee teammate, Waite Hoyt, shut out the Cardinals, and the new Mrs. Durocher cried over the defeat. An annoyed Frankie Frisch asked reporters, "Can you imagine picking a time like this for a wedding?"

But Rickey's reading of the situation had been astute. "After his marriage," said Lieb, "the Lip's mind was cleared for baseball; he was a veritable ball of fire on the Cardinals' infield, as the St. Louis club swept their last four-game series with the Reds."

Nine years later, the romance ended in a divorce court.

After the Giants lost to the Phillies, an unbelieving Harry Robert wrote in the *Philadelphia Evening Bulletin*, "It's one of the greatest stretch drives in history. Great races are traditional in the National League, but few have equaled this. And around it all, the buzzing of the fans. Yes, they're pulling for the Cards. They want to see the Deans pitch their team to a pennant and then fire at the Tigers in the Series."

J. G. Taylor Spink, writing in the *Sporting News,* seconded the motion:

> Dizzy Dean is the game's greatest showman since Babe Ruth. Has two names—Jerome Herman and Jay Hanner—in two different *Who's Who in Baseball*. It's his sense of humor. That's Dizzy. . . . He's never too busy to chat with hotel lobby fans and will give autographs anywhere at any time. He's just beginning to learn about clothes. The awkward figure of his rookie days is being transformed into a slender dude by the art of tailoring. He's also learning about money. In the old days he would buy an $80 overcoat from a fly-by-night peddler in a hotel lobby. Now the only persons he insults are those trying to make gyp sales to ball players. If Jerome Herman had had an education, he'd have made good at anything. He's generous to a fault. If a small boy wants an autograph and has no paper, Dizz will tear off a cuff.

After the Cardinals reduced the Giants' lead to a half game by defeating the Reds, with New York idle, Paul Gallico, writing in the *New York Daily News,* reminded his readers of something virtually every baseball fan in the city already know, and had not forgotten the entire season long: Bill Terry's disparaging response, back in January, to a question about the Dodgers' chances. "Brooklyn? Is Brooklyn still in the league?" the Giants manager had asked, with a snort.

Now, as fate would have it, Brooklyn and the Giants were facing one another in the two final games of the year. "If the Brooklyns can knock the Giants off in these games," Gallico wrote, "it will be the sweetest revenge for a cutting remark that anyone ever heard of. Those games at the Polo Grounds will probably be two of the greatest ever played. Here is the best baseball story of the year."

Stengel had reserved Van Lingle Mungo and Ray Benge, his two best pitchers, for the occasion. "The World Series will be an anti-climax to those two brawls at the Polo Grounds," Gallico concluded. "The most rabid, vituperative, hysterical rooter in the world, the Brooklyn fan, will troop across the bridge by the thousands, bringing cowbells, sirens, razzberries, whistles."

"By this time," said John Kieran in the *New York Times,* "Bill Terry may have some vague idea that the hand of fate is clutching at his epiglottis."

On Friday, September 28, Dizzy Dean shut out Cincinnati, 4 to 0, for his twenty-ninth victory. The next day, Paul led the Cardinals to a 6-to-1 win over the Reds, his nineteenth win of the year. True to his word, Frisch had vowed to pitch no one except the Dean brothers until the pennant was won. On that same Saturday, in the Polo Grounds, Brooklyn defeated the Giants, 5 to 1. A gleeful *Brooklyn Times-Union* ran a front-page headline that read:

BROOKLYN DODGERS 5; NEW YORK GIANTS 1
ST. LOUIS CARDINALS 6; CINCINNATI 1
YES, INDEED, MR. TERRY,
THE DODGERS ARE STILL IN THE LEAGUE

Now, on the very last day of the season, the only way for the Giants to win the flag was to prevail over the Dodgers while the Cardinals lost their game in St. Louis. That combination of circumstances would then set up a three-game playoff. A confident Dizzy Dean, who was scheduled to pitch the contest with the Reds, told reporters that "there ain't goin' to be any playoff."

The Cardinals were now in first place. True to his word, Dizzy pitched *another* shutout on one day's rest. At that point, it made no difference how the Giants fared, but they lost to Brooklyn anyway, 8 to 5, before a near-capacity crowd of forty-five thousand at the Polo Grounds. The panic-stricken Giants had ended their season by losing their last five games. Almost fittingly, given the near-tragic circumstances, the game concluded in semidarkness. Writing in the *Times,* John Drebinger suggested that the Brooklyn fans, who were not about to forget Terry's insult, were as much responsible for the Dodgers' victory as the players were.

"Once inside," he wrote, "they turned on a terrific din, augmented by whistles, horns, and bells, thus providing another unprecedented setting for a situation which already had set a record quite unparalleled in all baseball. For this probably marked the first time where a team making a last stand for a pennant came on its home field with as many jeers as cheers ringing in its ears."

The game in New York had begun an hour earlier than the one in St. Louis, because of the difference in time zones, so that by the time the ninth inning began, the Cardinals already knew the pennant was theirs. Yet Dean continued to pitch his heart out. Grinning and cocksure as always, he struck out the first two batters, then threw a fastball down the middle to little Sparky Adams, the Reds second baseman, who fouled out to Bill DeLancey. The moment the ball hit DeLancey's glove, Dean ran over to his teammate, snatched the ball, and dashed into the dugout just moments before the frenzied fans surged onto the field. They were cheering the Cardinals, of course, for winning their fifth pennant since 1926, and their first since 1931, but perhaps especially for Dean for making Major League history. The final game of the season not only marked his seventh shutout of the year, but his thirtieth win of the season. Together the Dean brothers had accounted for forty-nine victories, or more than half the Cardinals' wins that year.

Somebody yelled, "Brooklyn's in the league now!" Several Cardinal players shouted back, "And how!"

In the middle of the onfield jubilation, with fans swarming over the infield, a young boy solemnly walked out to place a four-pound chunk of ice on the pitching rubber. When a sportswriter asked him what he was doing, the boy replied that he was only following Dizzy's instructions.

"Dizzy told me this morning to put it there after the game," the youngster revealed. "Said it would be burning up if I didn't. Go ahead and feel it. Even the ice hasn't gotten it cooled down yet."

Back in the Cardinals locker room, everyone was backslapping and shouting, speechifying and popping champagne, with photographers flashing pictures and reporters asking questions and well-wishers keeping up a din. Martin, Buzzy Wares, and, of all people, Joe Medwick formed an impromptu barbershop trio and began singing, "I want a girl, just like the girl, that married dear old dad," with Medwick, of all people, providing the tenor.

Yet amid the festivities, two men remained strangely quiet: Frankie Frisch and Dizzy Dean. The two old adversaries sat side by side on a wooden bench, chatting confidentially, in striking contrast to Dizzy's hearing before Commissioner Landis only a few weeks earlier. Some observers remembered that, after the meeting with Landis had ended with Dizzy's reinstatement, he had refused to shake hands with Frisch or smile for the photographer.

Frisch declined to name the starting pitcher for the World Series. The next morning, the Cardinals boarded a train for Detroit, hoping to arrive in time for a morning workout on Navin Field.

In winning the pennant, said Drebinger in the *New York Times*, "the Cardinals have completed one of the most spectacular uphill drives in baseball history. In addition, they will bring into the forthcoming World Series as colorful an array as ever competed in the fall classic." In another piece, Drebinger elaborated, "Hopelessly beaten for the flag as late as Labor Day, the Cards' electrifying dash to the top stands almost without precedent in the Major Leagues. It was a spurt that took veteran fans back to the meteoric rise of the Braves of 1914, and something of a similar outburst by the Cards of 1930." He noted also that the Cardinals had battled their way to the pennant mostly while on the road, whereas the bewildered Giants, "heading for one of the most astounding collapses in baseball, hung stationary at the top." Even more curious, said Drebinger, the Cardinals, "while undeniably showing themselves as a great fighting team, spent about three-fourths of the year fighting among themselves before they finally struck upon the happy idea of uniting their energies in a common cause and fighting the enemy."

The awed sportswriter went on to exclaim that there were simply no legendary old-timers with whom the Dean brothers could be compared. "Blazing away in tireless rotation," he wrote, they seemed to pitch almost as if they were two Christy Mathewsons, two Walter Johnsons, two Lefty Groves. Dizzy Dean had finished the season with a 30–7 record and a 2.66 ERA.

In the words of an anonymous Associated Press reporter, filed on the last day of September, "Baseball's most amazing pennant rush since the campaign of George Stallings and his

'miracle men' of Boston [in 1914] ended in glorious triumph"
when the Cardinals secured the National League flag with a
rousing 9-to-0 triumph over the Cincinnati Reds. Oddsmakers
listed the Cardinals as 3-to-5 favorites to take the Series from
Mickey Cochrane's Detroit Tigers. No team had been named
such an overwhelming favorite in twenty years, back when
Stallings's Boston Braves upset the Philadelphia Athletics.

In the dismal Giants clubhouse up in New York, Jimmy Powers, a reporter for the *New York Daily News,* asked Bill Terry if
he had a farewell message for the Giants fans.

"Nope," the bitter Terry replied. "You can thank them if you
want—not me. In the tenth inning with everything lost they
booed me. I thought I was in St. Louis."

Asked if he would go to Detroit to see the Cardinals play the
Tigers in the World Series, Terry again shook his head and
said, "Nope. It would be humiliating."

The mood was just the opposite in the Brooklyn clubhouse,
Powers reported: "The din was deafening." Clad in a bath
towel wrapped diaper-fashion about his hips, manager Stengel
addressed his victorious troops:

"Farewell, my bonny men," he told them. "Some of you are
off to maim the gentle rabbit. Some of you will shoot the carefree deer. I bid you Godspeed, my lamby-pies, my brave young
soldiers. Go with Casey's blessing on your sweet heads."

The Detroit Tigers had ended their American League schedule on September 30 by sweeping a doubleheader on their
home field against the lowly Browns, St. Louis's other team,
which had never known the taste of a single pennant win and
victory celebration.

---— 7 ——---

IT AIN'T
BRAGGIN'

In the twenties and thirties, it was customary among sportswriters to bestow grandiloquent, vaguely literary, or at the very
least extravagantly menacing sobriquets on sports teams. The
mere nickname "the Gashouse Gang" probably provoked fear
in just about no one, unlike such classics of sports-page metaphor as the Four Horsemen of the Apocalypse of Notre Dame
football or the Yankees' Murderers' Row.

Not only was the Gashouse nickname inherently harmless,
even boyish, but there was also another, and much more decisive, reason that it conjured no feelings of trepidation or despair among those teams whose lot was to oppose the St. Louis
Cardinals in 1934: In that year, they were not even known as
the Gashouse Gang. In a remarkable demonstration of sports-
writing legerdemain, a chorus of columnists conspired to bestow one of the most memorable nicknames in all of sports to a
championship team—retroactively. After all, nearly every
player on the 1934 Cardinals had a folksy moniker of his very
own. It only seemed right that the most colorful team in the
history of baseball also become known to lore and legend by

something more evocative than the name of a twittering species of red-feathered bird.

The Gashouse nickname was not only a bit late in arriving, but no one since has been quite able to ascertain exactly what it meant, or who coined it, and when. It sounded good, and so sportswriters, players, and fans adopted it because, after all, *Gashouse Gang* had the virtue of being at least alliterative and seemed to suggest a gang of fellows at a funhouse, or having a gas, or being a gang of tough guys, or whatever. Who cared? The name stuck. The theories about what it meant and who thought it up came later. In 1935, the sports pages of America's major newspapers made a concerted effort to refer to the St. Louis Cardinals as the Gashouse Gang, but then Branch Rickey started to trade away some of the players who were an integral part of the Gashouse Gang. Nor was the 1935 version of the Cardinals to win the pennant. What had been a nickname in search of a team had arrived too late, and then was gone too soon.

Several people have claimed responsibility for coming up with the name. In his autobiography, *Nice Guys Finish Last,* Leo Durocher recalls how the uniforms of the 1934 Cardinals were always dirty. One day, after the Cardinals had arrived in New York for a series of games, he saw a cartoon by Willard Mullin in the *New York World-Telegram.* "It showed two big gas tanks on the wrong side of the railroad track," Durocher wrote, "and some ballplayers crossing over to the good part of town carrying clubs over their shoulders instead of bats. And the title read: 'The Gas House Gang.'" Durocher did not explain how or whether the cartoon image applied to the Cardinals, though that is clearly the inference if the St. Louis team was, in fact, in town. Nor is it clear in Durocher's account why or how the familiar, if somewhat inaccurate, term *gas tank* became the unfamiliar and obsolete *gashouse.*

Another widely circulated story about the origin of the Gashouse Gang name concerns the time Dizzy Dean and Durocher were chatting one day in 1934. "I don't know whether we can win in this league," Dean allegedly said, "but if we were in the other league we sure would win." Durocher allegedly replied, "They wouldn't let us in the other league. They would say we are a lot of gashouse players." The problem with this story is that it would be profoundly uncharacteristic of either Dean or Durocher ever to think that they could, under any circumstances, lose a baseball game. On a team crammed with overachievers, they topped the list.

Lee Allen, author of a juveniles' biography of Dizzy Dean and a baseball historian on the staff of the National Baseball Hall of Fame in Cooperstown, New York, also reported that Durocher was the man responsible for coming up with the name, although not in 1934, but the following year. In Allen's slightly different version of the story, the Lip was chatting with Frank Graham, a sportswriter for the *New York Sun*, as they sat on the visitors' bench at the Polo Grounds, where the Cardinals were playing the Giants. According to Allen, the Cardinals were enjoying a winning streak, and just then Dizzy Dean stopped by to observe that, in his opinion, the Redbirds could win the championship in either division, American or National.

"Oh, but they would never let us play in the American League," Durocher allegedly replied. "They'd say we were just a bunch of gashouse players."

Allen did not explain what Durocher could possibly have meant by the phrase. Did people who lived near or worked in gashouses even play baseball? If so, how was it different from the game of baseball played by, for example, workers in shoe factories or breweries? Allen only said that Graham used the phrase the next day in his column, other writers soon picked it up, and a nickname was born.

Like many other sportswriters of the day, Graham celebrated the generally shabby appearance of the 1934 Cardinals. The inference was that they resembled a gang of street toughs. "They don't look like a Major League ball club or as Major League ball clubs are supposed to look in this era of the well-dressed athlete," he wrote in the *Sun*. "Their uniforms are stained and dirty and patched and ill-fitting. They don't shave before a game and most of them chew tobacco. . . . They spit out of the sides of their mouths and then wipe the backs of their hands across their shirt fronts. . . . They are not afraid of anybody."

Graham added, "They don't make much money and they work hard for it. They will risk arms, legs, and necks, their own or the other fellow's, to get it. But they also have a lot of fun playing baseball."

But nowhere in the many thousands of words that Graham wrote for the *Sun* does the phrase "Gashouse Gang" make, in fact, its debut as a reference to the 1934 St. Louis Cardinals.

In other versions of the tale, Pepper Martin, not Durocher, uttered the famous phrase "a bunch of gashouse players," while also insisting that the Cardinals just might be good enough to play in the American League.

Still another widely circulated version of how the 1934 Cardinals arrived at their nickname concerns the day they arrived in New York to play the Giants after playing the Boston Braves in a rain-soaked game. Being the passionate, ever-sliding bunch that they were, their uniforms were stained with dirt and grime. Not having extra uniforms, and unable to wash the ones they had after their most recent game, they showed up at the Polo Grounds looking like, in the words of an anonymous New York sportswriter, "the gang from around the gashouse." The original source for this account is unknown.

John Devaney, author of *The Greatest Cardinals of Them All*, agreed with the conventional wisdom that the slovenly appearance of the 1934 Cardinals gave rise to their nickname. He then threw a curve, writing, "For they looked like mechanics who had just left the grease shop of a gas house (or what we now call a gas station)."

But that explanation raises another equally difficult question, namely, what the nickname "the Gashouse Gang" even meant. What was a gashouse? Was it spelled gashouse or gas house? And where, exactly, could such an edifice be found? Only Devaney identified a gashouse as a gas station. In most dictionaries, a gashouse is listed as a variation of the more popular *gasworks,* which in the *Merriam-Webster Collegiate Dictionary* is defined as "a plant for manufacturing gas, and especially illuminating gas." Illuminating gas was a synthetic mixture of hydrogen and hydrocarbon gases, and was used to light lamps in the days before electricity. The large cylindrical storage containers that were once a common urban sight were known as *gasholders,* or *gasometers.* Colloquially, they were called *gas tanks*—not *gashouses.* The size of a container depended on the quantity of stored gas, and its height rose or fell depending on the pressure released from the weight of the container's movable cap. In recent years, gas is more commonly stored in large underground reservoirs.

Before it was leveled in the late 1940s by the Metropolitan Life Insurance Company to make way for two residential complexes known as Stuyvesant Town and Peter Cooper Village, an area on Manhattan's Lower East Side was informally known as the Gashouse District. The name derived from the chemical fumes created by industries that made it one of the city's least desirable neighborhoods. Toughs from the Gashouse District were so nasty, and the pickings so few in their own neighborhood, that they reportedly preyed on petty thieves in nearby areas. Other street gangs of the time included the Fourth Avenue Tunnel Gang, the Car Barn Gang, Sweeney's Gadabouts, and the Jimmy Curley Gang, to mention only a few. Turf battles were frequent and violent. Despite its reputation for toughness, the gang from the Gashouse District does not appear to have been different from any other run-of-the-mill New York street gang.

Nevertheless, Mike Eisenbath, in *The Cardinals Encyclopedia,* supports the view that the Gashouse District gang was the muse that inspired the Gashouse Gang's name, writing, "The Gashouse District was a section of the lower East Side of Manhattan, an area that once had housed several large gas tanks. Historians have described the general area there as a rough neighborhood, with writer Frank Moss saying, 'Perhaps the most unique of all vicious drinking places is a 'dead house' on 18th Street in what is called the 'gashouse district,' a hangout for vagrants and bums of New York, Brooklyn, and New Jersey.' The neighborhood came to be known best for its wandering group of particularly cruel thugs: the Gashouse Gang." Moss was a journalist who published a history of New York in 1897 entitled *The American Metropolis.*

Numerous references in New York newspapers confirm the existence of a "gas house district" located around Eighteenth Street east of First Avenue. An item in the October 9, 1879, edition of the *New York Times* reports on a meeting of a political club located at 427 Second Avenue. The story then continues: "This is what is known as 'the Gas-house District,' because the hundreds of employees in the gas-works there have for years been practically compelled to vote the Democratic ticket."

In the November 15, 1894, edition of the same newspaper, this item appears: "Six boys were arraigned in the Harlem Police Court yesterday on charges of burglary. All belong to the 'Gas House Gang,' many members of which have been sent to the State prison and the penitentiaries."

In fact, there were many other gashouse districts in New York. According to the city's Heritage Resource Center, New York's five boroughs were home to probably more than a thousand gasworks in the first third of the century. By contrast, only about forty such plants operated in St. Louis.

Indisputably, then, the terms *gasworks, gashouse,* and *gashouse district* were reasonably current in the late nineteenth and early twentieth centuries in New York, although not nearly to the same extent in St. Louis. The manufacturing areas in North St. Louis, and on the Illinois side of the Mississippi, were mostly crowded with woolen mills, gunsmith shops, brass foundries, boiler works, soda water factories, milliners, boot factories, and scores of other establishments, and no one area ever came to be known as a "gashouse district."

By 1934, on the other hand, nearly a half century had passed since the phrase "gashouse district" had been current in New York. Moreover, the city had been electrified, and gaslights had become a thing of the past. Undoubtedly, the extensive area later razed by Met Life to make way for two middle-class housing projects remained, in its decline, an area known for its street toughs and other hazards. Most New York journalists, as well as such New Yorkers as Durocher and Frisch, were almost certainly familiar with the neighborhood, though for decades it went without a name. Officially, on most city maps, it was simply shown as part of the outer fringes of the exclusive Gramercy Park neighborhood. *

Curiously, Frisch was less certain than Durocher about how the name came to be. In his memoir ghosted by *St. Louis Post-Dispatch* sportswriter J. Roy Stockton, who was presumably as familiar with the minutiae of the Gashouse Gang legend as any other reporter, the Flash reminisced about a hard-fought game played between the Chicago Cubs and the Cardinals in 1935. In back-to-back plays, Martin and Orsatti had collided, respectively, with the catcher and then the pitcher covering home plate, and each had scored to bring the Cardinals the victory. That night, in Frisch's version, the defeated Cubs boarded a train for New York, and they were joined by Chicago baseball journalist Warren Brown, who teased the Cubs for having turned into their bunks so early.

"Are you boys afraid that Pepper Martin is on the train?" Brown bellowed. "You all had better stay on your side of the tracks, or the Gashouse Gang will get you."

Frisch concluded, "It was during that summer of 1935 that the Gashouse Gang name was pinned on the Cardinals. Perhaps Brown did it. Perhaps it was our uniforms. You can't play a game for all it is worth and keep your uniforms clean through a three-weeks' road campaign, with the sun broiling each day and saturating your clothes before the game even starts."

Though other theories about the origin of the Gashouse Gang name could be advanced, this final one must suffice. If nothing else, it adds to the weight of evidence that, regardless of who first uttered the phrase, it was probably picked up and popularized by New York journalists. They had witnessed at first hand the stark tragedy of the Cardinals coming from third place in 1934, like an onrushing locomotive, to win the championship, while the Giants—indomitable all season long—had collapsed in the last days of the season in one of the most astounding demonstrations of mass hara-kiri in baseball history. In *Diz,* his biography of Dizzy Dean, Robert Gregory declared that the Gashouse Gang nickname originated, in fact, during the 1934 World Series. Gregory wrote, apropos of game one, "Already on the stands in New York were early editions of the *World-Telegram,* and fans would read in Joe Williams' piece for October 4, 'I picked the Tigers but the Cardinals have got me worried. They looked like a bunch of guys from the gas house district who had crossed the railroad tracks for a game of ball with the nice kids.' That was the origin of the Cards' famous nickname."

A gashouse gang, in sum, was thoroughly dated New York slang for kids from a tough neighborhood. The name was pinned on the Cardinals even though there was no gashouse district in St. Louis, and even though the term *gashouse* had all but disappeared from common usage. Just as sportswriters had tried and failed to affix "Daffy" to Paul Dean, so the Gashouse Gang label also failed to stick to the 1935 club. If most fans were never quite sure what a gashouse gang actually was, nearly everyone at least agreed that the name applied only to that immortal, implausible, impossible gang of ballplayers known officially as the 1934 St. Louis Cardinals.

Over the years, Detroit's sports scribes had done their best to arm the Tigers with an extra layer of hyperbolic armor, imposing on its doomsday infield such soon-to-be-forgotten clunkers as the "First Line of Defense," the "Punch and Protection of Bounding Bengals," the "Tigers' Million-Dollar Infield," "Detroit's Big Guns," and even the almost-memorable "Infield of Dreams."

Then, in 1934, baseball writer Charles P. Ward of the *Detroit Free Press* christened the four Detroit infielders "the Battalion of Death." The name caught on with other sportswriters, and soon Motor City had its own legend in the making. This formidable quartet consisted of Hank Greenberg, still an awkward young slugger who was just beginning to reach his awesome maturity, at first base; the brilliant Charlie Gehringer at second; the smooth-fielding team captain, Bill Rogell, at shortstop; and Marv Owen, another exceptional fielder, holding down third. In the first week of September 1934, as the Tigers drove for the American League pennant, Rogell had fractured his ankle. He had his leg tightly wrapped and continued to play throughout the Series. "Hell," he later recalled, "in those days you didn't want to get out of the lineup. Someone might take your job."

Today the Tigers' superlative 1934 infield has been almost forgotten. Yet it had a claim to fame that the years have not eroded. If other foursomes were stronger defensively, there was never an infield, as H. G. Salsinger wrote in the *Detroit News,* "that produced as many hits as the Detroit infield. All four men on the infield are hitting above .300, and one of them [Gehringer] has been hitting above .400 for a good part of the season. We do not believe there was ever before an infield on which every man was a .300 hitter; at least no infield with the combined batting average that the Detroit quartet presents."

Salsinger went on to point out that, in the opinion of Detroit manager Mickey "Black Mike" Cochrane, "Owen was the best third baseman in baseball," and that Gehringer, "playing the best ball of his scintillating career, . . . is the best player in the American League, if not in baseball." That was quite a statement. Yet it was undeniable that very few other American Leaguers in 1934 were quite in Gehringer's class either as a fielder or as a batter. "You wind him up on opening day and forget him," his teammate Doc Cramer once said of the player nicknamed the "Mechanical Man." Cochrane elaborated, "Charlie says 'hello' on opening day, 'goodbye' on closing day, and in between hits .350." Whether the formidable Gehringer could trounce the intimidating Dizzy Dean remained to be seen.

During the 1934 season, the so-called Battalion of Death amassed a total of 462 RBIs, with Greenberg accounting for 139, Gehringer 127, Rogell 100, and Owen 96. That record still stands today. What added to their strength was that all four men were good friends, who respected each other both as individuals and as players and were to remain friends long into their retirement—in marked contrast to the contentious feuding and occasional brawling among the Cardinals. Moreover, all four had played all of their games that season in a single position—another record, then as now. If there was any weakness, it was a minor one: In 1933, Owen, who suffered from severe hay fever, allergies, and sinus problems, had had to curtail his batting practice in order to save his strength for each game. But in 1934, he had shown renewed vigor after consulting a host of specialists during the off-season. Finally, no fewer than three members of this infield were nominated for the 1934 MVP award—Gehringer, Greenberg, and Owen—and the first two were future Hall of Famers. Among the team's standout pitchers were Lynwood "Schoolboy" Rowe, Alvin "General" Crowder, and Elden Auker.

Some of the most colorful writers in sports journalism had also shown up in Detroit to cover the event, including Damon Runyon, Grantland Rice, John Lardner, Paul Gallico, and Westbrook Pegler. They would not be disappointed. The 1934 World Series that pitted the Gashouse Gang against the Detroit Tigers proved to be one of the greatest fall classics in the annals of baseball.

The Cardinals arrived in Detroit at 8:05 A.M. on October 2, the day before the Series was to begin, aboard the *Wabash Special*. A crowd of about three hundred fans, mostly men, waited to greet them. The last to step off the train, dressed in a chocolate-brown suit with matching vest, gray felt hat, dark brown shoes, and a camel's hair overcoat just like the one Babe Ruth always wore, was Dizzy Dean. He had been delayed by a game of gin he was finishing up with a porter. Two days earlier, Ruth had announced his retirement from baseball, and Dean and just about everyone else knew that he was now the biggest name and the most dominating player in the sport.

"Where's them Tigers?" he asked, with a grin, as he stepped off the train. He was 20 pounds lighter now, a paler version of the strapping, 189-pound athlete he had been only a month earlier. The grueling September schedule had clearly taken its toll.

Most fans hoped, and expected, that Dean would face off against Schoolboy Rowe in the opening game. Dean presumed as much himself. So had sportswriter Grantland Rice, who in anticipation of the Series had written another poem:

Who says romance is gray with age,
That men no longer battle odds,
When two raw kids from brush and sage,
Still face the lightning of the gods?
Can life be stupid, drab, or slow
With Dizzy Dean and Schoolboy Rowe?

Rowe had won an astonishing sixteen straight games that year, while compiling an overall record of 24–8. Back on September 20, when it had looked as though the New York Giants would capture the pennant, Detroit manager Mickey Cochrane had been asked about his first-game pitching choice.

"That's easy," he answered. "Rowe. I don't care who the other manager picks. It may be bad bridge to lead with your ace, but it's good baseball, and that's what I'm going to do. If the Giants win, they'll use Hubbell, won't they? If the Cardinals should nose out the Giants, they'll use Dizzy Dean, won't they? That's sound judgment. So we'll use Rowe. Why, if we used any but our best we'd be in the position of conceding the game, and the Tigers aren't conceding anything."

Two weeks later, he had changed his mind. Now that the Tigers were facing the Cardinals, Cochrane announced the day before the Series, "I don't intend to pitch Rowe against

Dizzy. If Diz pitches tomorrow, Alvin Crowder will work for Detroit. If anybody else pitches for St. Louis, it will be Rowe for us."

Many sportswriters and fans instantly pounced on his words, seeing in them, as though in code, the white flag of surrender. At the very least, by not starting Rowe, Cochrane had ceded the all-important psychological edge to his fearsome rivals.

Dean, himself a master of psychological intimidation, only added to any sense of insecurity the Tigers might be feeling by boasting to anyone who would listen that he was going to lead the Cardinals to a world championship. Such utter self-confidence and terrorization of a future opponent was perhaps not to be witnessed again in the world of sports until 1964, when a young upstart boxer from Louisville, Kentucky, named Cassius Clay—afterward known to the world as Muhammad Ali—made it loudly clear to one and all that he intended to dethrone the fearsome heavyweight champion Sonny Liston in their title match in Miami Beach.

Dean's arrogance quickly became a severe irritant to Detroit players and fans alike, and something of a distraction for sportswriters as well. As he made his way from the train to a waiting cab, besieged by autograph seekers and photographers, Dean predicted that the Cardinals would sweep in four straight games, so long as he was allowed to pitch each game.

"The way I sees it," Dizzy later explained to J. Roy Stockton of the *St. Louis Post-Dispatch*, "braggin' is where you do a lot of poppin' off and ain't got nothin' to back it up. But I ain't braggin'. I know me 'n' Paul is gonna win four games in this here Series—if Detroit is good enough to win a couple when we ain't pitchin'—and you might just as well be honest and tell the public all about it. They pays our salary and it's nothin' but fair that we tell 'em just what's goin' to happen."

Today that long-winded explanation has been abbreviated to "It ain't braggin' if you can do it" and lives on in books of quotations and sports histories.

The Associated Press reported that Detroit was "gripped by Series hysteria" as the Motor City awaited the arrival of "rubber-armed" Dizzy Dean, his kid brother, Paul, and their Cardinal teammates. The Series would be the first in Detroit since 1909, and the first between two of the westernmost clubs since the White Sox scandal of 1919, when eight members of the Chicago team conspired to fix the outcome of the fall classic against the Cincinnati Reds. The seating capacity at Navin Field was forty-seven thousand, "not nearly enough." Thousands of fans crowded the box office, clamoring for tickets, and "heaven be with you if your choice was the Cards and a real husky Detroit rooter happened to hear you." Not since the heyday of Ty Cobb had the town seen such baseball excitement.

"All the old-time glory of the World Series blazes again," Damon Runyon reported in the *New York American*, noting that "crowds wait at the ball yard gates, crowds hang around the hotel entrances and jam the lobbies, arguing baseball to the point of acrimony. The whole city is alive, personally interested, boiling with civic pride, hoping for a massacre of the St. Louis Cardinals."

"The sky darkens," Jimmy Powers added in the *New York Daily News*. "The street lights bloom. Calliopes parade the downtown district playing 'The St. Louis Blues' . . . The Deans are on every lip. Vaudeville actors insert allusions to them in impromptu acts, movie organists compose parodies of popular songs in their honor. The papers carry headlines of the size usually employed to announce a declaration of war. They tell hourly bulletin movements of the two grinning, roistering, record-breaking farm boys."

With Detroit celebrating its first pennant in twenty-five years, railroad lines were reporting heavy traffic from all parts of the country to "the scene of the hostilities," in the words of James P. Dawson, a *New York Times* correspondent. He reported that hotels were so overbooked that they were unable to honor many reservations, and that vehicles "of all sizes, descriptions, and vintages" were clogging the surrounding highways. The Tigers' front office had to send out 30,999 letters of regret to fans whose request for tickets could not be met, though to accommodate the heavy demand an extra 1,500 tickets for standing room were put on sale. Reserved seats were priced at $6.60, and 20,000 general admission seats went for $1.10 each. Speculators were quoting $25 for a pair of $6.60 tickets.

So intense was the interest of Detroit fans in the Series that a newsreel unit of Universal Studios had made plans to provide several major movie theaters in town with a play-by-play print of the game within an hour of the last out. Hal Totten, the baseball expert of the National Broadcasting Company, was to provide commentary. A messenger service had also been hired to relay reels inning by inning to a local film-developing laboratory, and planes had been reserved to fly copies of the complete prints to all major cities in the United States and Canada, with bonuses for any pilot who broke a commercial speed record.

When the Cardinals arrived at the Book-Cadillac Hotel, where they were staying, an even bigger crowd was on hand to greet them, including a band blaring away a hot trombone version of "Tiger Rag" (with sing-along Detroit fans changing the lyrics from "Hold that tiger" to "Hold them, Tigers"). Jumping out of his cab, Dean pretended to conduct the music, took a bow, then grabbed a toy tiger someone tossed to him. Twisting it by the tail, he and Paul went inside to enjoy a late breakfast with humorist Will Rogers and Damon Runyon. Neither Dean had met either man, but Dizzy had heard Rogers on his radio show. He knew virtually nothing about Runyon's reputation as a Broadway storyteller, much less that the Hearst newspapers he wrote for promoted him as "the world's greatest reporter." To Dizzy, he was just another sportswriter—there were so many of them, all clamoring for an interview.

Hungry from the long train trip and the morning's exertions, Dizzy ordered three eggs, bacon, biscuits, gravy, milk, orange juice, and coffee. Rogers wryly observed that only two kinds of people could eat that much: opera singers and cotton pickers. He himself was on a diet in preparation for an upcoming film and limited himself to a glass of grapefruit juice. Perched in front of Runyon, whose racy use of slang and underworld jargon had culminated in his enormously popular collection, *Guys and Dolls,* published only three years earlier, was a fancy cup holding a soft-boiled egg.

Using just a fork, as usual, Dean cut the bacon into pieces and mixed them and the gravy into the eggs, then layered his biscuits with butter and jelly.

"Looks good, don't it, Will?" he asked, digging in. Pointing to Runyon's forlorn egg, he added, "Them things taste better when they're fried like mine, Damon. Ain't that right, Will?"

They then got down to talking baseball. Rogers, who hailed from Oklahoma, figured that the Cardinals were certain to win, because they had more players from southwestern states than the Tigers did. He then went on to extol the Dean brothers and Pepper Martin in particular because, he thought, they were all Oklahoma natives like himself. To his mind, that very fact all but assured a Cardinals victory. Dean, who knew how to bend a truth when it suited him, did not bother to correct the humorist about his birthplace and wholeheartedly agreed with his analysis, such as it was.

Runyon begged to differ. A man who preferred New York's nightlife to the wildlife that Martin liked to hunt in the Oklahoma hills during the off-season, he predicted in his column the next day that the Tigers would take the Series in six games.

Runyon did compliment the Dean brothers, though, as two handsome young men who "looked more like a couple of kids off Broadway than lads from a little country town." He also noted that one of the brothers did all the talking, while the other brother said nothing at all.

After breakfast, Dizzy and Paul relaxed in one of their bedrooms, lounging on the beds and smoking cheap cigars. The next man up for an interview was Grantland Rice, who had heard that some St. Louis fans had presented the pair with three-carat diamond rings enameled with the Cardinals' insignia on either side. When Rice asked Dizzy to hold out his ring for a closer inspection, Dean asked, "You got any this swell at home, Granny?"

He then asked the esteemed sportswriter to do him a favor.

"You know Frisch," he said. "Go tell him I want to pitch the whole Series, all them games. Go fix it up for me, Granny."

"You can't win four straight games," Rice replied.

"I know I can't," Diz admitted, "but I can four outta five."

As Rice got up to leave, a host of local big shots came by to pay their respects—Senator Gerald P. Nye, boxer Barney Ross, and announcer Graham McNamee, who had broadcast the first game that Dizzy ever heard on radio. A few well-wishers remarked that they were placing thousand-dollar bets on the Tigers if Dizzy did not pitch.

"Save your money, boys," Dean assured them.

A large group of other journalists soon filed into the room. Some found chairs to sit in; others plopped themselves on the floor.

"I know what you want," Dean told them. "You want me to pop off and brag about me 'n' Paul. Well, I ain't goin' to do it. But I will say I'm goin' to plow that ball through there tomorrow and Paul here is goin' to fog it through when his time comes. Ain't that right, Paul?"

"You're tellin' the truth there, Diz," Paul answered with a grin. It was the most he had spoken all morning.

"What we wham down at them Tigers," Dizzy continued, "is liable to be tough to get a hold of. Paul there's gotta fastball that'd skin a rabbit from the kitchen to the barn and mine ain't no freight train, is it, Paul?"

"No, it ain't, Diz. It's faster than mine."

"Naw, Paul, it ain't faster than yours, but I guess mine's a little meaner 'cause I got a wickeder hook and my change a pace is so slow that when I follow it with a fast one it just naturally seems like a .44."

In an adjoining room, Pat Dean was giving an interview to a reporter for the *Detroit Times*. She denied rumors that she was giving herself airs because of Dizzy's success and said she was worried that he was not getting enough rest. "He won't last five years at the rate he's going," she predicted, with the accuracy of a woman who knew him better than anyone.

Later Paul wandered down to the gift shop to buy some postcards, while Dizzy settled into a sofa in the lobby to chat with old-timers Tris Speaker and Rabbit Maranville. Eventually, an official strolled in to announce that the team bus was scheduled to depart soon for the ballpark.

"I ain't gonna ride no bus," Dizzy announced. "I wanna walk."

He was halfway out of the hotel when Casey Stengel walked in, and a group of grateful Cardinals greeted him with hugs. The garrulous Brooklyn manager had all but handed the championship to the St. Louis team when his lowly Dodgers had defeated the once high-and-mighty New York Giants just the previous weekend.

"Your felicitations are all very well, gentlemen," Stengel told them, "but I can't deposit them at my bank. You should have voted me a full share of that World Series swag."

Dizzy wholeheartedly concurred, telling Stengel to demand his cut from team owner Sam Breadon. "He don't deserve what he's gettin'," he said. "He didn't do nothin'. Take his."

By now, the crowd outside the hotel had grown to more than two thousand. Some hung from statues on the grassy islands on Washington Boulevard, Western Union boys sat astride their bicycles, and others simply pressed forward, hoping for a glimpse of the fabled Dizzy Dean, who of course had snubbed them earlier that summer by not showing up for the exhibition game. As he walked past a phalanx of policemen, Dean asked, "Can you boys show me where the ball park is?"

The policemen obliged by lining up their squad cars and motorcycles, with Dean prancing at their head as he marched like a major domo down Michigan Avenue for almost a mile, with pedestrians cheering him on and sirens wailing. When he arrived at Navin Field, he told the assembled policemen and onlookers that he would not mind if they booed him. Their jeers, he assured them, might even help the desperate Tigers, who needed all the support they could get.

On the field, Rowe was rehearsing his windup for movie cameras, while Greenberg stood posing at the plate for photographers. Sitting far up in the stands was Tom Rowe, School-boy's father, who had journeyed by bus for forty-six hours from El Dorado, Arkansas, to see the game. Only fifty-nine, he looked like an old man, worn out from years of farming, and he kept a chew of tobacco constantly in the corner of his mouth. Schoolboy had greeted him with a filial kiss fully on the lips. Also in the stands was Rowe's fiancée, Edna Mary Skinner, an attractive schoolteacher from El Dorado. Tiger fans had first heard about Skinner during Rowe's phenomenal winning streak, when he explained to reporters, "I eat a lot of vittles, climb that mound, wrap my fingers around the old baseball, and say to it, 'Edna, honey, let's go.'"

On the day his streak ended, he appeared on NBC radio and talked again about his favorite foods, then whispered into the microphone, "Hello, Ma. Hello, Edna, how'm I doin'?"

Mrs. Rowe later chastised him for not calling her "mother," as she had raised him, but he explained that he was only reading from a script provided to him by the radio station. But those scripted sweet nothings were to prove the bane of the Series so far as he was concerned, once the rabid player-baiting Durocher got wind of them.

Rowe was also perhaps the most superstitious ballplayer in the Majors. Robert Gregory noted:

> No one else in baseball believed so much in good-luck charms. On the day he was trying for his seventeenth straight, his pocket contained a Canadian penny, two trinkets from China, and a copper coin from the Netherlands. Inside his shirt were four feathers plucked from the tail of a three-legged rooster. A jade elephant figure was in his glove. Beneath his hat was a rabbit's foot, taken from a rabbit said to have been shot in a graveyard at midnight. But Rowe lost the game anyway, and when he got back to the Tigers' hotel in Philadelphia, he heaved them all— like a failed witch doctor—from his sixteenth-story window. Now getting psyched up for the Series, he had begun a new collection, to which Cochrane contributed some beads and two miniature shoes. Not that Cochrane didn't believe in black magic, too. He just didn't have room for them. Already in his pocket were five coins, a rabbit's foot,

a copper crucifix, and the carved ivory cross that Tommy
Armour carried when he won the British Open.

Rowe's superstitions were widely reported in the press, and
Dizzy Dean wasted little time trying to put a hex on his presumed opponent. Passing Rowe in the field, soon after his arrival at the stadium on this day before the first game, Dean
quipped, "If I was a four-leaf clover, you could have me,
Schoolboy."

Greenberg was still posing at the plate when Dean approached, took a fungo bat from Tiger coach Del Baker, gently
nudged Greenberg aside, and stood wiggling his rear end with
the bat poised over his right shoulder. As if on cue, a mass of
photographers soon crowded around, urging him to take a few
practice swings.

Dean sauntered good-naturedly toward the mound to talk
to Tiger coach Carl Fischer, who had been throwing the ball
to Greenberg.

"Heave me a few, fella," he called out, "and you can put all
the stuff you got on them."

When the first ball came whizzing toward the plate, reporter
Paul Gallico later wrote, "all you could hear was the snapping
of shutters and the grinding of the movie cameras." Dean hit a
liner to left field, then two more. Taking off his coat, he yelled
out to Fischer, "Let's see what you got, boy."

By now, many of the Cardinals players had lined up on their
side of the field, enjoying every moment of the spectacle. Along-
side the first-base line, only a few Tiger players were gloomily
observing the pregame sideshow. Many of them had never seen
Dean in person before and knew him only by his reputation.
Here, indeed, was baseball's wunderkind in all his outsize ec-
centricity, and they could not help but be a little bewildered.

"There we were," Tigers outfielder Jo-Jo White later recalled. "The kid's having fun and swinging away like a sandlotter and we're watching, afraid we'll miss something. Only Diz would ever barge in on fellows like that and put on his show."

On the next pitch, Dean whacked the ball into center.

"You're showing them your strength, Diz," Pepper Martin impishly called out from the sidelines. "Miss a couple."

Removing his vest, Dean spit on his hands, waved his bat, and shouted at Fischer, "Ain't you got nothin' more than that? Bear down, boy."

The abject coach wound up and threw his best pitch, and Dizzy sent it sailing into right field, while cracking the bat. Tossing the bat aside, he snatched up his vest and ambled off, saying, "I done broke this thing all to pieces," then adding over his shoulder, "Boy, I love to hit."

Martin and Paul Dean joined him on the field, and the three of them then performed an impromptu Indian war dance, whooping and hollering. Gallico observed, "The Cards look like winners. Dizzy Dean is all ice."

Even the Tigers eventually had to admit to themselves that watching Dean putting on his act was all fun. Good-naturedly, they later welcomed him when, in typical fashion, he wandered into their clubhouse while they were getting dressed, as was often his custom with opposing teams. Introducing himself to the different players, he asked those who were afraid of his fastball to identify themselves, so he could toss them only curves. Then he asked muscular Hank Greenberg if he wanted to feel the right bicep, without charge, of a thirty-game winner.

"This Dizzy Dean they're all talking about," Tigers star Goose Goslin later admitted to a reporter, "told the boys what he's going to do to them, but after listening for a while I kind of liked the kid. There's no real harm in him."

For the rest of the day, Dizzy Dean was the toast of the town, mobbed everywhere he went by hordes of curious onlookers. "There ain't nothin' to bein' a hero in a swell town like Dee-troit," Dizzy had to admit.

———— • ————

By now, Dizzy Dean had assumed the status of an almost mythical hero, a true American legend in the making.

"I have seen Matty pitch," wrote Bill Corum in the *New York Journal-American*, referring to Christy Mathewson, "and Walter Johnson, and Cy Young, Rube Waddell, Eddie Plank and Three Finger Brown, Bill Dinneen and Addie Joss, Big Ed Walsh and Chief Bender, Grover Cleveland Alexander and Wee Willie Sherdel—and none of these great stars ever turned in such a feat as the Dean brothers have just completed."

Other sportswriters similarly reached for lofty comparisons, suggesting that the Cardinals' splendid come-from-behind pennant victory was the most dramatic finale seen since the last days of World War I. Not to be outdone, the *New York Daily News* proclaimed Dizzy and Paul Dean the best brother act since Romulus and Remus.

In the public square outside the hotel where the Cardinals were staying, some St. Louis fans were chanting, "We want Dean. We want Dean." But they were drowned out by a triumphant "Tiger Rag" being blasted from loudspeakers mounted on a truck provided by a local radio station.

Following hallowed baseball tradition, Frisch had refused to name his pitcher for the opening game of the World Series. But Dizzy Dean was not fooled and confided to sportswriter J. Roy Stockton, "Frisch is sayin' that he don't know who's goin' to pitch that first game. But he ain't foolin' me none. I told him this afternoon there wasn't no use kiddin' hisself. There's only one man to pitch the first game, and that's old Diz. Frank, I guess, is tryin' to use what Doc Weaver calls si-kology. He don't want old Diz nervous on the eve of battle. But he's silly if he thinks he can fool me. I ain't no kleptomaniac or whatever you calls it, what goes around gettin' nervous. Who won the pennant? Me 'n' Paul. Who's goin' to win the World Series? Me 'n' Paul. Certainly. Si-kology, my foot!"

Frisch had two important factors to consider, though. One was that, if Dean started, he would be going to the mound after only seventy-two hours of rest. While Frisch no doubt wanted to give his ace pitcher that honor, he also needed him to be at his very best when he did pitch. Also, the Tigers were heavy with left-handed batters, including Gehringer, switch-hitter Rogell, Goslin, White, and Cochrane. Conventional baseball si-kology suggested that Frisch might want to start with his crafty southpaw veteran Bill Hallahan on opening day, figuring that the surprise choice might not only cause the Tigers to lose that game but also leave them too disoriented to recover when they opposed Dizzy Dean in the second game. Also, though Hallahan had posted a rather indifferent record, he had tamed the Tigers in two exhibition games earlier that year—including the one in Detroit that Dizzy Dean had declined to show up for. Another impressive Cardinals pitcher was Tex Carleton, who was sometimes called "the third Dean" because he shared with Dizzy and Paul the same rangy, beanpole physique. In the previous year, in fact, many fans and sportswriters had judged him to be a better pitcher than Dizzy. This season he had gotten off to a lame start, due to ill health. Late in the season, though, he had shown flashes of his old form.

One Cardinals pitcher who was just hopeful to be sent in as a relief pitcher was Dazzy Vance, now past forty, who told reporters in his Nebraska drawl, "Yes, boys, in the general confusion it looks as though the old master finally did sneak into a World Series."

Manager Mickey Cochrane was equally confidant that his Tigers would take the Series but was mum about who his starting pitcher would be, despite his earlier boast that it would be his ace, Schoolboy Rowe, no matter who the Cardinals nominated to oppose him. If Rowe got the nod, Drebinger predicted in the *New York Times*, the result would be "one of the greatest World Series pitching duels in history." Like Dizzy Dean, Rowe had also had his share of alleged health problems. During the spring, he had faced a steady stream of boos while complaining of what some sportswriters called "sore arm hypochondria." By season's end, though, he had developed into the sturdiest right-hander in the league.

If the Cardinals held a slight advantage in the pitching department, the Tigers had the clear edge on the attack. Greenberg, Goslin, and Gehringer, collectively known as the "G-men" after the federal law-enforcement agents of that era, were all dreaded long-ball hitters. Nor was there any weak spot in the rest of the offensive lineup—unlike the Cardinals lineup, whose superb shortstop, Leo Durocher, was almost useless at the plate. Orsatti and Rothrock were also soft spots on the Cardinals offense.

Summing up, Drebinger observed, "Inasmuch as World Series history is replete with instances where high-grade pitching holds the advantage over the hitters, the final edge must be given to the Cards." In another pregame dispatch, Drebinger took the measure of the city's fever-pitch excitement: "In every hotel and theater lobby, in every store, and on every corner, all one hears is baseball, the Series itself, and who will be tomorrow's starting pitchers. And whenever the talk veers to pitchers—which it invariably does almost at once—all one hears is a single name . . . the Deans, Deans, Deans, and then more Deans."

Another *Times* correspondent, John Kieran, summarized the upcoming contest even more succinctly, saying it all came down to "just three men. Two Deans and one Rowe." All three hailed from Arkansas. Unlike the unschooled Deans, though, Lynwood T. Rowe had gone to both high school and college, where he had set new athletic records in a variety of events. He was a discus thrower, a ten-second sprinter, and an outstanding tennis player. He could hurl a javelin more than two hundred feet. He had won a scholastic golf championship. He was the star on both his college football and his college basketball teams. Now, in 1934, he was only in his third season in professional baseball and stood on the very threshold of greatness. The logic of Detroit fans' sentiment was simple: In the face of such demonstrable talent and dedication, what hope was there for the Cardinals? One Rowe was more than enough for two Deans.

Bill Terry, the defeated Giants manager, who had announced that he was not going to watch the Series, was rumored to be returning to his home in Memphis, where he worked in the oil business during the off-season. Although taking full blame for his team's spectacular tailspin at season's end, he predicted that the Cardinals would win the Series. The only Yankee who planned to travel to Detroit and then St. Louis to take in the Series was Babe Ruth.

Both managers were also Series veterans. Frisch was making his eighth appearance in the classic, and Cochrane his fourth. Both had also been mentored by two of the greatest managers of all time: Frisch under McGraw, and Cochrane under Connie Mack. Each man had a range of interests outside baseball. If Frisch was well read, something of a wine connoisseur, and passionate about gardening, Gordon Stanley Cochrane was a licensed airplane pilot and played a mean saxophone. Clearly, both were extraordinarily accomplished and brought not only baseball savvy but worldly savoir faire to this October showdown in two industrial cities in America's heartland.

The 1934 World Series would also be the first since 1919 in which a team from the East was not one of the competitors. Both Detroit and St. Louis had been especially ravaged by the Depression, Charles C. Alexander noted, "Detroit as a result of massive layoffs prompted by a plummeting automobile market; St. Louis because of the collapse of the Plains wheat-belt economy and the decline of the Mississippi River traffic, among other factors." In the first full year of the New Deal, it seemed only appropriate to many observers that "two cities that desperately needed its help should make it into the Series."

On the eve of game one, the odds remained 3 to 5 for the Cardinals to win the Series, and 7 to 10 for them to take the opening game. No doubt, the bettors were assuming that Dean would be the starting pitcher. More than three thousand fans camped out along the streets leading to Navin Field on the night before the ticket office opened for business. The glare of bonfires and the smell of roasting hot dogs filled the air. The Chamber of Commerce reported that this was the first time in twenty-five years that packing boxes and empty fruit crates had sold for as high as fifty cents apiece. That was the price demanded by entrepreneurial residents who lived near the ballpark as they tried to induce all-night campers to buy a crate for a pillow.

On the day the Series opened in Detroit, Monroe Dean, the father of Dizzy and Paul, awoke at 4 A.M. and made himself his usual breakfast of cornmeal mush, biscuits, and black coffee. Monroe still lived in Houston, just a few blocks from the railroad tracks, sharing a bare apartment with his oldest son. After quitting his job as a peanut vendor at Buff Stadium, Elmer, who was now twenty-six, had been supporting himself by doing odd jobs for a tire shop down the street.

Monroe's plan was to take a bus to St. Louis later that morning to see his sons play the third, fourth, and fifth games of the World Series. If all went as he expected, he would be sitting in a box seat when Dizzy and Paul led the Cardinals to victory during his visit; and if somebody asked for his own autograph, he would not mind obliging.

"Them boys won't forget their Popper," he told a group of reporters. "When they know I'm gettin' low, they send me what they can. But they ain't makin' them big wages yet." All he hoped for, he allowed, was enough cash to set up a fresh vegetable stand out by the highway. "I wouldn't need another thing," he said.

At Dizzy's request, Elmer was staying behind, and Monroe had made arrangements for his oldest boy to listen to the Series on the radio at the gas station next door. At the moment, the cost of a new radio was just out of Monroe's reach.

Monroe had last seen Dizzy pitch in 1932. Dizzy had asked Branch Rickey to bring his father to St. Louis for the Series in an airplane, but Rickey sent him a thirteen-dollar bus ticket instead.

"That's fine with me," Monroe said. "I'd rather go on a bus and see somethin' of the country."

After Monroe boarded the Greyhound bus, the driver told his passengers that Dizzy Dean's father was an honored guest, sitting in the front seat and smoking a cigar. When the first Series game began, somebody switched on a portable radio, and cheers went up every time Dizzy retired a batter. Monroe had constructed a homemade scorecard and paraded up and down the aisle, displaying it, at the end of each inning. A hundred miles outside St. Louis, on the edge of the Ozarks in Rolla, Missouri, Monroe said good-bye to his fellow passengers and got into a waiting automobile that Dizzy had dispatched to collect him. Several aging farmers, having heard that the father of the famous pitcher was going to descend from the bus as soon as it arrived at the depot, were waiting in Rolla to shake Monroe's hand and wish him well.

———

To no one's surprise, of course, Frisch had finally named Dean the starting pitcher.

Manager Mike Cochrane started the Tigers off at a disadvantage by choosing Alvin Crowder, and not his own well-rested, number-one pitcher, Schoolboy Rowe. As for Dean, whatever other reasons Frisch might have had for starting him, including wanting a victory on his opponent's home turf at the start of the contest, "a final convincing argument was that Dizzy insisted on starting himself," as John Kieran of the *New York Times* pointedly observed. The defeatist Tiger attitude seemed to be: Why waste Rowe against Dizzy Dean, who was unbeatable? Perhaps, as several sportswriters suggested, both the Detroit players and the forty-three thousand spectators in the stands were also acutely aware that the invading St. Louisans had just spent the past three weeks stealing the thunder of the New York Giants.

On October 3, the first day of the Series, with an estimated ten thousand fans lining the streets, trying to buy tickets, one angry group tried to form a flying wedge to crash to the head of the line. Twenty-five mounted policemen drove them back.

Dean looked palpably tired. Not only was he pitching his third game in six days, but the trip up to Detroit from St. Louis and the ensuing round of publicity—talking to reporters and fans, posing with Babe Ruth and other luminaries for the benefit of photographers—had clearly also taken their toll. Yet he had not lost his sense of humor. During infield practice, he sauntered over to the Detroit dugout to tease Hank Greenberg.

"How come you're so white?" he taunted the slugger. "You're shakin' like a leaf. You afraid Ol' Diz is going to pin your ears back?"

Frisch, meanwhile, ordered his coaches to hit a series of grounders at him that he allowed to bounce off his chest. He wanted to test the texture and resiliency of the ground area around second.

The weather that day was cool, but not chilly, with the game scheduled to begin at precisely 1:20 P.M. Yet, for reasons unknown, the start of the game continued to be delayed. Dean and Crowder then alternately returned to the mound to resume their warm-ups, until finally Frisch marched over to the box where Commissioner Landis was sitting and appeared to demand that the game begin immediately. On a lighter note, baseball comedian Al Schacht, draped in a tiger's skin, wandered onto the field and jumped on Dizzy's back as a photographer snapped their picture. Finally, Detroit mayor Frank Couzens threw out the first ball, and the first game of the 1934 World Series got under way.

Within the first three innings, each member of Detroit's Battalion of Death was to make an error. The first came in the opening round when, with two out, Frisch hit a grounder to crack third baseman Marv Owen, who bobbled the ball. Medwick, who was to share honors with Dean as the star of the game, strode to the plate and smashed a sharp single into left field—the first of his four hits. Crowder retired Rip Collins to keep the inning scoreless.

Crowder, called the "General," fared less well in the second inning. With one out, Orsatti singled. Durocher obliged the Tigers defense with a second out. Dean slapped a grounder to shortstop Billy Rogell. But when Rogell tossed the ball to second for a simple force-out, Charlie Gehringer—perhaps the best second baseman in the game—dropped it. Martin, the hero of the 1931 Series, then whipped a grounder to third baseman Owen, who came up with the ball but unfurled a wild throw to first. Suddenly, the Cardinals had the bases loaded.

Orsatti and Dean scored when Jack Rothrock lined a single into center field.

The Tigers gave the Cardinals a bad scare in the bottom half of the second, though not as a scoring threat. After Goslin singled, he took off for second with two strikes on Rogell. De-Lancey's bullet throw to second bagged the Goose, who came crashing into the Flash with such force that Frisch slumped to the ground. All the Cardinal players rushed to their fallen leader, and for a time it was uncertain whether he would be able to continue to play. But the old Fordham star, who had no doubt absorbed much worse in his football-playing days, shook off the injury, and after a few moments indicated that he was ready for play to resume.

In the third inning, the Detroit infield again helped the Cardinals build their lead. Medwick led off with his second straight single. Collins grounded to first baseman Greenberg, who threw the ball to second for a seemingly routine force-out. But Rogell's return went wide of the mark, and by the time the ball had been retrieved, Collins stood on second.

The comedy of errors continued. Bill DeLancey hit a grounder to Greenberg, who fumbled the ball badly, and Collins scored from second. Three Cardinal runs had crossed the plate and five errors had been committed. Yet Crowder had not allowed a single earned run.

"In the meantime, Dizzy was struggling along rather laboriously in the eyes of the discerning critics," noted Drebinger of the *New York Times*. Dean had allowed Gehringer to single in the first, and Goslin in the second. He retired two in the third before Detroit was finally able to score a run. Jo-Jo White drew a walk, which Dean, Frisch, and several Cardinals on the bench vigorously protested. Cochrane belted a single to left, Gehringer punched another to center, and finally Detroit was on the scoreboard. Almost as important, the fans, virtually speechless until now, found their voice and erupted in cheers. Best of all, Orsatti had erred on Gehringer's hit, so that the latter now roosted on second, and Cochrane occupied third.

"At this point," said Drebinger, "Dean got very annoyed. He frowned fiercely, glared at Greenberg, and on four pitches struck lanky Hank out. The crowd fell back with a groan."

The score now stood at 3 to 1.

Medwick increased the Cardinals' lead in the fifth by sailing a homer into the new yellow pine bleachers on the left wing of Navin Field. In the last of the fifth, Cochrane pulled Crowder and sent in a pinch-hitter. The tactic failed. Firpo Marberry took over pitching for the Tigers, but in short order Dean hit a double into deep left center and then scored when Martin followed with a single to center. Rothrock sacrificed, and Frisch fouled out, but Medwick and Collins each singled to bring in another Cardinal run. Marberry, the fastball pitcher who had been on the mound only ten minutes, was pulled.

Elon "Chief" Hogsett, a left-hander and a Chippewa Indian, then went in to pitch. Durocher, one of the fiercest kibitzers in the game, kept up a ferocious volley of insults during the warm-up. The next batter up was DeLancey, who completed the Cardinals' rout of the Tigers with a towering double to left that scored Medwick and Collins. In the last half of the inning, Greenberg managed to hit a single, then took off for an extra base when Orsatti bobbled the ball. Goslin knocked a single into center, giving Detroit its second run. By this time, though, only a few vociferous diehards in the stands still cheered the Tigers on. Everyone else in the stadium knew the situation was dire. There was a last gasp of hope in the eighth when Greenberg lofted a high Dizzy Dean fastball into the left-field bleachers. But Dean, who seemed to have gotten his second wind and was now throwing with better control than at the beginning of the game, allowed the Tigers only one more hit. Gerald Walker was the last Tiger up in the bottom of the ninth, and he struck out. The final score was 8 to 3.

As he strode off the field after the ninth inning ended, Dizzy remarked to reporters, "Shucks, this was nothin'. Wait 'til they see my brother Paul tomorrow."

After the game, the WABC-Columbia radio network transmitted a shortwave interview with Dizzy Dean to the Second Antarctic Expedition organized by Rear Admiral Richard E. Byrd. In January of that year, Byrd had led a landing party to the site of Little America and had reestablished the camp with massive amounts of radio and other equipment. In characteristic fashion, Dean managed to combine genuine humility with overweening self-assurance. That, after all, was his charm. Although admitting to "big Byrd down in Little America" that he "didn't have a thing on my fast ball or my curve ball," Dean went on to say, "I think if they pitched me the whole four days, I would win all four of them." Perhaps still smarting from the censure he had endured for missing an exhibition game in Detroit earlier that year, he also tossed out an insult, adding that the Tigers were not nearly as good a team as he had expected them to be.

———— -◆- ————

Early in the morning of game two, Henry Ford sent a chauffeured limousine to the Book-Cadillac Hotel to collect Pat and Dizzy Dean and Paul Dean. They were taken to the automobile tycoon's mansion in the suburb of Dearborn, where they had breakfast with Ford, his son Edsel, and the comedian Joe E. Brown and his wife. Later the Deans visited the Greenfield Village School, which Edsel had attended, and spoke briefly with the clearly delighted students. In a reverse, Dizzy also asked for Henry Ford's autograph on a baseball. The Deans and Browns then needed a police escort to clear the way for them to make it back in time for the game at Navin Field. The older Ford decided to remain home and listen to the contest on his radio, and Edsel attended the game, sharing his father's box with Will Rogers.

While the other players warmed up on the field, Dizzy Dean wandered over to the sidelines, autographing scorecards, posing for photographs, and chatting with fans. Later he ambled over to the brass band behind home plate, picked up a tuba, and began oom-pahing with reasonable competence to the tune of "Wagon Wheels." Still restless, he strutted over to the Detroit dugout and apologized to the players, saying, "I sure am sorry I pitched so poorly in that game yesterday. I'll try to show you my real good stuff the next time out."

Shortly before game two, Al Schacht and Joe E. Brown staged a "prizefight" behind home plate, with movie star George Raft posing as the referee and catching a few fake punches himself. After the actor counted Schacht out in the second round, he took his seat with Father Charles Coughlin, the Detroit-based radio broadcaster and virulent critic of President Roosevelt's economic and social policies.

It was ironic that Coughlin and Henry Ford—two of the country's most rabid anti-Semites—were fans of the Tigers, because baseball's first Jewish star, Hank Greenberg, was a team stalwart. The Tigers first baseman had grown up in the Bronx, New York, home of the Yankees, who had, in fact, tried to sign him up. Greenberg, though, preferred not to play in the shadow of Lou Gehrig and went to Detroit.

In an era of blatant anti-Semitism, Greenberg faced a unique challenge, noted baseball historian Paul Katzeff: "The atmosphere was especially hostile in Detroit, home of both the hate-mongering priest Father Charles Coughlin, who made his notorious broadcasts from a station in the area, and Henry Ford, who wrote a book blaming Jews for the world's problems." As Katzeff also reported, opposing teams also occasionally indulged in ugly bench jockeying: "Some opposing players, according to the *Denver Post*, tried to bait Greenberg at the plate with the taunt, 'Hitler is waiting.'"

As expected, Schoolboy Rowe was pitching for the Tigers. Dizzy was annoyed that Frisch had selected Bill Hallahan to oppose him, thinking the nomination should have gone to his brother Paul. As soon as the Schoolboy took to the mound, the entire Cardinals bench, led by Durocher, began chanting, "How'm I doin', Edna? How'm I doin', Edna?" The Cardinals' derisive chorus was to follow the Tigers ace throughout the Series.

As events proved, the six-foot-four Rowe was doin' just fine. His mighty right arm needed twelve innings, though, to bring the Tigers to victory and tie the Series. In the first three innings, Schoolboy nearly flunked out, giving up six hits to the feisty Cardinals. For a while it looked as though the St. Louisans were about to get a stranglehold on the Series with their second straight victory. But then "Rowe suddenly swung sharply about on this crisp, sunny afternoon," as Drebinger reported in the *New York Times*, "to turn in as brilliant an exhibition of pitching as ever was witnessed in World Series competition." From the fourth to the twelfth inning inclusive, he allowed only one Cardinal to get on base. Despite his exceptional performance, though, Rowe was able to prevail only with a little help from Lady Luck.

The day also turned out to be a windy one, with unpredictable gusts blowing through the infield, and Rowe was known to dislike throwing on days when a little turbulence might deprive him of complete control, or might carry a pop fly just outside the range of an infielder.

Sitting in the stands among the crowd this day was Giants manager Bill Terry, who had decided that, after all, he could not stay away. He had to pay to get into the stadium.

In the top of the first, with two men out, Frisch sliced a single just inside the third-base line for the Cardinals' first hit. But Medwick, who had hit for four straight the previous day, struck out. In the bottom half, with two out, Gehringer dribbled a shot toward first. Hallahan raced over to cover the base, but dropped the ball. Yet the doughty left-hander, a veteran of two previous World Series, kept his professional composure and retired Greenberg.

The Cardinals scored their first run in the second inning when DeLancey zinged a single behind Gehringer at second. He scored on Orsatti's triple into left field. Durocher hit a high pop fly that Greenberg easily bagged behind first base. In the third inning, the Cardinals let loose another barrage against Rowe. Martin hit a single to center. After Rothrock sacrificed, Frisch flied to White in center for an easy out. Medwick then slashed a single to left. Goslin made a heroic but futile throw to the plate, but Martin scored as Medwick pulled up at second. The Cardinals now led, 2 to 0. Collins smashed another single to left, and it looked as though the St. Louisans would score another run. But this time Goslin's masterful long throw took one bounce right into Cochrane's waiting glove to tag out a sliding Medwick. The collision, the second of the Series, sent the catcher sprawling, and for a time a worried Detroit team was not sure whether their manager would stay in the game. But like Frisch, who had been knocked down by Goslin in game one, Cochrane had only had the wind knocked out of him and soon signaled that he was able to resume playing by limping back to the dugout.

Goslin's strong, accurate throw may also have been a game-saver. If Medwick had scored, the Cardinals would have gone ahead by three runs.

Over the next nine innings, Rowe pitched at the top of his form, retiring twenty-one straight batters. Billy Rogell saved his teammate's streak in the seventh when he made a spectacular diving catch of a low, whistling liner by DeLancey.

Meanwhile, Hallahan and his teammates had kept the Tigers scoreless until the fourth inning. Then, with one out, Rogell hit a high fly toward the center-field bleachers. Orsatti twisted around and headed back, then realized too late that the wind was buffeting the ball. Turning back again, he made a desperate headlong dive to make the catch, breaking his sunglasses and suffering a cut over his left eye, but the ball bounced just in front of him, and Rogell got a double. After Owen grounded to Frisch, Pete Fox pulled another double that bounced just inches from the left-field foul line, and Detroit was on the scoreboard. Rowe struck out.

In the ninth, the Tigers scored again when Fox opened the inning with a single to right. Rowe sacrificed, bringing up Gerald Walker, who was pinch-hitting for White. Walker hoisted a high pop fly along the first-base line. DeLancey elected to allow Ripper Collins to go after it. But the wind that Rowe so feared carried the ball back to the plate, and the ball rolled foul where it fell. With a new lease on life, Walker smacked a smoking single to right center that brought Fox racing across the plate to tie the score amid a deafening din from the Detroit fans. After a conference at the mound, Frisch signaled for left-hander Willie Walker, an ex-Giant, to come in as a replacement for Hallahan. Walker was known to have "a good move to first base," in baseball parlance, and he soon proved it with a snap throw that trapped Gerald Walker between bases. After he was chased down, as seven Cardinals closed in as backups, Cochrane struck out, sending the game into extra innings. The score was now 2 to 2.

In the tenth, Frisch fumbled a grounder by Gehringer, who then stole second. Unruffled, Walker retired Greenberg and

Goslin on flies to the outfield, and then walked Rogell. The inning ended on Owen's fly ball to Orsatti in center.

In the top of the eleventh, Willie Walker fanned for Rowe's twenty-second straight out. Martin cracked a double into center. But the Cardinals lost another chance to score again when Rothrock struck out and Frisch grounded out. In the bottom of the twelfth, Walker retired Cochrane, then lost control of his usually unerring delivery by walking Gehringer and Greenberg. The moment of truth had arrived. Frisch and the other Cardinals huddled with their pitcher, urging him to get the ball across the plate. He did exactly that, and the Goose blasted it for a single into center. Fielding the ball, Orsatti fired it home in desperation, but it arrived seconds after Gehringer had raced across the plate.

In its postmortem, the *St. Louis Post-Dispatch* noted, "Bill Hallahan was at his best. He pitched so well that a shutout would have been his portion, a shutout for his fourth World Series victory, a total never reached by a left hander in October championship competition, if the Cardinals had not missed two simple fly balls that high school boys could have caught."

Back in the clubhouse, a furious Frisch chased the newspapermen out the door, roaring, "Get the hell out!" Later, after he had cooled down, he told the reporters, "It was a tough one to lose. You can't take anything away from Rowe. He pitched a great game. But I feel sorry for Hallahan."

The dejected Hallahan's own assessment was simple and to the point: "Brutal," he allowed.

The only consolation Frisch might have permitted himself—and certainly, at that point, it was the last thing on his mind—was that he set a new record every time he went to bat. He now held the record for the most World Series games played, at forty-five, and most times at bat, at 175.

After twenty-five years of frustration and disappointment, the Tiger faithful were feeling as giddy and glorious as Frisch was dejected. Not since the era of the immortal Ty Cobb had they savored such sweet victory. Rowe's final strikeout had sent thousands swarming into the streets. The windows of the city's downtown skyscrapers opened as office workers dumped heaps of confetti, torn paper, and tickertape into the swirling air. Everybody with a car horn, whistle, or hand bell joined in the giddy hubbub. The bedlam in the downtown area lasted for nearly two hours, with many stores closing down as crowds wound their way through the streets. Thousands more jammed Washington Boulevard near the Book-Cadillac Hotel, and another mob scene awaited both the Tigers and the Cardinals at Union Depot, where they were scheduled to board a train for the overnight twelve-hour journey to St. Louis 513 miles away.

Down in Eldorado, Arkansas, Schoolboy Rowe's hometown, the city's high school had arranged for its students to assemble in the school auditorium to listen to the game over the loudspeakers. When the game was over, they gave a thunderous ovation to their 1930 all-state quarterback who had just defeated St. Louis in the World Series thriller. That evening, two railroad coaches filled with Detroit fans departed for St. Louis, with the Tigers' victory still echoing in the bar car long into the night. Another contingent heading for St. Louis consisted of forty fans from Okemah, Oklahoma, another of the Dean family's many hometowns during their cotton-picking days.

8

BY THE BREATH
OF THE GODS

A huge crowd greeted Dizzy Dean and company at Union Station in St. Louis when the train arrived at 7 A.M. on the morning of October 5. Cardinal pennants depicting two resolute redbirds perched on a bat flew gaily all over the city, and posters bearing the same red-on-white image could also be seen in shop windows. During the season, support for the team had been apathetic, but now St. Louis was clearly in the grip of World Series fever.

At game time, the temperature hovered in the high seventies. A capacity crowd of thirty-four thousand people jammed into antique Sportsman's Park under a blue sky. A slight breeze caused the flag in center field to flutter just barely. The fans knew that Paul Dean was scheduled to pitch that day against Detroit right-hander Tommy Bridges, and they expected Paul to exact a terrible revenge on the Tigers. Bookmakers also continued to favor the Cardinals to win the Series, 7 to 10. Only once since 1920 had the team that won the opener failed to win the Series. The exception was the Cardinals themselves, who in 1931 lost the first game but emerged as the world champions anyway.

Monroe Dean now sat among the fans in Sportsman's Park. His middle son had clearly inherited his raw-boned features. Monroe and Will Rogers were observed having a long, quiet conversation in Dean's box, and no doubt the two men, having spent much time in Dust Bowl Oklahoma, had much to talk about. "He says I look like him, and doggoned if I don't," Rogers remarked as he returned to his seat.

The Tigers' leadoff man was Jo-Jo White, who lifted a high foul ball over the box seats on the left side of the field. "Through the bull pen squad and into the boxes charged Jersey Joe Medwick," wrote Drebinger in the *New York Times*. "He gave a queer flip with his glove, like a cook making an excellent catch of a flapjack, and came up with the ball in his grasp." Medwick's balletlike grab turned out to be the finest play of the game, even though the contest had just started.

Paul Dean pitched competently, if not exceptionally, and was often in trouble. Yet the Tigers failed to capitalize on their scoring opportunities, particularly in the early innings. The Cardinals' offense was also in good form. In the bottom of the first, Pepper Martin crashed a triple off the screen in front of the right-field pavilion, then dove headlong into third to beat the throw relayed from the outfield. Rothrock sent a fly ball deep into center field toward the flagpole, and after the catch Martin trotted home for the Cardinals' first run. In the bottom of the second, Collins opened with a single, and DeLancey followed up with a double that sent Ripper sweeping around to third. Bridges then cracked Orsatti squarely between the shoulder blades with a pitched ball, knocking him down. After he regained his feet, he walked slowly to first, and the bases were now filled. Poor Orsatti had become the marked man of the World Series. Not only did he have a bad cut over his left eye and a sore neck from his desperation dive of the previous day, but he was also now limping from a bad charley horse.

After Durocher fouled out to Greenberg, Paul Dean sent a long fly to Fox in right, and Collins scored the Cardinals' second run after the catch.

The two teams traded hits, with little consequence, in the third inning. Then in the fourth, said Drebinger in the *Times,* "Daffy tempted the fates as no pitcher in World Series competition had ever done without being practically skinned alive. With Owen out of the way, Fox singled to left, and to the utter consternation of the onlookers Dean walked Bridges, who had never been regarded as any great shakes as a hitter. To put him on, therefore, with the head of the batting order again swinging into action, certainly appeared suicidal on the very face of things."

Dean's control thus far had appeared somewhat uncertain at best, and on occasion almost absent. But he got White to foul out to Martin for the second out. He then walked Cochrane, filling the bases.

The Cardinals were now confronted with their biggest crisis of the game. Gehringer was in the batter's box, and he had so far proved to be the Tigers' most effective hitter. An uneasy Frisch signaled for Dazzy Vance to begin warming up. But the inning ended on an anticlimactic note when Gehringer grounded to Frisch, and the Tigers' drive sputtered to an end.

In the fifth, the Tigers again failed to capitalize on their chances. On a 3–2 count, Greenberg drew a walk. Goslin, the second batter, also took a 3–2 count before flying out to Collins. Vance again started warming up, while several Cardinals gathered around Paul Dean, giving him advice and urging him to remain calm. After two balls and a strike, Rogell singled to center and Greenberg raced to third. Owen came to bat, missing a strike with such force that he nearly fell down. He then struck out, and Dean also fanned Fox on four pitches, retiring the side. The two Tigers stranded on base now brought the team's total to eleven in five innings.

In the bottom of the fifth, the Cardinals administered the final blow. Martin sailed the first pitch against the right-field pavilion screen for a double. Rothrock tripled over Goslin's head into deep left field, scoring Martin. Anxious Tigers gathered on the mound for a hurried conference. Frisch was next up, and the infield closed in, expecting a bunt, but the Flash plastered a single over Gehringer's head, scoring Rothrock. Hogsett relieved Bridges, got Medwick to hit into a double play, and later retired the side.

The next three innings passed more-or-less uneventfully. In the top of the ninth, White got a single, and Cochrane and Gehringer each popped out. Dean seemed on his way to a shutout when Greenberg hit a triple with terrific force over Orsatti's head in deep center field and into the wall. White scored. But the game ended when Goose Goslin, the hero of the previous day's contest, lifted a high fly into shallow center field. Frisch twisted back and caught it with a dramatic flourish. The final score was 4 to 1.

The Cardinals manager was mobbed by his players when he was finally able to reach the clubhouse. His crowd-pleasing catch had ended the game on a spectacular note, and many of the Cardinal players were now telling anyone who would listen that the Series would be won in the next two engagements. The jubilant players were also shaking Paul Dean's right arm off. The younger Dean admitted that he had been unable to get his curveball to break properly, but Dizzy had a different explanation for Paul's wobbly performance. Feigning a serious mood, Dizzy told the assembled sportswriters that Greenberg's triple in the ninth inning had come off a floater that Paul, feeling sorry for the poor Tigers, had wafted up to the plate in a charitable moment.

The mood in the Tigers clubhouse, in contrast, was gloomy, and the atmosphere seemed supercharged with desperation.

Plenty of Detroit injuries only compounded the team's predicament. Cochrane had been badly bruised after a collision at
home plate with Medwick, shortstop Billy Rogell was lame,
and third baseman Marv Owen had been hit on the back with a
pitch. Cochrane requested all reporters to remain outside. He
did send word, though, that he was going to change the batting
order for the next day's game, dropping Greenberg from the
fourth to the sixth position. Elden Auker, the starting pitcher,
was to oppose the Cardinals' Tex Carleton.

"The Tigers have the look of losers," Westbrook Pegler reported in the Chicago *Daily News,* "whereas the Deans are
overbearing even when mediocre."

Elden Auker was a lanky twenty-four-year-old from Norcatur,
Kansas, and a former all-star at Kansas State College. Like Tex
Carleton, Auker was a right-hander, though he threw with a
somewhat underhanded motion that some wits claimed was the
result of spending so much of his early career in a cyclone cellar,
where he could not swing his arm freely over his head. Both
Auker and Carleton were making their World Series debuts.

Before game time, Babe Ruth, who was clearly rooting for
the American Leaguers, went to have a serious chat with
Cochrane in the Tigers clubhouse, pointing out the team's mistakes and suggesting remedies. Cochrane later vowed to reporters that if the Tigers ever got the lead, they would hold it.

Moments before the game began, Dizzy Dean marched across
the field with a police escort to stand in front of the box on the
first-base line that held the governors of Missouri, Kansas, and
Oklahoma. As he posed with them for photographers, a band
played "Happy Days Are Here Again." Then it was game time.

In this fourth contest of the Series, everything seemed to
break down for the Cardinals: pitching, hitting, and fielding.

As for Detroit in the first game, nothing went right. Worse, in the course of the game, the Cardinals' star player, Dizzy Dean, suffered a severe injury that might have damaged him permanently and ended his career. The injury also then cast a cloud over the Cardinals' strategy, since he was scheduled to pitch the next day.

A frustrated Tigers offense struck back savagely in this fourth encounter, amassing fourteen hits, four of them by Greenberg. The Cardinals committed five errors, three by Pepper Martin. As Drebinger remarked in the *Times,* the game proved to be "as weird and bitter a battle as ever graced an event to decide the baseball championship of the world."

Detroit failed to score in the first two innings. When Gehringer singled against Carleton in the first inning, an overly confident Sam Breadon pushed back his cream-colored fedora and remarked to his box seat companions, "There goes his chance of a no-hit game." That was an understatement.

In the bottom of the second, the Cardinals drew first blood. Medwick, the first batter up, singled sharply to center, and then Collins sent the ball caroming off the pavilion screen in right field for a double. Medwick held at third. Auker threw four bad pitches to DeLancey for a walk. With the bases loaded, Orsatti lifted a high fly ball into left. After Goslin caught it, Medwick raced home. Durocher flied out to Fox, and Carleton hit a grounder to Rogell, who threw to Gehringer, forcing DeLancey at second.

The Cardinals, led by a confident Carleton, seemed well in control of the game. In the top of the third, the "third Dean" easily retired the first two Detroit batters. But then something went amiss. Cochrane knocked a single near the first-base line and turned it into a double, snatching off his cap to keep it clean as he slid into second. Carleton now seemed to lose control, walking both Gehringer and Goslin to fill the bases. Frisch and a few other players gathered solicitously on the mound to counsel the pitcher, who assured them that he felt fine. Frisch waved to the bull pen, and the ancient veteran, Dazzy Vance, began warming up. On the very next play, Rogell punched a single over second, scoring two men.

Frisch called a time-out, and again went to the mound. Carleton told him he still felt fine, and Frisch replied, "Well, you may feel all right, but I feel terrible. Please go away from here." Vance, the one-time strikeout king of the National League, shuffled to the mound. "The old Dazzler," in the words of John Keiran in the *New York Times,* though he had been in and around the Major Leagues "since the Civil War," was now getting his first chance at World Series glory.

What awaited the old-timer was a series of misfortunes, beginning with Greenberg, who bounced a grounder just out of Durocher's reach. The hit scored Goslin and put the Tigers up 3 to 1. Owen hit a grounder to Martin, whose hurried throw to first was too high, and the runner reached first safely. The fans, who had cheered Martin only the day before for leading the attack against the Tigers, booed him this time. Vance ended the inning by striking out Fox.

In the bottom of the third, the Cardinals chipped away at Detroit's lead when Frisch slammed a single to center, Medwick walked, and Collins drove in Frisch with his second hit, a single to center.

Then Vance's real troubles began. In the fourth inning, he struck out Auker but walked the fleet-footed Jo-Jo White, who promptly stole second. When DeLancey's throw "whirled through a mass of flying colors at that bag," as Drebinger noted in the *Times,* "Jo-Jo picked himself up and continued for third."

In his incomparable style, the gifted *Times* sportswriter went on to chronicle what happened next: "[White] seemed to bear a charmed life, for though Orsatti's throw from center field to third base arrived in time for a putout, Martin dropped the ball for the first of his afternoon's three errors. The spectacle of the ball flying around in all directions must have reminded Vance of his merry days with the Dodgers. At the moment, however, it proved far more serious. For the Dazzler hurled a fast one that got away from DeLancey for a wild pitch and White scored." Vance then struck out Cochrane and retired the side on Gehringer's easy infield grounder. White had made his grand tour on a walk, a steal, an error, and a wild pitch.

Then came fifteen minutes of thrilling, superior baseball. Orsatti opened the fourth with a single to center. Predictably. Durocher grounded to Owen, who tossed the ball to Gehringer at second for the force-out. But Orsatti crashed into the Detroit second baseman with such vehemence that he was knocked down as the ball bounced into the air. Cochrane protested furiously to the umpires, to no avail. The Cardinals now had runners on first and second, Gehringer was charged with an error, and the crowd was delirious. Pinch-hitter Spud Davis came to bat and thwacked a single to right field, bringing home Orsatti and advancing Durocher to third.

The crowd's euphoria knew no bounds when Dizzy Dean himself was sent in to run for the slow-footed Davis. Taking his position, he gave Davis a friendly pat on the chest, and bowed courteously to the threesome of governors with whom he had posed before the game. Never before had Sportsman's Park echoed with such noise and racket. Dean's mere presence on the field seemed a virtual guarantee that the day would belong to the Cardinals.

Auker took his time with Martin, the next batter up. His patience appeared to have paid off when the Wild Horse of the Osage hit a grounder to Gehringer, who flipped the ball to Rogell at second. Touching the base to dispose of Dean, Rogell twisted about to throw to first for the double play. Instead the ball went crashing straight into the forehead of the onrushing Dizzy, one of the fleetest runners on the Cardinal team, and then bounced into right field. "Dean plunged headlong over second base," said Drebinger in the *Times*, "out as cold as a mackerel."

Dean lay unconscious for several long moments as players from both teams gathered around him and an anxious hush fell over the crowd. When he had revived somewhat, several of his teammates helped him to his feet and half-carried him off the field. There was some good news, though. In the mix-up, Durocher had scored from third base for the Cardinals' second run of the inning. The score was now tied, 4 to 4. It was the closest the Cardinals were to come to winning. The blow that had felled Dean, now recovering in the clubhouse, seemed to sap the energy and strength of the Redbirds as well. When play resumed, Rothrock flied out on the first pitch, and then Frisch grounded out on the first pitch.

Not only did the fire seem to go out of the Cardinals, but Auker's confidence was also improving, inning by inning. In the bottom of the fifth, he allowed Medwick to single into right, but he then retired the rest of the side with little problem. In contrast, Vance, who had waited fourteen years for his first chance to appear in a World Series, lasted only one and a third innings and gave up two hits. Willie Walker took over the mound for the Cardinals in the fifth.

In the seventh, the Tigers broke the tie and followed up with a barrage of runs in the eighth. Walker's luck began to run out in the seventh when Gehringer, the first batter up, blasted a single to center. Goslin sacrificed to second, and Rogell blazed a grounder to Durocher, who shot the ball to Martin in time for a putout of Gehringer at third. In the scuffle, Martin dropped the ball, and the Tigers now had men at first and third. Martin was credited with an error. Greenberg sent a towering fly into right center. Badly misjudging it, Orsatti just managed to get his glove on the ball but could not hold onto it, and Greenberg wound up with a double. Gehringer scored, putting the Tigers ahead. The bottom of the seventh started with an announcement that Dizzy Dean was all right—though, in fact, no X-ray had yet been taken, and the Cardinals had only Dean's own word for it that he was not seriously injured. Despite renewed hope among the hometown crowd, the Cardinals went down in order.

The top of the eighth inning turned out to be a long, brutal ordeal for the host team, and a nightmare for Walker. After White walked, Cochrane attempted a sacrifice bunt in front of the plate. Fielding the ball, the pitcher decided to try for White dashing toward second; instead, the ball went flying past Durocher into center field. With men now on first and second, Gehringer sacrificed, and White and Cochrane each moved forward a base. Walker then purposely walked Goslin to fill the bases. With a 2–1 count, Rogell singled past Durocher into center, scoring two men, and advancing Goslin to third. Next up was Greenberg, who hammered the first pitch to the front of the right-field pavilion, where a fan barely missed grabbing the ball before it fell to the field. Goslin and Rogell scored as Greenberg raced to third. But after Frisch protested to the umpires, the slugger's hit was ruled a double under ground rules because the fan had touched the ball. Rogell was recalled to third, and Greenberg was sent back to second.

Frisch then replaced Walker with the venerable Pop Haines, a veteran of the Cardinals' first World Series back in 1926. Owen crashed the first pitch into right field for a single, bringing home Rogell and advancing Greenberg to third. On a 3–2 count, Fox missed a third strike, and a double steal was on that only added to the Cardinals' misery. Owen instantly dashed for second, drawing DeLancey's throw to Frisch, which was too late, and simultaneously Greenberg raced for home, beating Frisch's return throw. Worse, DeLancey let the ball get away.

Owen took third on the error. A blessed end to the inning came for the Cardinals when Auker was called out on strikes. The score was now 10 to 4.

Neither team scored again. Jim Mooney was sent in to pitch for St. Louis. The last man at bat was Frisch, who hit into a double play to end the contest. The game also concluded on a hopeful note for the Tigers, who now knew they would enjoy a home-field advantage for the sixth and possibly seventh games of the series; and on a dire one for the Cardinals, whose premier player had suffered a blow that would propel most mortals onto the injury list. Dizzy, in fact, recovered almost instantly on returning to the clubhouse, and even managed to quip that he hoped the bump on his forehead did not ruin his pretty face. Manager Frisch, however, was being questioned by reporters, who wondered about the wisdom of exposing Dean to the risk of injury as a mere pinch runner when he was scheduled to pitch the next day.

Showing he was still as tough as nails, the old warhorse gruffly replied, "What happened to Dean today will not happen again in 15 years. It was just one of those things. Dean is a great base runner; that is why he went in." Then Frisch added his tongue-in-cheek clincher: "And, after all, he broke up a double play."

Displaying a remarkable lack of concern, Frisch later supplied a postscript: "[Dizzy] assured me he was all right before he left here and I'll pitch him tomorrow. That was my original plan—to use Dizzy Sunday and call on Paul Monday if that was necessary. Well, a Monday game now is necessary, and the pitching schedule is unchanged. Dizzy told me he felt all right, and he walked out of here with Paul apparently all right."

As a precaution, though, Frisch ordered Paul Dean to accompany his brother to St. John Hospital, just a few blocks from the Deans' lodgings at the Forest Park Hotel, and have him X-rayed.

As for his own plans, Frisch said, "I'm going out to a quiet retreat where I can enjoy a glass of beer and relax. I need it."

Many years later, noting that Frisch had received a great deal of criticism for sending in a thirty-game winner to pinch-run, Hallahan tried to set the record straight. "Well, here's how it happened," he said. "We needed someone to run. And while Frisch was looking up and down the bench trying to decide who to put in, Diz ran out there, on his own. Somebody said to Frisch, 'Dizzy's already out there.' Frisch took a look, and sure enough, there was Dean, standing on first base. Frisch frowned; he didn't like the idea. But the guy was already on the field, so he said, 'Okay, let him be.'"

Dr. Robert Hyland, the team physician, examined Dizzy at the hospital. The X-ray results showed that he had not sustained a fracture, though Hyland declined to say whether Dean should be allowed to play the next day. Dean was ordered to return to his hotel room and stay there for the rest of the night.

Understandably, all was bedlam in the Tigers clubhouse. An elated Mickey Cochrane announced that, if Dizzy Dean pitched for the Cardinals, he would start Bridges. If Dean did not play, Schoolboy Rowe would be sent in to finish the Cardinals off. "Then," he added, "it will be all over but the shouting."

Grantland Rice, writing in the *New York Sun,* summarized what had happened that day: "The shadow of a national sporting tragedy missed Sportsman's Park by the breath of the gods yesterday as the Tigers clawed and maimed five pitchers to trim the Cardinals. . . . The throw that floored Dizzy would have knocked down two elephants. The wonder is that the entire top of his head was not shot away at such close range."

Paul Gallico, in the *New York Daily News,* took a much harsher view, writing, "Yesterday we saw what was probably the greatest managerial World Series boner in the history of baseball. Frankie Frisch took a million-dollar asset and used him on a 10-cent job."

———

A photograph hangs in the Baseball Hall of Fame in Cooperstown, New York, that captures forever the magnificent competitive spirit of Mickey Cochrane. Taken during the sparsely attended opening game of the 1933 City Series between the Philadelphia Phillies and the Philadelphia Athletics, it shows an airborne Cochrane leaping toward home plate to tag out a sliding Pinky Whitney as the umpire looks on.

The 1933 season marked Cochrane's ninth under manager Connie Mack, but that year the fabled A's dropped to third place after taking the pennant in 1931 and finished behind the Yankees the following year. The team was in deep financial trouble, and Cochrane himself was suffering from financial woes that would culminate in a nervous breakdown within only a few years. An uneducated farm boy from Oklahoma, he had lost heavily in the stock market after the 1929 crash. On quite a few occasions, while sitting in the dugout during a game, he had had to excuse himself to take an urgent call from a broker. Yet he had earned enough money to help out several of his friends who had also suffered financially in the crash. Most notably, he put up some of his own stock as collateral to enable his teammate Cy Perkins to obtain a loan to cover a margin call, and he also cosigned another loan to Perkins for twenty-five thousand dollars from the Franklin Trust Company, a major Philadelphia bank. Up through 1933, banks continued to fail at a discouraging rate, and in those days depositors were not yet federally insured.

Cochrane's entanglement in a plummeting stock market and as a cosignatory on assorted loans reached a crisis in the 1931 World Series against the Cardinals. Making matters worse,

Cochrane's professional life as a catcher was being made miserable by the fleet-footed Pepper Martin, who stole five bases during the seven-game Series, which the Athletics lost. On October 5, 1931, when game three was played, the Franklin Trust closed. During the game, Cochrane's broker visited the ballpark to arrange for the liquidation of stock holdings that had been used as collateral for loans. Soon after the Series ended, J. G. Taylor Spink, publisher of the *Sporting News*, remarked in his "Casual Comment" column, "It is understood that Mule Haas, Mickey Cochrane, and several other of the Athletics were [more] worried about the dough that they had tied up in the banks of Philadelphia that blew up just before the Series than anything else. Cochrane is said to have lost $80,000 and Waite Hoyt is understood to have been touched for a wad."

"Cochrane wound up batting a miserable .160 for the Series with only four hits in 25 at bats," noted Charles Bevis in his biography of Cochrane. Moreover, "Mickey's tribulations with Martin's stolen bases dogged him for the rest of his life. It really rankled him that the blame was placed 100 percent on his shoulders by most baseball fans, writers, and even his own teammates. Although he received support from the Philadelphia press, which implied these writers knew of his real troubles, others were not as understanding."

In its October 8, 1931, edition, after the Athletics had lost the Series to St. Louis in seven games, the *Philadelphia Inquirer* noted that "Mickey is sick at heart—his faith in human nature crushed. For days he's been subject to a poison pen attack—an insidious anonymous letter writing campaign which Mickey, accustomed only to praise, has felt to the bottom of his heart."

The Depression continued to grind down ball players and ball clubs alike. Connie Mack's Athletics were in deep financial trouble. Attendance had dropped at Shibe Park from a high of 720,000 in 1930 to fewer than 300,000 in 1933. A staggering payroll only added to his troubles, making the Athletics the costliest team in the majors. As loan repayments became due in the dark days of 1932 and 1933, Mack sold three players for $100,000 to the Chicago White Sox to help pay off a $700,000 loan. Like Cochrane, Mack also had severe personal financial problems. He and his sons were rumored to have lost heavily both in the stock market and in real estate.

By August 1933, reports were circulating that Mack was going to trade Cochrane. The rumored buyer was Tigers owner Frank Navin, but he had his own problems with dwindling attendance and thought that hiring Babe Ruth as his manager might bring back the crowds. Ruth was definitely interested in a manager's job—as long as it was with the Yankees. Yankee owner Jake Ruppert had just the opposite agenda: He could not wait to get rid of the aging Bambino, who was a drain on both his payroll and team morale. The quarrelsome Ruth had become so estranged from Lou Gehrig and manager Joe McCarthy that neither of the two men was now on speaking terms with the Yankee slugger.

By the end of 1933, though, a persistent Navin had finally persuaded Ruth to consider taking the manager's job with the Tigers. But Ruth's asking salary and insistence on having a percentage of the gate receipts were more than Navin was willing to cede. Somewhat reluctantly, he instead offered the job of player-manager to Cochrane, who accepted it with Connie Mack's urgent blessing. The purchase cost Navin $100,000, a huge amount of money at the time.

All through the 1934 season, the Tigers and Yankees fought it out for first place. Cochrane was well liked by his players, and—unusual for the time—he both liked and socialized with them. Cochrane was not only an outstanding ballplayer but also a hero and role model to millions of people during the Great Depression, especially in Detroit, where unemployment in the auto industry was extremely high. Some parents even named their children after Cochrane, including an Oklahoma family named Mantle.

One result of Cochrane's driving leadership was that attendance had risen dramatically, and the twenty-five-year wait for a championship season seemed about to end. In late September, the Tigers finally clinched the pennant after winning three of four games against the St. Louis Browns, and then watching as the Yankees lost to the Red Sox. Cochrane, even though Gehrig led the American League in batting, homers, and RBIs, won the Most Valuable Player award, and finished with a respectable .320 batting average. In *Iron Horse,* his biography of Gehrig, Ray Robinson dryly commented, "Despite the Triple Crown, Lou was bypassed when it came time to name the league's most valuable player. Mickey Cochrane was selected. That Cochrane was the playing manager of the pennant-winning Tigers was, without a doubt, the decisive influence, for the writers determinedly believed their own stories about inspirational value and intangibles of leadership."

Like almost everyone else, Cochrane expected his Tigers to oppose the Giants in the 1934 World Series. Then the Cardinals won the pennant, and Cochrane began to have second thoughts about sending Schoolboy Rowe, the best Detroit pitcher, up against the best pitcher in the world. Later, when St. Louis was established as the favorite, he remarked, "We're not afraid of the Deans."

But he was, and Dizzy knew it. The Cardinals pitcher, a master of psychological warfare, wasted no time going on the offensive. At the start of game one, after Cochrane announced that Al Crowder would start for the Tigers, Dean wandered across the field to watch his opponent warm up on the sidelines, then shouted to Cochrane, "Mickey, the General ain't got nothin'. You better find Schoolboy and get him ready."

"Go to hell, Diz," Cochrane replied.

During a postgame radio interview, the victorious Dean resumed the attack, opining that Cochrane "used great judgment because he figured if I was at my best, no one could beat me. I don't blame Mickey, but I would've been tickled to death if he started Schoolboy."

Joe Medwick added to Cochrane's woes in game two. In the third inning, with two out, Collins hit to Goslin, who threw to Cochrane at home plate to prevent Medwick from scoring. The throw arrived well ahead of Medwick, who torpedoed feet first into the Tiger's manager for spite, inflicting two deep spike wounds in Cochrane's leg.

Before game four, a sarcastic Cochrane said with a sneer to his assembled players in the clubhouse, "You guys are a great team. You are in a pig's eye." Reasonably proficient in psychological warfare himself, Cochrane goaded his team to rip Frisch's Cardinals for fourteen hits.

On the eve of game five, Cochrane decided to start Bridges again, even though he had had only one day's rest. Cochrane wanted to beat Dizzy Dean on his home turf and guessed that a highly motivated Bridges wanted to exact revenge after having been sent to the showers in game three after lasting only four innings.

After he suited up for the game, Dizzy had only one thing to say to his manager.

"Give me the ball," he told Frisch, "and I'll go out and get 'em for you."

As for the massive bump on his forehead, Dizzy quipped, "The doctors X-rayed my head and found nothing."

No slouch in the humor department himself, Detroit shortstop Billy Rogell would later say of the play that felled his opponent, "If I'd have known his head was there, I would have thrown the ball harder."

While Dizzy was taking his final warm-ups, just before game time, Rogell strode to the mound to offer his hand and good wishes to the Cardinal pitcher. A flock of photographers rushed onto the field to record the event for posterity, or at least for the next day's newspapers, and Dizzy good-naturedly draped an arm around Rogell's shoulder and removed his cap to display the bump on his forehead. The cheering crowd soon erupted into wild laughter when a fan raced from a nearby box to present Dizzy with a medieval-style iron helmet.

Dizzy's first throw was a strike, and another cheer went up from the crowd of almost forty thousand. Their hero had obviously survived the crack on his head and was back in form, and that blazing fastball was like a shot fired across the enemy's bow. It all but foretold the Tigers' fate in the fifth game of the World Series—they were doomed. After all, they were up against the self-proclaimed greatest player in all of baseball. His younger brother had just whupped them, and now he was going to whup them, too. He easily retired the side. The only interesting thing that happened when the Cardinals came up to bat was that a photographer had to be chased off the field.

In the second inning, though, Greenberg walked, then scored from first when Fox, with one out, doubled to center. Over the next three innings, the game seesawed back and forth, with few hits for either side. Dean, though not in top form, pitched ably. In the fourth inning, he fanned Greenberg on four pitches and Fox on three. But in the sixth inning, with the count 3–2, Gehringer electrified the crowd with a vaulting home run onto the roof of the right-field pavilion. Goslin, the second batter up, flied out to Medwick, but Rogell hit the first pitch to center field for an apparent single. Chick Fullis allowed the ball to whistle through his feet, and Rogell wound up on third. He scored after Greenberg flied out to Rothrock. The score now stood at 3 to 1.

In the bottom of the seventh, DeLancey duplicated Gehringer's feat, smashing a home run onto the roof of the right-field pavilion amid an ear-splitting din from the crowd, but the next batter up grounded out, ending the inning. In the eighth, Dean was replaced by a pinch-hitter, but the Cardinals again failed to score. In the bottom of the ninth, St. Louis threatened once more when Frisch, the first batter up, singled into deep right field. After Medwick fouled out, Collins walloped the first pitch off the right-field pavilion screen for a single as Frisch raced to third. Umpire Brick Owens then called two straight strikes on DeLancey. As Cochrane looked on, a livid DeLancey let Owens know exactly what he thought of the plate umpire's eyesight.

"You'uh givin' them the fuckin' game," he drawled.

"That will cost you $50," Owens calmly replied.

"Make it a hundred, why don't you?" DeLancey sneered.

"One hundred it is."

"Fuck you, make it two hundred," DeLancey snarled.

"Two hundred it is."

Cochrane then stood up, removed his mask, spit, and wisely said to DeLancey, "Listen, kid, you better pipe down or you'll be playing this Series for nothing."

As he headed for the showers after striking out, DeLancey grumbled, "Fuck 'em anyway."

Orsatti, batting for Chick Fullis, was next up and grounded to Rogell to end the inning and give the victory to the Tigers, who now took the Series lead for the first time. Bridges had pitched a nearly flawless game, scattering seven hits, and not giving up a single base on balls. He had been backed up by a self-confident team that bore little resemblance to the jittery band of players who had committed one misstep after another in games one and three. In particular, Cochrane had distinguished himself with several extraordinary defensive plays at the plate.

President Franklin Roosevelt, on a weekend cruise with friends on the Potomac River, had listened to the game on the radio. An American League fan, he won a dollar bet on the game.

As both teams prepared to board a train that evening for the return trip to Detroit and game six on the following day, John Drebinger, writing in the *New York Times*, summed up the mood of the St. Louis team and their fans: "For St. Louis the Series virtually ended today and very sadly, indeed, with a feeling of considerable apprehension in the air that the Cardinals, who started out so gaily, are heading for complete disaster just around the corner." It seemed almost a foregone conclusion that the Cardinals could not possibly win because they would be facing Schoolboy Rowe, who had pitched the Tigers to a twelve-inning victory in the second game. Mickey Cochrane's strategy was beginning to look like genius.

"I'll start Rowe for sure tomorrow," Cochrane crowed to reporters, as his team whooped it up in the clubhouse. "We have them on the run now and want to get it over."

By contrast, Frisch's decision to send in an overworked Dizzy Dean, who had just sustained a near concussion, on only one day's rest, seemed in retrospect a terrible misjudgment at best, and more likely a signal that the Cardinals were growing desperate. Another indication of Frisch's poor judgment was his decision to replace Orsatti with Fullis in the outfield. Frisch had decided that the former had frequently misjudged high fly balls on windy afternoons. But Fullis had committed two errors: The first, in the second inning, had allowed Detroit to score its first run, and the second, in the sixth inning, was directly responsible for the Tigers' third run.

In the gloomy Cardinals clubhouse after the game, a scowling Frisch approached Dizzy Dean, who had insisted on pitching, and quietly murmured, "Nice game out there, you son of a bitch."

"My head hurt a little," a subdued Dean replied, without looking up, "but I have no excuses."

In fact, he had pitched the entire game with a fierce headache pounding in his skull.

The three strikes umpire Owens had called on DeLancey in the ninth inning seriously aggravated a latent ill feeling between the two teams, and it was only to escalate in the ensuing days. Back at their hotel, while the Tigers players were packing up before catching the train to Detroit, Bill Klem, the senior National League umpire, and Detroit's Goose Goslin encountered one another in the lobby and nearly came to blows.

Once the Cardinals boarded the train, Frisch walked up and down the aisle, giving them an old-fashioned pep talk and punching his fist into the air for emphasis.

"We'll pull this thing out," he promised them. "We've been down before, this year, and we always came back. We're a better team than they are."

"To hell with Schoolboy Rowe," Pepper Martin scowled.

"We'll tie a knot in his neck," Rip Collins put in.

"We'll knock 'em off the way we did the Yankees in '26," Pop Haines reminded them, even though he and Bill Hallahan were the only ones on the team who had any memory of that stirring victory over the Bronx Bombers.

"It's in the bag," Dizzy drawled. "Paul'll fog it by them tomorrow, and I'll settle their hash the next game."

In another railroad car, Cochrane was similarly prowling the aisle, telling his players that they had the Cardinals where they wanted them: in the doghouse. The only problem was, he reminded them, the doghouse door was open.

Detroit rooters and bookies alike could not have agreed more that the Tigers now had the edge. Jubilant fans in Motor City immediately began forming lines for seats for the next day's game. The next morning at 7 A.M. a surging crowd greeted Mickey Cochrane and his gang at Union Depot. At the Book-Cadillac Hotel, where the Cardinals were staying, a band dedicated to keeping the visiting Cardinals awake around the clock was playing "Tiger Rag" over and over and over. Several grumpy Cardinals players threw wastebaskets and other objects out the window in an effort to make the noisemakers go away.

Bookmakers now established the Tigers as 1 to 3 favorites to win the sixth game and take the Series.

The World Series was generating so much excitement around the country that, according to an Associated Press item, it was interfering with Vice President John N. Garner's daily afternoon siesta. A Tigers fan, he had skipped an entire week's worth of naps, while vacationing at his home in Uvalde, Texas, to listen to each game on the radio.

In other news that day, German immigrant Bruno Hauptmann was indicted for the murder of the infant son of Charles Lindbergh.

Dizzy spent the morning of game six, as he had a few days earlier, at the home of Henry Ford. Most players went straight to their hotel for a few hours of rest after the train pulled into Detroit, but Dean had hopped into a waiting limousine for the trip to Dearborn, and he showed up at the Cardinals clubhouse an hour late. Frisch was furious.

"Aw, Frank," Dean replied, in his patented tongue-in-cheek manner, "I'm tryin' to get Henry to buy this ballclub, and I'll get you a raise if he does."

The Redbirds manager also announced that if DeLancey's fine for his run-in with umpire Brick Owens was upheld, he would pay it himself. "And the American League has never even heard me swear," he added with a grin.

Babe Ruth also once again avowed to reporters before the game that he was retiring from baseball, at least as a player, though he was still hopeful of securing a position as a manager. "I have no intention of sitting on the bench or being around merely for pinch-hitting purposes," he said. "That doesn't appeal to me at all." He did admit, though, that he no longer harbored any hope of replacing Joe McCarthy as skipper of the Yankees the next season. In a face-to-face meeting, Jacob Ruppert, the Yankees owner, had made it clear to a disappointed Ruth that McCarthy was his man for the 1935 season.

All that now stood in the way of a Tigers victory and the World Series championship was Dizzy's little brother, Paul, the quiet, self-effacing half of the double-barreled Dean phenomenon. Once again, Umpire Owens was destined to be the center of controversy, only this time the Tigers were the ones who insisted he needed to see an ophthalmologist.

The Cardinals scored quickly in the first. After Martin popped to Owen, Rothrock banged a double into right field. Frisch lined a ball straight into Owen's waiting glove, but Medwick brought Rothrock home with a long single to right. Both the Cardinals and the Tigers continued to play spirited ball, on both offense and defense, in the bottom of the first, and in the second. In the third inning, the Detroit fans generously cheered Paul Dean as he approached the plate; on the first pitch he grounded to Greenberg at first. The game was temporarily stopped when some fans were asked to remove their overcoats from the railings along the box seats, and then delayed for a few minutes more when some young fans perched like crows on the right-field fence were ordered to leave, with the crowd booing their displeasure at this seemingly mean-spirited order on so jubilant an occasion. Rowe retired the next two batters.

The Detroit pitcher received a deafening ovation when he came up to bat. Dean struck him out, then gave up his first walk when he passed White on four straight pitches. On the next pitch, to Cochrane, White dashed to second and arrived safely when Frisch went sprawling and dropped the ball, which rolled onto the infield grass. Wasting no time, White sped on to third. With the count 2–1, Cochrane fouled six times in succession, prompting DeLancey and Dean to confer at the plate. After fouling off another ball, Cochrane beat out a hit to Collins, sliding into first before Ripper's throw reached Dean, who was covering the base. White crossed home plate, tying the score at 1 to 1. The game was then briefly held up, with players from both teams clustering around first base, because Dean had accidentally spiked Cochrane on his knee during Cochrane's slide. Dean and DeLancey warmed up during this interval. After lying on the ground for five minutes, Cochrane got to his feet, with the help of other players, and limped about the field. Finally, he signaled that he was ready to resume playing. Gehringer flied out to Rothrock, ending the inning.

In the top of the fifth, St. Louis added two more runs. Durocher sent the first pitch just out of Gehringer's reach, though the second baseman was able to at least knock the ball down. Dean sent a sacrifice bunt to Greenberg at first, advancing Durocher. As Greenberg leisurely ambled to first to make the out, Dean suddenly burst forward in a bid to reach the base safely, but Greenberg beat him by a step, while the crowd laughed. Durocher scored on Martin's single to left. Martin took second on the throw to the plate. Goslin's throw to Cochrane was off the mark, going past the pitcher, and Martin then advanced to third on the error. Next up was Rothrock, who grounded to Rogell, who threw him out at first, but Martin scored. Frisch ended the Cardinals' half of the inning when he fouled out. The score now stood at 3 to 1.

Detroit struck back in the bottom of the sixth. After White walked, Cochrane hit a low liner over first. Collins knocked the ball down but could not field it, and it rolled into foul territory for a single as White raced to third. On a 3–2 pitch, Gehringer grounded to the pitcher's mound, but Dean let the ball roll through his legs for an error. White scored, Cochrane pulled up at second, and Gehringer was safe at first. On the first pitch, Goslin attempted a sacrifice bunt, but DeLancey picked up the ball in front of the plate and forced Cochrane at third by just inches. Gehringer now stood at second, and Goslin at first, with only one out. Rogell flied out to Orsatti, but Greenberg tied the score at 3 to 3 when he lashed the first pitch to left for a single, scoring Gehringer. Owen, the next batter up, hit sharply into the hole, but Durocher grabbed it and made a long throw to first to retire the side.

"That was the play that kept me in the big leagues," Durocher was later to recall.

When the Cardinals came up to bat, Orsatti flied out, but Durocher and Dean teamed up to restore the Cardinals' lead. The shortstop doubled into deep center field. On the first pitch, Dean brought him home with a single past Greenberg into right. The next two batters grounded out.

In the bottom of the sixth, reported James P. Dawson in the *New York Times,* "Fox hit the first pitch for a Texas Leaguer double in short left, Medwick, Durocher, and Orsatti all failing to get under the ball." Rowe sacrificed and Fox took third. When White grounded to Durocher, the shortstop threw to DeLancey, who tagged Fox out. With Cochrane at bat, De-Lancey then threw White out at second on an attempted steal.

Detroit just barely missed taking the lead in the bottom of the eighth. Cochrane, his knee still aching, grounded to Frisch and was easily thrown out at first as he limped down the line. But Gehringer beat out a bounder to Frisch, and barreled on to third when Goslin singled to right. Both base runners held at their bases when Rogell flied out to Orsatti, but now slugger Hank Greenberg strode to the plate. Several players then consulted with Dean at the mound, and it was decided to pitch to the slugger. The first pitch was a called strike. Greenberg then "lifted a high foul fly back of first," said Dawson in the *Times,* "which Collins raced over and caught, making what seemed like an impossible clutch."

Cochrane came in for more physical punishment in the top of the ninth. After DeLancey fanned on three pitches, Orsatti singled to center. When Durocher also singled to center, Orsatti reached third; Durocher took second on the unsuccessful play at third. When Dean grounded to Gehringer, Orsatti took off, crashing into the Detroit catcher, who somehow managed to hold onto the ball for the putout. Rowe retired the side by striking out Martin. In the bottom of the ninth, Paul Dean retired the Detroit batters in order, with Rowe flying into deep center for the final out. The Cardinals had won, 4 to 3. The World Series was now tied at three games apiece.

Both teams had played often spectacular defense, and the cheering crowd had shown its appreciation for both Cardinal and Tiger fielders alike, from Martin's leaping catch that deprived Goslin of a hit in the first inning, to Goslin's own magnificent running catch of DeLancey's long ball in the same inning, to Orsatti's running catch of Rowe's shot in the third. In that inning, Orsatti had made all three putouts. His total of seven putouts in the game was just one short of the record. In the near disastrous seventh inning, Collins had made an amazing catch of Greenberg's foul near the right-field boxes to shut down an impressive Tiger rally.

Perhaps the happiest man in the Cardinals clubhouse was Leo Durocher, whose three hits amounted to more than he had racked up in the previous five games combined. "Boy, do I feel great!" he yelled, as congratulatory players crowded around him. "Gosh, it feels great to be a slugger!"

Irrepressible as always, Dizzy Dean told Bill Corum of the *New York Evening Journal,* "You know, that lick on my head sort of set me thinkin', and I just thought to myself, I know what I am goin' to do: I am going to send my little brother after them rascals. And he brought 'em home with him, too, didn't he?"

The misery in the Detroit clubhouse was deepened by the injury Cochrane had sustained when he slid under Paul Dean's foot in the third inning. In the ninth, he had been shaken by the hard-driving Orsatti. Nor did Cochrane make any attempt to conceal his resentment at having lost the ball game. "The Cards did not beat us," he complained. "Umpire Owens did." Later he added, "We were beaten by umpires and hitters like Dean and Durocher. That's a hot one, isn't it?"

Cochrane was later taken to a hospital to be X-rayed. Though tests showed that he had escaped serious injury to the bone or any chip on the kneecap, the ligaments beneath it were pulled, and his leg now bore a nasty gash. While Cochrane was still at the hospital, Schoolboy Rowe also showed up unexpectedly. Soon after the Tigers had checked into the hotel that morning, someone had accidentally slammed a door on the pitcher's right hand and he wanted to have it examined by a doctor since there was a good possibility he might be called on to pitch the following day.

"I soaked my hand in water as hot as I could bear it just before the game," he later recalled. "It was painin' me and I was worried but not enough to miss my turn."

In his postgame analysis, Drebinger of the *New York Times* congratulated Paul Dean for having restored the Cardinals, "as garrulous and belligerent an outfit as ever catapulted itself into this fall classic of the diamond, back into the struggle." With both teams deadlocked at three victories apiece, that struggle now stood, in the reporter's opinion, as "one of the most remarkable in World Series history."

Unable to contain his obvious admiration for the Cardinals, Drebinger went on to say, "This St. Louis team, in fact and in deed, seems to be a throwback to the legendary days of baseball when men fought for the mere relish of fighting and with anything that came ready to hand."

As Dizzy Dean might have said, he hadn't seen nuthin' yet.

9

TIGER RAG

Just before the start of the seventh game, Pepper Martin asked the band to play a few old-fashioned pieces, and the musicians obliged with several tunes dating back to the Gay Nineties. The biggest crowd of the Series, 45,551, was on hand.

But Martin's good mood was in sharp contrast to the tension and sour disposition of many of the fans. The stress was also visibly affecting many of the players. As Goose Goslin prophetically told a reporter, "Everybody seems to be mad at everybody else in this Series, with all hands sore at the umpiring, which has been terrible. So watch out for fireworks."

While Elden Auker was warming up, Dizzy, in a taunting mood as ever, wandered to within earshot of Cochrane and yelled, "He jes' won't do, Mickey."

Bookmakers again installed the Cardinals as 7 to 10 favorites.

An embarrassing moment occurred just before the start of the game. A delegation of well-meaning Detroit fans rolled a huge horseshoe-shaped floral display up to home plate. Unaware of baseball's many superstitions, they were unsuccessful in inducing Cochrane or any other Tiger players to come out and accept the gift. After a few moments, the group hauled away its gift in silence.

Now that six grueling games had been played, and the seventh was about to begin, the thirty-five-year-old Frisch was beginning to feel his age. As the Cardinals took to the field, the manager said to Durocher, "How about playing a little closer to second and giving me a hand. I'm getting pooped."

Irascible as ever, Durocher unhesitatingly replied, "Go get yourself a wheelchair if you can't cover your territory. I'm not going to make myself look bad just to make yourself look good."

That exchange, observed Durocher's biographer Gerald Eskanazi, "was a foreshadowing of Leo's inevitable exit from St. Louis." It was one thing for the Cardinals shortstop to ride the opponents from the bench, or even criticize other teammates in his capacity as captain. But dressing down the manager in such fashion was beyond the pale.

Auker started off in the first inning by throwing three wide balls to Martin, but he then calmed down and struck him out. Rothrock doubled to center, but the Detroit pitcher easily disposed of the next two batters. In Detroit's half of the first, the only excitement occurred when manager Cochrane grounded to manager Frisch, who threw him out. The second inning was similarly uneventful.

Then came Detroit's Waterloo, in the third inning. The beginning was inauspicious. Durocher flied out. The fans generously cheered Dizzy Dean as he went up to bat; he fouled a ball behind the plate, which Cochrane, with equal generosity, ignored, though he could have caught it by reaching over the box seats where it dropped down. Dean repaid his kindness by smacking the ball into left. Galloping on to second, he beat Goslin's throw by inches. Martin, who was next up, also beat out a slow roller to Greenberg, reaching the bag again by inches before Auker, who was covering, took the first baseman's throw. Dean, after hesitating, had dashed to third. The fleet-footed Martin stole second on Auker's first pitch. Though

Cochrane's throw got away from Gehringer, Dean held third. A nervous Auker walked Rothrock on four pitches, and now the bases were filled.

The count against Frisch reached 2–2, as the Fordham Flash fouled off four balls, including one down the right-field line and another down the left-field line. He hammered the next pitch straight down the middle for a double, clearing the bases, and the Cardinals now led, 3 to 0. Auker was yanked, and the lanky figure of Schoolboy Rowe emerged from the bullpen. The cheers were deafening. At last, the Series' two premier pitchers were to oppose one another, in a final winner-take-all showdown.

Detroit's euphoria was short-lived. The Gashouse Gang was in top form, putting on a display of sheer baseball talent and raw determination that quickly overwhelmed the helpless Tigers. Medwick grounded to Rogell on the first pitch and was thrown out, while Frisch took third. Collins bashed the first pitch to left for a single, scoring Frisch. DeLancey hit a long ball off the right-field screen for a double, scoring Collins from first. Elon Hogsett replaced Rowe, who had lasted not even a full inning. Hogsett walked Orsatti. Durocher then had the unusual experience of batting twice in the same inning in a World Series game. With the count 2–1, he singled to right, filling the bases.

Dean was the next man up, and beat out a grounder to Owen for a single. DeLancey crossed home plate, bringing the score to 6 to 0, and now the bases were again filled. Dean had distinguished himself not only as a pitcher thus far in the game, but as a batter who had the rare distinction of getting two hits in one inning in a World Series game, driving in one run and scoring another. Hogsett walked Martin on four straight balls, forcing in Orsatti with the seventh Cardinals run, and still leaving the bases loaded. Hogsett was relieved, and a desperate Cochrane signaled for Tommy Bridges. The inning finally ended when Bridges got Rothrock to ground to Gehringer, who tossed the ball to Rogell to force out Martin at second.

The fourth inning passed uneventfully. In the fifth, Dean was the third batter up after both Orsatti and Durocher flied to Goslin. The magnanimous crowd cheered him as he toed the plate, but laughed uproariously when he fell down after missing the first pitch for a strike. He then missed a second and a third strike, and as the crowd applauded, Dizzy laughed and took the ball from Cochrane. Umpire Owens called for it to be returned. Absentmindedly, Dizzy handed him the bat instead and started walking to the dugout until he realized his mistake, retrieved the bat, and returned the ball. In the bottom of the inning, Detroit managed to get two hits but was stalled by Durocher's acrobatic fielding when he scooped White's grounder and, while still in midair, tossed the ball to Collins to retire the side.

The Cardinals scored two more runs in the sixth inning. Martin singled to left and then dashed to second when Goslin fumbled the ball. After Rothrock and Frisch flied out, Medwick bounced a triple off the bleachers in right center, scoring Martin.

Then came the most controversial moment in the Series, and one of the most notorious in all of baseball. As the hard-charging Medwick rounded second, he saw Mike Gonzalez, the third-base coach, give the sign indicating he could approach the base standing up. But third baseman Owen reached down to make a phantom tag. Not knowing that the third baseman did not have the ball, Medwick slid hard. Owen raised his foot to get out of the way, brought it down on Medwick's leg, then tumbled down on top of him. Medwick struck back with a vicious kick, and in seconds the two were tussling in the dirt, swinging wildly at one another, until they were separated by umpire Bill Klem and several players. After dusting himself off, Medwick, with a grin, offered to shake hands. Owen refused, cursed at Medwick, and waved him off. However, the scene was apparently misunderstood by the Detroit fans, who thought that Medwick's extended hand was an invitation to engage in more combat.

"I admit he slid hard," Frisch later recalled in his autobiography. "Joe always played hard. But it wasn't a dirty slide. But Marvin Owen, the third baseman, thought Joe was carrying one of his spiked shoes too high as he slid, and perhaps accidentally or perhaps in retaliation, Owen took the high throw and came down on Joe's leg harder than Joe thought was necessary. So Medwick kicked at Owen's leg."

Frisch was a no-nonsense man with a genuine sense of what was right and wrong, and his eyewitness view and postgame analysis was probably as objective as any.

Medwick scored when Collins collected his fourth hit of the day, and Collins took second when White fumbled the ball. But the frustration of the Detroit fans now found an outlet in their resentment of what they perceived as Medwick's poor sportsmanship. As he trotted back to the Cardinals dugout, he was roundly jeered, and some fans tossed programs and assorted bits of litter onto the field as a sign of their contempt. DeLancey went down swinging for the third out. The score now stood at 9 to 0.

As the Cardinals took to the field in the bottom half of the sixth, the irate Detroit fans were still in an unforgiving mood, especially the seventeen thousand who were packed solidly into huge wooden bleachers built especially for the Series. As Medwick took his position in left field, those fans showered him with oranges, bananas, tomatoes, potatoes, lemons, apples, cigar stubs, and empty soda bottles. Medwick stood in left field with his hands on his hips, glaring straight ahead. Attendants had to clear the field four times, with the announcer imploring the fans through the loudspeakers to desist so that the game could continue. All four umpires took up positions to keep the players on the two teams apart.

An impatient Medwick, temperamental at the best of times, finally chose not to ignore the detritus being thrown at him, and to taunt the Detroit fans into further frenzy by picking up an apple and playing catch with Pepper Martin and Ernie Orsatti. After all, at this late stage of the game, it was virtually a foregone conclusion that the World Series was theirs, and a little premature celebrating seemed in order.

At one point, Durocher strolled to the outfield and said, "Aw, it's nothing, Joe. Don't let it bother you."

"Nothing, hell," Medwick barked. "If you think that, you play left field, and I'll play shortstop."

"I don't know where they were getting all that stuff from," Gehringer later recalled. "It was like they were backing produce trucks up to the gate and supplying everyone."

One person completely unconcerned about all the ruckus was Dizzy Dean, who stood around the infield in his bright red windbreaker while the fans were pelting anyone within range with anything they could get their hands on. Occasionally, Dean threw a few warm-up pitches, and then continued to wander aimlessly about.

At last, Commissioner Landis, who was sitting in his box on the third-base line, rose and summoned Owen, Medwick, Frisch, and the umpires. In open court, he asked the Cardinals outfielder if he had committed an overt act.

Perhaps not fully confident that he understood what the commissioner meant, Medwick merely replied, "It was just one of those things that happen in a ball game."

Landis then rephrased his question, asking Medwick if Owen had done anything to him that might cause him to retaliate by kicking the Detroit player. Medwick replied, "No."

Landis then asked Owen if he knew of any reason why Medwick should have spiked him. Owen replied that he did not.

Landis then ordered Medwick to leave the field for his own safety and to avoid having the game, as well as the Series, end in a forfeit. He made no attempt to patch things up between the two players, since in his view that was not a priority. Medwick bitterly protested. He had accumulated eleven hits during the Series. Now, by leaving the game, he would lose another turn at bat and a chance to tie the World Series record, which stood at twelve.

"It's a good thing Joe didn't have a bat in his hands," Frisch later recalled. "He would have killed some of those fans." Frisch himself also bitterly complained about Landis's decision, to no avail. Owen apparently did not contest the decision, but after the game he told reporters that he did not think Medwick should have been removed.

"It was one of the most disorderly scenes ever witnessed at a World Series game," said James P. Dawson in the *New York Times*. Medwick finally had to leave the field under the escort of five policemen, crossing from the third-base to the first-base line. Amid the cries and boos, someone in the upper stands flung a cushion that landed at his feet. His place was taken by Chick Fullis. The delay of game had lasted twenty minutes. When the game was finally resumed, the Detroit side was retired in order.

The Cardinals then took out their own wrath and frustration on the Detroit fans. The Gashouse Gang had no intention of showing the humiliated Tigers any mercy after their star slugger had been banished from the field. They were only innings away from becoming the champions of the world, and they were going to do it at the expense of a thoroughly defeated and demoralized Detroit team; and perhaps, too, some of the

Cardinals players were motivated not a little by the earlier in-hospitable rowdiness of those fans who had kept them awake the previous night, parading around the Book-Cadillac Hotel into the wee hours with honking horns and blaring music. Now it was the Cardinals who were having the last laugh, play-ing their own version of "Tiger Rag" while amassing seventeen hits. After Orsatti flied to White, Durocher sailed the first pitch to the front of the bleachers in right center for a triple.

Dean was then thrown out at first, while Durocher held at third. Martin grounded to Gehringer, who fumbled the ball for an error. Durocher scored. Martin stole second, for the second time in the game, on the second pitch to Rothrock, who banged a double to left center, scoring Martin. The inning ended when Frisch flied out. By the time the Tigers came to bat at the bot-tom of the seventh, some fans were already beginning to file out of the stadium. When Greenberg, the second batter up, struck out, Dean laughed derisively. The humiliation of the Tigers had become a joke.

The exodus of fans continued as St. Louis came up to bat at the top of the eighth. Firpo Marberry was now pitching for the Tigers, and he was able to retire the side with no trouble. In the bottom of the inning, Detroit left one man on base, but posed no real threat.

In the ninth inning, manager Cochrane took himself out of the game and sent Ray Hayworth in to catch. He also dis-patched General Alvin Crowder to the mound. The Cardinals were retired in order.

With hope running out, and the odds of pulling out a victory almost astronomical, the brave Tigers did their best to launch an offense. Gehringer, the first man up, singled to left. Goslin grounded to Collins, who threw to Durocher for the force-out. Hoping for a double play, Durocher shot the ball to first, but the bid failed because Dean, who took the throw, was mistakenly standing not on the bag, but on Collins's foot. Goslin raced to second when Rogell singled to right. But it took Dean only four pitches to strike out Greenberg. On the last pitch, Dean turned his back and laughed again, not even bothering to look as the ball whizzed toward the plate. With a mighty swing, the slugger connected only with the air. The final batter up was Owen. On a 2–1 count, he hit to Durocher, who flipped the ball to Frisch at second, forcing Rogell, and sealing the Cardinals' victory. As in 1907, 1908, and 1909, the Detroit Tigers had once again failed to prevail over their National League opponents in the World Series. Dizzy Dean's 11-to-0 shutout was the worst that had been suffered by a losing team in World Series history.

As they whooped and hollered their way into the clubhouse, the Cardinals were acting like a bunch of schoolkids, said James P. Dawson in the *New York Times:* "Trainer Doc Weaver was lifted bodily and tossed under the running shower, clothes and all. Dizzy Dean, a pith helmet on his head, held an inflated rubber tiger by the tail, gripped the tail between his teeth, exerted a Strangler Lewis headlock on the tiger, and posed for clicking photographers." Lewis was the current world heavyweight wrestling champion.

"We did it, didn't we?" Dean yelped. "I knew we would from the start. I felt great out there this afternoon. Had a lot of fun. Let them get a couple of hits, and, then, I decided to stop foolin' around and get those strikes past 'em. Boy, was that Greenberg wild? I just had to laugh when he missed those third swings."

Among the visitors who stopped by to offer their congratulations were Cochrane, Will Rogers, American League president Will Harridge, and Landis. In the Tigers clubhouse, the mood was understandably bleak. Most of the players had plans to disperse to their homes immediately, and they would not see one another again until the spring. Detroit's loss did not prevent one enterprising fan from unstrapping the bag at second base and then dashing across the field and out the right-field gate. Other fans dug up home plate as policemen looked on impassively. Souvenir hunters tore the bunting to shreds, while hundreds of pillows rented from a concessionaire were ripped to pieces and thrown from the grandstands.

The police escorted the victorious Redbirds back to the Book-Cadillac Hotel. As they were about to enter the elevator, roommates Medwick and Hallahan observed two suspicious-looking men, who followed them in. When the two players got out at their floor, the two men also exited, and trailed them down the hall. Clearly, something was afoot. Medwick and Hallahan made it safely to their room, but then they heard a knock. When they opened it, one of the men who had been following them asked, "Which of you is Joe Medwick?"

"He is," Medwick said, pointing to Wild Bill.

"I am *not*," Hallahan exclaimed. *"He is."*

The men explained that they were plainclothes detectives assigned to protect Medwick until he left town. Fortunately for Medwick, the team had a 9 P.M. train to catch that would get them to St. Louis in the morning.

But there was still time for a bit of celebrating. Amid the merriment at the hotel, Breadon announced that Frisch would return as manager of the Cardinals in the 1935 season. He also strongly denied a persistent rumor that the Cardinals were for sale. Though the Dean brothers had won a combined forty-nine games, Breadon also admitted that he had given no thought to awarding them, or anyone else on the team, a bonus. Each player was to receive a check for $5,389 as his share in the Series jackpot. The players also voted to donate $3,000 to their clubhouse attendants, and $1,000 to Charley Gelbert, whose Cardinals career had been halted by a hunting accident. Each Detroit player was awarded $3,354. In addition, the seven-game show earned each club a total of $144,238. Commissioner Landis did slightly better, taking in $154,811, before expenses.

The bitterly fought 1934 World Series marked an unprecedented record for Frisch. When he took the throw from Durocher for the final putout in game seven, he had completed his fiftieth game in the October classic. Babe Ruth, who had appeared in ten Series to Frisch's eight, had appeared in only forty-one contests. Frisch had also piloted the Cardinals to their third championship since Rogers Hornsby first did it in 1926. Among other records, the Cardinals also posted the highest-ever batting average—.279—for a seven-game Series, as well as driving in the most runs, sending the most men up to bat, and getting the most base hits and triples. The margin of Dizzy Dean's closing shutout victory, 11 to 0, was also one for the books. The batting champions of the Series were Joe Medwick of the Cardinals and Charlie Gehringer of the Tigers. Each had collected eleven hits in twenty-nine times at bat, and had missed tying the Series record by one.

In a pair of columns wrapping up his views on the 1934 season and its thrilling finale, John Drebinger of the *New York Times* dubbed the Cardinals "the most astonishing ball club of modern times." The St. Louis club's pennant race and victory over their American League rivals, in his view, was the most exciting championship contest in at least twenty years. After wresting the flag from the Giants, the Cardinals "plunged into the World Series like a herd of steer into a children's playground." He admitted that the Cardinals had played baseball that was at times plain marvelous, and at other times plain bad. "But at all times they played a fierce, aggressive game such as a World Series has not witnessed in a long time." Parenthetically, he noted that "Dizzy the elder enjoys a decided flare for showmanship, but he is far from being as flighty upstairs as frequently pictured. On the contrary, ball players in the National

League, and to this the Tigers will add their testimony, agree that Dizzy is one of the craftiest pitchers to come to the top in the majors in years."

Seconding Drebinger's words were a host of other writers, including the anonymous correspondent for the *Literary Digest,* an influential mass-circulation magazine, who wrote that Cochrane's Tigers had been "smeared gleefully by one of the wildest, most astounding ball clubs that ever reached and won a World Series. . . . No mortal dramatist could have written a climax for the World Series of 1934 after the first six acts had been played—six of the maddest games in the wildest World Series in the history of the game."

As the Cardinals traveled down the rails from Michigan to Missouri, celebrating all the way, the city of St. Louis was holding a spontaneous victory party of its own. Soon after Dizzy Dean's last pitch, fans poured into the downtown area, jamming the street and creating an incessant din with car horns, sirens, and music. Some of the more enterprising noisemakers tied abandoned washing machines or the rim from an automobile's extra tire to car bumpers and added a note of chaotic cacophony by dragging them up and down the streets.

The next morning, the train pulled into St. Louis's Union Station bearing the world champion St. Louis Cardinals, and thousands of fans were waiting to greet and cheer them. When Dizzy Dean, the hero of the Series, finally appeared on the platform set up for the occasion, he was still wearing his white pith helmet and carrying his much-abused stuffed tiger. Its long tail had now been tied into four knots, each one symbolizing a Detroit defeat. As he held the tiger aloft, Dean then choked it again as the crowd wildly cheered and applauded.

"This hat," Dean cried out, "is to wear when I go fishing down in Deanville, Florida, which used to be Bradenton."

The celebration went on all day and far into the night. In the victory parade through downtown, its streets still littered with debris from the previous day, the lead car carried Mayor Bernard F. Dickmann, Dizzy and Pat Dean, Paul Dean, Mr. and Mrs. Breadon, and Mr. and Mrs. Frisch. Mr. and Mrs. Rickey and all of the players, many with their wives or girlfriends, followed behind in a long cavalcade of cars. Medwick was particularly popular with the fans lining the streets. At one point, a boy ran up and, holding out a piece of fruit, cried, "Wanna banana, Joe!" The fruit thrown by Detroit fans to express their anger and frustration had become the victors' symbol of conquest. The revelers also kept asking the band to keep playing a particular favorite, and the musicians happily obliged. The tune, of course, was "Tiger Rag."

Club officials, the players, and their wives later assembled for a dinner party at the Coronado Hotel. Afterward, the mayor invited some of the group to be his guests at a horse show, though many of the players immediately left for home. Two players who had not been able to attend the celebratory dinner were Dizzy and Paul Dean. As soon as the parade ended, they had gathered up their belongings and hurried to the airport. They were scheduled to appear on an all-star team in an exhibition match the next day against the Kansas City Monarchs in Oklahoma City.

———

The day after the game, Commissioner Landis fined umpire Bill Klem fifty dollars for his use of "over-ripe words" in his altercation with Goose Goslin in a hotel lobby. It was the first time in his fourteen years as baseball's highest official that Landis had been obliged to chasten an umpire in such a manner. He also fined DeLancey fifty dollars for similar language that the Cardinals catcher had directed at umpire Brick

Owens during the Series, though the fine marked a significant reduction from the two hundred dollars originally levied as the two men quarreled at the plate. A hearing about the incident in the seventh game involving Medwick and Detroit third baseman Owen was postponed, though Landis did indicate that he did not blame the crowd for the near riot that had ensued after Medwick slid into third.

"As I saw the incident at third base," he said, "Medwick came sliding hard into the bag, then kicked his feet up at Owen. I did not see Owen make any gesture previously toward Medwick, but I do not say he didn't. I have yet to find two men who agree exactly what happened or who is to blame."

Landis then slipped away for a fishing vacation in northern Michigan.

Elsewhere in Michigan that day, Schoolboy Rowe and his fiancée, Edna Skinner, asked for and received a waiver of the state's law requiring a five-day waiting period after obtaining a marriage license so that they could be wed immediately.

———

During the pennant drive in late summer, rumors had first surfaced that Sam Breadon wanted to sell the St. Louis Cardinals. The team owner had had to issue denials more than once. Even during the World Series victory celebration, reporters prodded him on his intentions, and Breadon insisted that the team was not for sale. In fact, though, he had been negotiating to sell the franchise to Lewis Haines Wentz, a Ponca City, Oklahoma, oil millionaire with Pittsburgh connections. Wentz and Branch Rickey had known one another for years. In mid November 1934, Breadon finally went public, admitting that his general manager and Wentz had recently met in a downtown hotel to see if they could come to terms. Breadon's alleged "take it or leave it" asking price was understood to have been between

$1,000,000 and $1,250,000. Breadon now owned 77 percent of the Cardinal stock. But all talk of a sale had since been postponed "indefinitely." Asked when he and Wentz might resume their talks, Breadon replied, "I have no idea."

Wentz, a self-described ardent baseball fan, claimed that he wanted to own a professional baseball team for the sheer love of the game, and not because of "any silly idea that there's a lot of money to be made out of it." Years earlier, Wentz had bid unsuccessfully on the Pittsburgh Pirates. The November 1934 press reports about the possible sale were not quite correct, however. Breadon had put a much higher valuation on the Cardinals' farm system than Wentz did, and the disagreement on its worth was the reason the talks had ultimately ceased. If Wentz had succeeded in buying the club, he would have brought former Pirates manager Fred Clarke from Pittsburgh to run the club.

Also in late November, local newspapers speculated that the sale of the team was perhaps being held up by the Cardinals' stalled contract negotiations with the Dean brothers. Baseball writers pointed out that the team had a much higher market value with Dizzy and Paul on board than if they were to bolt for another city.

Dizzy himself had announced, in no uncertain terms, that he wanted $25,000 for his services in 1935. Rickey had offered him $15,000, and $7,500 to Paul. Dizzy also told reporters that he wanted to know more about Wentz's intentions. Dean later met with Breadon and Rickey and afterward told reporters that the matter of his salary had not been discussed. No, he said, "I may buy the team myself. Me 'n' Paul ought to have enough money pretty soon to buy it, and before I get through with all these conferences I may make Sam Breadon an offer he can't refuse if he's half the businessman I think he is. I wouldn't mind owning a ball club with a couple of pitchers on it like me 'n' Paul." Some days afterward, he added that a Hollywood studio had offered him $35,000 to make a film based on his life.

In early December, Dean signed a contract, but the terms were not disclosed. Rumors again circulated that Wentz, now satisfied that the Dean brothers were again on board, had resumed his negotiations with Breadon.

"Boy, am I happy" was all Dizzy Dean would say before heading out for a game of golf. "I can hit that ball a mile." Adding to his happiness, he had just signed a deal with an advertising agency for fifteen thousand dollars and had celebrated by buying a new car. Paul Dean, meanwhile, had still not been signed.

Also in early December, the Cardinals declared a dividend, and in a surprise announcement revealed that Branch Rickey had sold his remaining holdings in the club, estimated at 10 percent. The buyer was Clarence Howard, a local entrepreneur who already owned a minority share in the team. "I certainly do not intend to leave the club," Rickey said. "I have a three-year contract with it. I have no other job in mind, and haven't had." The dividend amounted to $100,000. Breadon, as the majority shareholder, collected $77,000 of that amount.

A few days later, the owners and business managers of the various teams in the National League convened for their annual winter meeting at the Waldorf-Astoria Hotel in New York and agreed to a limited experiment with something that was all the rage in the minor leagues: night baseball. Desperate to increase attendance, which had dropped precipitously with the onset of the Depression, the officials agreed that each team would be permitted to hold seven games under the lights during the upcoming season. In Breadon's case, though, there was a qualifier. Sportsman's Park, where the Cardinals played, was owned by the St. Louis Browns, and he would need their permission if the Cardinals were to experiment with night baseball. Breadon would have to wait until November 1936, in fact, when new owners took over the Browns and announced their intention to install lights in the stadium and bring night baseball to St. Louis.

In late December 1934, Paul Dean married a young woman named Dorothy Sandusky, identified in several news reports as "a 19-year-old local beauty contest winner." The marriage took place in Russellville, Arkansas, and culminated a two-month courtship. Asked what he thought his brother Dizzy might say about the rushed marriage, Paul replied, "It's none of his business, anyhow."

On the second to last day of the year, John Drebinger of the *New York Times* looked back over the momentous 1934 baseball season and proclaimed it to be one that would be remembered for as long as the game was played. The year was marked by two especially sad occasions. Babe Ruth, "perhaps the greatest" of all baseball luminaries, had announced that, at the age of forty, he could no longer continue as a regular player. Another "sad blow" was the death of John McGraw, the legendary manager of the New York Giants. The great Lou Gehrig had also set an all-time endurance record for consecutive games played, while also winning the American League's batting championship. Drebinger further noted the masterful managerial debuts of Bill Terry, who had succeeded McGraw, and of Mickey Cochrane of the Tigers. Also not to be overlooked was the stellar performance of the Tigers' "young pitching giant," Schoolboy Rowe, who had pitched for sixteen straight victories to tie an American League record. "But scarcely had the nation adjusted itself to this new setup for its coming fall classic, than events of an even more spectacular nature began to happen in the National League. A flamboyant swashbuckling Cardinals team, which for four-fifths of the way had regaled the country with the eccentricities of its pitching Deans, Dizzy and Daffy, while rowing boisterously within its ranks, suddenly squared about to make one of the most heroic pennant bids in baseball history."

Drebinger likened the Cardinals' late-season pennant drive to a shell shot from a howitzer: "The ensuing World Series was by far one of the most colorful and tempestuous classics seen in years. Valiantly, a well-rested Tigers team sought to fight off this strange combination from St. Louis. But the two Deans and an unconquerable spirit proved too much."

EPILOGUE

Dizzy Dean's fame, both as a personality and as an athlete, made him one of the highest-paid players in baseball at a time when most Americans were still mired in the joblessness, poverty, and desperation of the Depression. After the Series, Cardinals treasurer Bill DeWitt—who also doubled as Dean's personal business manager—released a statement listing Dean's other post-Series earnings that year:

CHRISTY WALSH SYNDICATE, PART PAYMENT (WRITING ABOUT WORLD SERIES)	$500
BREAKFAST CEREAL ENDORSEMENT	$300
HARMONICA ENDORSEMENT	$250
APPEARANCE AT ROXY THEATER, NEW YORK	$1,625
APPEARANCE IN MOVIE SHORT	$2,350
RADIO APPEARANCE WITH AL JOLSON (FIVE MINUTES)	$900
USE OF NAME ON HATS	$500
RADIO APPEARANCE WITH KATE SMITH (FIVE MINUTES)	$600
MAKING A RADIO TRANSCRIPTION	$100
USE OF NAME ON CHILDREN'S SCHOOL WRITING TABLETS	$500

USE OF NAME ON TABLE BASEBALL GAME	$250
FIRST PAYMENT ON $15,000 ADVERTISING CONTRACT	$2,500
USE OF NAME ON A WATCH	$100
DIZZY'S SHARE OF ME 'N' PAUL SWEATSHIRT CONTRACT (FOR TWO MONTHS)	$1,000
USE OF NAME ON PANTS	$438
ENDORSEMENT OF A TOBACCO PRODUCT	$250
ENDORSEMENT OF A BOYS' BASEBALL SUIT	$374
APPEARANCE IN ONE CIGARETTE COMIC STRIP	$500

Even the opportunity to earn a lucrative income in the off-season proved to be something of a grind for the ever-restless, impulsive Dean, who later wisecracked, "Doggone, but I'm gettin' tired of havin' to take in all this money. I never knew dough could be so much trouble. Old Bill DeWitt sure is earnin' his 10 percent. Boy, he's wearin' a path to the old bank. It's Diz, please take a thousand for indorsin' watches. And please, Diz, take this check for baseball caps. And now I'm liable to have to go in the toothpaste and shavin'-cream business. Doggone, I'm gettin' tired of it all. For two cents, I'd jump the club and go fishin' up to Novus Scofus."

Instead of going fishing, though, Dean had gone on to earn another seventy-five hundred dollars on a barnstorming tour. Many of the postseason games that he and Paul played were against the great Negro teams that flourished before the integration of baseball in the late 1940s. Dizzy pitched several times against Satchel Paige, who was known as "the black Dizzy Dean." Paige had magnificent speed and a curveball that he liked to call "the back dodger." Asked once about the ethical nature of some of his pitches, Paige drawled, "I never throw an illegal pitch. The problem is, once in a while, I throw one that ain't been seen by this generation."

Dean and Paige were eventually to gain enormous respect for one another. Sometimes Dean won, and at other times Paige was the winning pitcher.

After the Cardinals won the 1934 championship, Dean and his wife, Pat, bought a house in Palma Sola Park, an exclusive community in Bradenton, Florida, and lived there until the late 1930s. A neighbor remembered that Dean hung a white wooden board outside the house with a hole just slightly larger than a baseball cut into the middle. Passersby often saw him trying to throw a baseball through the hole. Locals also sometimes observed him pumping gas at a Standard gas station that he owned on the corner of Fourth Avenue and Tenth Street West.

The Gashouse Gang, though, turned out to be a one-year wonder. The Cardinals actually won one more game in 1935 than in 1934, but they finished behind the Chicago Cubs. Dizzy posted a 28–12 record that year, and even Wild Bill Hallahan recovered sufficiently from his poor showing in 1934 to win fifteen victories against eight defeats. Paul Dean won another nineteen games in 1935 but injured his arm in the spring of 1936. By age twenty-two, he had won thirty-eight games, but was to win only twelve more in the remainder of his career.

Then a string of setbacks struck the club. Catcher Bill De-Lancey, a power hitter and a very promising rookie in 1934, came down with tuberculosis, his career cut tragically short. DeLancey died on November 28, 1946, his birthday, at the age of thirty-five. In the opinion of some observers, he might have developed into one of the greatest catchers of all time.

Dizzy was injured in 1937. Frank Frisch got too old to play and also became a fairly inept manager. The Cardinals' salvation lay in its far-flung farm system pioneered by Branch Rickey, and the team later added such stellar players to the lineup as Enos Slaughter, Terry Moore, and Johnny Mize. But the Gashouse Gang never won another pennant.

In 1938, Dizzy was traded to the Chicago Cubs for $185,000 plus three players. Rickey knew that Dizzy's sore arm was about to wear out. Neither Dean ever pitched in another World Series game for the Cardinals, nor did the Cardinals win another pennant until 1942.

Branch Rickey traded Leo Durocher to Brooklyn during the 1937–1938 winter season. By that time, the Lip and Frisch were barely on speaking terms, and Durocher had given Rickey an ultimatum: Him or me. Durocher lost.

The Cubs won the 1938 pennant, with Dizzy Dean aboard, though he managed to win only seven games, with one defeat. St. Louis slumped to sixth place that year, from fourth the previous season. Frisch was let go in September 1938, after twelve years with the club. Two years later, he returned to baseball as manager of the Pirates.

Joe Medwick and Pepper Martin both left the Cardinals at the end of the 1939 season. Pepper took over the management of a Cardinals farm team in Sacramento, and Medwick was traded to the Dodgers. Like Dizzy Dean, Medwick had been loudly complaining that he was not being paid adequately. He found out about the trade only when he read about it in a New York newspaper while the club was on the road.

In 1941 Dean became a play-by-play broadcaster for both the St. Louis Cardinals and the St. Louis Browns. On the last day of the 1947 season, before a crowd of sixteen thousand—almost record-breaking for a Browns game—the thirty-seven-year-old Dean donned a Browns jersey and walked out to the mound for the first time in six years. After pitching four scoreless innings, he smacked a double but came up lame at second base. His wife, Pat, then screamed at Browns manager Muddy Ruel to remove him from the game before he hurt himself.

As a baseball broadcaster, Dizzy Dean became even more famous than he had been as a player. He called the outfield "the pasture," described line drives as "blue darters," and liked to ruminate about the condition of a pitcher's "soupbone." He said "slud" instead of "slid" and noted that "the runners are returning to their respectable bases."

In 1952, Hollywood released *The Pride of St. Louis,* starring Dan Dailey as Dizzy, Joanne Dru as Pat Dean, and Richard Crenna as Paul. Also in the early 1950s, Dean became the voice and face of a fledgling television show, *The Game of the Week,* produced by the upstart American Broadcasting Company. By 1955, the show had become so popular that the much larger Columbia Broadcasting System took it over, and Dean was eventually joined in the broadcasting booth by another ballplayer turned announcer, Pee Wee Reese. The show attracted an enormous audience, who loved Dean's cornpone humor and mangling of the language. He soon became "something of a national folk hero," as Charles C. Alexander noted in *Our Game*: "Only a minority of viewers complained that the action on the field was often secondary to the rumination of Ol' Diz on everything from quail hunting to the Gashouse Gang."

Once, while broadcasting a game with Reese, Dean spotted a young couple in the grandstand. "Look-a-there, Pee Wee," he remarked. "Those young folks are smooching after every pitch. He's kissing her on the strikes, and she's kissing him on the balls."

Reese later denied that Dean made any such remark, but so many people claimed to have heard it themselves that, whether or not he had, that entirely characteristic observation took on the status of an urban legend.

Sometimes, when the action on the field was slow, Dean would amuse his listeners by singing a song. One of the favorites in his repertoire was "The Wabash Cannonball," which he later, in fact, recorded. He was also known to provide a play-by-play analysis of a blowing hotdog wrapper, or to inform

Reese mid-game that he was heading out for a half-hour or so to get himself a steak sandwich.

Dean was only forty-four when he was elected to the National Baseball Hall of Fame, in 1953. His once lean frame had grown heavy, his hair had turned prematurely silver, and he often wore a ten-gallon hat.

Dizzy and Pat later retired to her hometown of Bond, Mississippi, a lumber mill town near Biloxi. He had proved to be an astute businessman, investing in oil, and he also owned extensive property in Texas. He died a millionaire in 1974.

———————

The relationship between Sam Breadon and Branch Rickey was like a marriage that had begun well and then run into a series of small problems that both parties were eager to resolve. But Rickey never quite got over Breadon's abrupt dismissal of him as field manager in 1925, when Rogers Hornsby had been named in his stead. Breadon's decision had been a necessary and wise one, and perhaps in time, deep in his heart, Rickey himself came to share that view. But at some deeper level, he felt betrayed, and the two men were never to be close again.

As Breadon grew into his job as Cardinals owner, he also made a number of important decisions without consulting Rickey—the purchase of Grover Cleveland Alexander in 1926, for instance, after he had been placed on waivers by the Cubs.

By the late 1930s, the rift between the two men was irreparable. The Cardinals owner was furious that Rickey had sent Medwick to the Dodgers. In turn, Rickey was angry that Breadon had recently agreed to allow a local brewery, Hyde Park Beer, to sponsor the radio broadcasts of Cardinals games. Breadon ignored his protests.

In October 1942, Rickey resigned from the Cardinals and soon afterward accepted a job as general manager of the Brooklyn Dodgers. The 1942 Cardinals, the last St. Louis team created during Rickey's tenure, was among the very finest in the club's history; it won the pennant and then went on to take the World Series in five games against the New York Yankees. The Cardinals also won the pennant in 1943 and 1944, when they faced their cross-town rivals, the St. Louis Browns, and again won the championship; and they reigned as world champions again in 1946, after they defeated the Boston Red Sox in seven games.

In late 1947, Breadon sold his controlling interest in the St. Louis Cardinals and their far-flung farm system to former postmaster-general Robert E. Hannegan and Fred M. Saigh, Jr., a St. Louis attorney, for a reputed three million dollars. In 1953 they sold the team to August A. Busch, Jr., the principal owner of the Anheuser-Busch brewery. The St. Louis Cardinals were the last Major League team to become fully integrated, and they were not to win another pennant until 1964. That year a thrilling young pitcher named Bob Gibson led the Cardinals to a world championship in a seven-game contest against their old foes, the New York Yankees. Like Dizzy Dean, thirty years earlier, he lost one game in that spirited Series and won two. Gibson knew how to throw just the right pitch, Dean opined, "99 times out of 10."

Notes

Preface

xi *from 1930 to March 1933*: Alexander, *Breaking the Slump*, page 15.

1. The Impossible Dream

6–7 *one and the same?*: Stockton, pages 225–226.

8 *If they were only white*: Lipman, page 11.

13 *my business manager*: Polner, pages 74ff.

13 *virtually illiterate*: ibid.

15 *on the game as Branch Rickey*: Lieb, page 62.

17 *had become powerhouses*: Golenbock, page 85.

19 *Speakers, and Mathewsons*: Stockton, page 20.

22 *he so sorely lacked*: Polner, page 80.

24 *a ball and chain*: ibid., page 83.

25 *You're ruining me*: Hood, pages 35ff.

26 *that he did not*: Polner, pages 89–90.

26 *spiked at $350,000*: Stockton, page 230.

2. Me 'n' Paul

29 *promise and personality*: The date and place of Dizzy Dean's birth has been the subject of a considerable amount of celebrated confusion. The *Sporting News Register,* various baseball encyclopedias, and sports historian Lee Allen, to cite only a few examples, say he was born on January 16, 1911, in Lucas. Robert Gregory and Vince Staten, Dean's two

principal biographers, correctly note that he was born on January 16, 1910, in Lucas. Other official and unofficial accounts list his birthplace as Holdenville, Oklahoma, and Bond, Mississippi. Not surprisingly, Dean himself was responsible for the numerous conflicting versions about when and where he was born. See in this book, for example, the account on pages 149–150 of his conversation in the back of a New York taxi with J. Roy Stockton, the sports editor of the *St. Louis Post-Dispatch,* who had asked Dean to explain the discrepancies.

30 *as tough as my father did*: Allen, page 23.

31 *and few agree*: For example, the estimable Frederick G. Lieb mistakenly claimed that Jay had an older brother named Jerome Herman, who died, and that the family superimposed the name of the deceased sibling on his own, and in time the name Jay Hanna faded away; Lieb, page 157. Handing out "exclusives" to journalists and editors was so deeply ingrained a habit that almost nothing Dean said could be accepted at face value. Similarly, he told Harold Johnson, the editor of the 1933 edition of *Who's Who in Baseball,* that he had learned how to pitch while he was a student at Oklahoma City Teachers College.

32 *the next guy popped up*: Lieb, page 157.

37 *"Your usual will do," Brought said*: Shapiro, page 43.

37 *hard-throwing Private Dean "Dizzy"*: There are numerous conflicting accounts of how Jerome Dean acquired his nickname. Most concur that Brought was the first to call him Dizzy, but few agree on the circumstances. For example, Robert Gregory gave this less plausible version: "In late August 1927, Brought was marching two platoons past the barracks when he saw Diz out back flinging freshly peeled potatoes at garbage can lids. Brought rushed over and made himself immortal with the angry yell, 'You dizzy son of a bitch.' It stuck, spreading first to the kitchen, then throughout the battery, to the regimental field, and on April 17, 1928, after his 17 strikeouts against the St. Mary University Rattlers, the San Antonio papers referred to him for the first time as 'Dizzy' Dean, the 'star twirler'"; Gregory, page 32. The newspaper reference, however, is accurate.

38 *valuable major leaguers*: Stockton, page 23.

39 *in full view of the players*: Polner, page 93.

42 *for thirty dollars a week*: As with so many other biographical details concerning Dean's early life, the story of how he was able to buy his way out of the army exists in numerous different versions. Dean himself promulgated the tale about being rescued from the army by his father, Monroe, in an article published in *Liberty* magazine in 1938. "It was a shock to me," Dean claimed, "to see tears come to his eyes as he shook my hand and to hear his voice tremble as he said, 'I'll buy you out, son, the first good cotton year I get.' He made good on that promise, and not long afterward. Made good on it, although he took almost every dollar he got out of his first good cotton crop. . . . He'd sold his cotton crop prematurely and at a low price so he could buy me out." In fact, though, as Vince Staten suggested, the San Antonio Public Service company most likely bought him out. "Many company teams in that era had semi-pro and former pro players on their rosters," Staten wrote, "guys who worked for the company so they could play on the company baseball squad"; Staten, pages 36–37. Dizzy told Brought that Monroe had given him the money probably on the advice of the San Antonio Public Service, which perhaps wished to avoid being accused by the government of poaching its enlisted men.

43 *took up the refrain*: Allen, page 30.

44 *how the how are you?*: Stockton, pages 40–41.

45 *still in the future*: Gregory, pages 41–42.

45 *only a pack of cigarettes*: Staten, page 53.

46 *You tell me*: Gregory, page 49.

47 *guzzle cups of raw whiskey*: Lieb, page 144.

48 *I ever struck out*: Gregory, page 130.

49 *subduing the Pirates 3 to 1*: Hood, page 60.

49 *get out of this game*: ibid.

50 *all of his 1931 salary*: Gregory, page 55.

53 *Dean just got sent down*: Like so many other anecdotes in the Dean anthology, Myers's remark has also been attributed to several other players.

55 *why I wanna marry her*: Gregory, page 64.

55 *a great big boy:* she explained, ibid., page 65.

57 *suffered with him*: Lieb, page 156.

57 *Loyd and Earl, to school*: Loyd and Earl were presumably the sons of one or both of Dizzy's stepbrothers or of his stepsister Carol.

59 *the exhibition game is off*: Lieb, pages 159–160.

62 *in the winter months*: Frisch, page 166.

62 *when he struck out seventeen Cubs*: That record would stand until October 2, 1938, when Bob Feller of the Cleveland Indians struck out eighteen Detroit Tigers.

63 *he promptly obeyed*: Allen, page 16.

69 *to pour it on scrambled eggs*: Gregory, page 144.

3. THE GANG'S ALL HERE

74 *reaction on big-league baseball*: Alexander, *Breaking the Slump,* page 4.

75 *than at any time since*: Hood, page 6.

76 *massage and Mercurochrome*: ibid., page 9.

79 *a case in point*: Neyer and Epstein noted, "By the late 1930s, the Cardinals either owned or were affiliated with teams scattered across the continent, from hell to breakfast. At its peak in 1940, the Cardinal empire numbered 33 clubs at all levels: major (1), AA (3), A-1 (1), B (4), C (4), and D (20!). Of the 32 minor league teams, the Cardinals owned 15 outright, and had working agreements with the other 17. Stan Musial, Terry Moore, Enos Slaughter, Marty Marion, Johnny Beazley, the Cooper brothers . . . all were products of Rickey's far-flung system. All those players meant two things for Rickey: pennants, and extra cash in his pocket. Every time the Cardinals had a youngster ready for the big leagues, Rickey would sell one of his veterans to another club and, as stipulated in his contract by then, he pocketed 10 percent of the sale price"; Neyer and Epstein, page 168.

79 *the worst of the Depression*: Alexander, *Breaking the Slump,* page 24.

80 *Young replied*: Devaney, page 58.

81 *from the beginning*: ibid., page 60.

82 *which we lost*: Frisch, page 50.

83 *to take a rest*: ibid., page 51.

84 *as Frank Frisch did in 1927*: Hood, page 44.

84 *Napoleon Lajoie, and Rogers Hornsby*: ibid., page 45.

85 *and affection for him*: Frisch, pages 52–53.

86 *a bat signed by John J. McGraw*: Barthel, *The Fierce Fun of Ducky Medwick,* page 7.

86 *something out you'd like*: ibid., page 11.

90 *Frisch, my manager, would tell me*: Hood, page 227.

91 *home runs in a World Series game*: *Philadelphia Inquirer,* October 12, 1931.

91 *middle finger on his left hand*: Harry Brundidge, *St. Louis Star-Times,* July 21, 1931.

92 *decided was his destiny*: Barthel, *Pepper Martin,* page 13.

93 *only bath in the creek*: Stan Baumgartner, *Philadelphia Inquirer,* October 4, 1931.

93 *lives of the fans in the grandstand*: Wilbur Adams, *Sacramento Bee,* February 22, 1944.

93 *smooth out the infield*: *New York World-Telegram,* May 21, 1931.

94 *how he could slug that ball!*: Bill Bryson, *Des Moines Register,* July 6, 1955.

94 *and he has a wonderful arm*: *St. Louis Post-Dispatch,* October 7, 1931.

94 *listening to him talk nonstop*: Harry Brundidge, *St. Louis Star-Times,* July 21, 1931.

94–95 *from one day to the next*: *Philadelphia Inquirer,* October 14, 1993.

95 *swore at pitchers in his sleep*: Chieger, page 90. For much of the material about Martin's early life, I am indebted to Thomas Barthel's *Pepper Martin: A Baseball Biography.*

97 *declined the offer*: Hood, page 53.

98 *filled the bill in fine style*: Lieb, page 161.

99 *help us win pennants*: Hood, page 50.

103 *convince Sam Breadon to make a trade*: ibid., page 51.

107 *Going to play ball*: ibid., pages 53–54.

4. The Gashouse Follies

114 *Thanks, Mr. Frisch*: Gregory, page 135.

117 *hold that lead, gutless*: Eskenazi, page 73.

118 *until the day he died*: Gregory, page 145.

119 *going out of his mind*: Devaney, page 19.

120 *according to Polner*: Polner, pages 106ff.

123 *was a better tactician*: Gregory, page 141.

126 *from George Raft movies*: ibid., page 143.

137 *almost losing consciousness*: Frisch, page 89.

147 *as if to cool off*: Gregory, page 158.

150 *I'll keep all three of 'em*: Stockton, page 35.

152 *three pitched balls*: ibid., pages 50–51.

152 *would be up around his ears*: Allen, pages 12, 14.

5. Dizzy in the Dock

156 *surprised him now and then*: Frisch, page 110.

157 *and he's right*: Eskenazi, page 74.

158 *greatest peanut salesman you can imagine*: Staten, page 119.

160 *keeping us in the pennant race*: Gregory, page 166.

177 *uniforms for a league game*: Frisch, pages 170–171.

180 *than were the rest of the Cardinals*: ibid., page 172.

6. Casey's Revenge

183 *significantly better terms*: Allen, page 15.

184 *and managerial career*: Gregory, page 180.

189 *love to drive that Dutchman nuts*: Stockton, page 47.

191 *to clear up all [Durocher's] debts*: Eskenazi, pages 75–76.

191 *ended in a divorce court*: Lieb, pages 169–170.

7. It Ain't Braggin'

202 *and a nickname was born*: Allen, pages 18–19.

203 *what we now call a gas station*: Devaney, page 14.

204 *cruel thugs: the Gashouse Gang*: Eisenbath, page 47.

206 *before the game even starts*: Stockton, page 74.

207 *origin of the Cards' famous nickname*: Gregory, page 213.

207 *the almost-memorable "Infield of Dreams"*: Viola Owen, "The RBI Record of the Battalion of Death: No Four Infielders

Ever Had More Than These 1934 Tigers," *National Pastime,* January 1, 2001, pages 40–44.

208 *Someone might take your job*: Bak, page 268.

208 *that the Detroit quartet presents*: Viola Owen, *National Pastime,* pages 40–41.

219 *won the British Open*: Gregory, page 11.

220 *and put on his show*: ibid., page 12.

222 *Si-kology, my foot!*: Stockton, page 55.

225 *make it into the Series*: Alexander, *Breaking the Slump,* pages 93–94.

232 *noted baseball historian Paul Katzeff*: "Hank Greenberg Kept His Eye and Bat on the Ball; Have Faith: Baseball's First Jewish Star Battled Hard throughout a Hall of Fame Career and Served His Country in WWII," *Investor's Business Daily,* February 24, 2005.

8. By the Breath of the Gods

250 *'Okay, let him be'*: Honig, page 192.

251 *an urgent call from a broker*: Lieb, "Fireball Cochrane." See Bevis, *Mickey Cochrane,* page 87.

252 *were not as understanding*: Bevis, page 90.

254 *intangibles of leadership*: Robinson, page 208.

255 *"Go to hell, Diz," Cochrane replied*: Bevis, pages 120ff.

259 *settle their hash the next game*: Hood, page 133.

263 *Durocher was later to recall*: Eskanazi, page 83.

9. Tiger Rag

268 *beyond the pale*: Eskanazi, page 82.

270 *to make a phantom tag*: Hood, pages 134–135.

273 *killed some of those fans*: ibid., page 136.

275 *he missed those third swings*: *Literary Digest,* October 20, 1934, page 36.

276 *until he left town*: Hood, page 136.

278 *in the history of the game*: *Literary Digest,* October 20, 1934, page 36.

281 *on board to run the club*: Lieb, page 175.

Epilogue

289 *quail hunting to the Gashouse Gang*: Alexander, *Our Game,*
   page 223.

291 *when they faced their cross-town rivals*: The story of the
   Browns' one and only appearance in a World Series is told
   in a book the author warmly recommends, since he is its
   coauthor, along with Brett Topel: *The Boys Who Were Left
   Behind: The 1944 World Series between the Hapless St. Louis
   Browns and the Legendary St. Louis Cardinals* (Lincoln: University of Nebraska Press, 2006).

BIBLIOGRAPHY

BOOKS

Alexander, Charles C. *Breaking the Slump: Baseball in the Depression Era*. New York: Columbia University Press, 2002.

_____. *Our Game: An American Baseball History*. New York: Holt, 1992.

_____. *Rogers Hornsby: A Biography*. New York: Holt, 1996.

Allen, Lee. *Dizzy Dean: His Story in Baseball*. New York: Putnam, 1967.

Auker, Elden, with Tom Keegan. *Sleeper Cars and Flannel Uniforms: A Lifetime of Memories from Striking Out the Babe to Teeing It Up with the President*. Chicago: Triumph Books, 2001.

Bak, Richard. *Cobb Would Have Caught It: The Golden Age of Baseball in Detroit*. Detroit: Wayne State University Press, 1991.

Barthel, Thomas. *The Fierce Fun of Ducky Medwick*. Lanham, MD: Scarecrow Press, 2003.

_____. *Pepper Martin: A Baseball Biography*. Jefferson, NC: McFarland, 2003.

Bevis, Charles. *Mickey Cochrane: The Life of a Baseball Hall of Fame Catcher*. Jefferson, NC: McFarland, 1998.

Broeg, Bob. *The Pilot Light and the Gas House Gang*. St. Louis: Bethany Press, 1980.

Broeg, Bob, and Jerry Vickery. *St. Louis Cardinals Encyclopedia*. Chicago: Contemporary Books, 1998.

Burns, Kenneth, and Geoffrey C. Ward. *Baseball: An Illustrated History*. New York: Knopf, 1994.

Chieger, Bob. *Voices of Baseball*. New York: Signet, 1983.

Creamer, Robert W. *Baseball and Other Matters in 1941*. Lincoln: University of Nebraska Press, 2004.

Devaney, John. *The Greatest Cardinals of Them All*. New York: Putnam, 1968.

Durocher, Leo, with Ed Linn. *Nice Guys Finish Last*. New York: Simon & Schuster, 1975.

Einstein, Charles, ed. *The Fireside Books of Baseball*. New York: Simon & Schuster, 1987.

Eisenbath, Mike. *The Cardinals Encyclopedia*. Philadelphia: Temple University Press, 1999.

Eskenazi, Gerald. *The Lip: A Biography of Leo Durocher*. New York: Morrow, 1993.

Feldman, Doug. *Dizzy and the Gas House Gang: The 1934 St. Louis Cardinals and Depression-Era Baseball*. Jefferson, NC: McFarland, 2000.

Fleming, Gordon. *The Dizziest Season: The Gashouse Gang Chases the Pennant*. New York: Morrow, 1984.

Frisch, Frank, as told to J. Roy Stockton. *Frank Frisch: The Fordham Flash*. New York: Doubleday, 1962.

Golenbock, Peter. *The Spirit of St. Louis: A History of the St. Louis Cardinals and Browns*. New York: HarperCollins, 2001.

Gregory, Robert. *Diz: The Story of Dizzy Dean and Baseball during the Great Depression*. New York: Viking, 1992.

Honig, Donald, ed. *The October Heroes: Great World Series Games Remembered by the Men Who Played Them*. New York: Simon and Schuster, 1979.

Hood, Robert E. *The Gashouse Gang: The Incredible, Madcap St. Louis Cardinals of 1934*. New York: Morrow. 1976.

Kavanagh, Jack. *Dizzy Dean*. New York: Chelsea House, 1991.

Leptich, John, and Dave Baranowski. *This Date in St. Louis Cardinals History*. New York: Stein & Day, 1983.

Levenson, Barry. *The Seventh Game: The 35 World Series That Have Gone the Distance*. New York: McGraw-Hill, 2004.

Lieb, Frederick G. *The St. Louis Cardinals: The Story of a Great Baseball Club*. Carbondale: Southern Illinois University Press, 1988.

Lipman, David. *Mr. Baseball: The Story of Branch Rickey*. New York: Putnam, 1966.

Mooney, Roger. "The Boys of Bradenton." *Bradenton Herald*, February 22, 2004.

Neyer, Rob, and Eddie Epstein. *Baseball Dynasties: The Greatest Teams of All Time*. New York: W. W. Norton, 1993.

Okrent, Daniel, and Harris Lewine, eds. *The Ultimate Baseball Book*. Boston: Houghton Mifflin, 2000.

Polner, Murray. *Branch Rickey: A Biography*. New York, Atheneum, 1982.

Rader, Benjamin G. *Baseball: A History of America's Game*. Urbana and Chicago: University of Illinois Press, 2002.

Rains, Rob. *Cardinal Nation*. St. Louis: Sporting News, 2002.

Rickey, Branch, with Robert Riger. *The American Diamond: A Documentary of the Game of Baseball*. New York: Simon & Schuster, 1965.

Robinson, Ray. *Iron Horse: Lou Gehrig in His Time*. New York: Harper Paperbacks, 1991.

Seymour, Harold, et al. *Baseball: The Golden Age*. New York: Oxford University Press, 1989.

Shapiro, Milton J. *The Dizzy Dean Story*. New York: Julian Messner, 1963.

Shouler, Kenneth. "Baseball's Greatest Teams." *Cigar Aficionado*, July-August 2002.

Smith, Curt. *America's Dizzy Dean*. St. Louis: Bethany Press, 1978.

Sporting News. *Cardinal Nation*. St. Louis: Sporting News, 2002.

Staten, Vince. *Ol' Diz: A Biography of Dizzy Dean*. New York: HarperCollins, 1992.

Stockton, J. Roy. *The Gashouse Gang and a Couple of Other Guys*. New York: A. S. Barnes, 1945.

Strong, Mark. *Cardinals Collection: 100 Years of St. Louis Cardinals Images*. Wilmington, OH: Orange Frazer Press, 2002.

Thorn, John, and Pete Palmer, eds. *Total Baseball: The Official Encyclopedia of Major League Baseball*. Kingston, NY: Total Sports Publishing, 2001.

Tiemann, Robert L. *Cardinal Classics: Outstanding Games from Each of the St. Louis Baseball Club's 100 Seasons 1882–1981*. St. Louis: Baseball Histories, 1982.

Tygiel, Jules. *Past Time: Baseball as History*. New York: Oxford University Press, 2000.

PUBLICATIONS

In writing about the 1926, 1931, 1932, 1933, and 1934 seasons, as well as the Cardinals' 1934 spring training, the 1934 World Series, and incidental news items, I have relied principally on the following newspapers: *Brooklyn Times-Union, Brooklyn Eagle, Detroit News, Detroit Free Press, Detroit Times, New York American, New York Evening Journal, New York Journal-American, New York Post, New York Sun, New York Times, New York World-Telegram, St. Louis Globe-Democrat, St. Louis Post-Dispatch, St. Louis Star Times,* and *Sporting News.* Specific magazine and newspaper articles are cited in the endnotes. I am also indebted, for background purposes, to the annual collections of articles published in *The Baseball Research Journal* and *The National Pastime* by the Society for American Baseball Research.

ACKNOWLEDGMENTS

I am deeply thankful to Andrew Blauner, my agent, and Lisa Kaufman, my editor, who made this book happen. The editorial staff at PublicAffairs is proof that no writer is an island. I am particularly indebted to the following for their invaluable—in fact, indispensable—help: David Patterson, Melissa Raymond, Laura Stine, Margaret Ritchie, and publisher Susan Weinberg. This book also could not have been written without the indefatigable assistance of the staffs of the main branches of the New York, St. Louis, and Detroit public libraries, and of the Missouri Historical Society in St. Louis. I also owe a fond thanks to the many independent booksellers around the country who kept me supplied for months on end with half-forgotten baseball histories and memoirs. Brett Topel, my baseball guru, was as always an invaluable font of baseball perspective and information. Lastly, my wife, Pat, an old Brooklyn Dodgers fan, still gave this book about a team from her husband's hometown the kind of loving, professional close reading that only she can give.

INDEX

JOHN HEIDENRY is a native of St. Louis and was the founding editor, in 1977, of *St. Louis* magazine and the *St. Louis Literary Supplement*. He was most recently executive editor of *The Week* and before that was acting editor of *Maxim*. He is the author of several books, including *Theirs Was a Kingdom: Lila and DeWitt Wallace and the Story of the Reader's Digest* and *The Boys Who Were Left Behind: The 1944 World Series Between the Hapless St. Louis Browns and the Legendary St. Louis Cardinals*.